Derby Hospitals NHS Foundation Trust

Library and Knowledge Service

The A–Z of the M...

Derby Hospitals

Dr Nicholas Taylor
MB ChB MRCPsych

Specialist Registrar in Forensic Psychiatry
Reaside Clinic, Birmingham

PASTEST
Dedicated to your success

WITHDRAWN

© 2004 PasTest Ltd
Egerton Court
Parkgate Estate
Knutsford
Cheshire, WA16 8DX

Telephone: 01565 752000

First edition 2004

ISBN: 1 904627 42 0

A catalogue record for this book is available from the British Library.

PasTest Revision Books and Intensive Courses

PasTest has been established in the field of postgraduate medical education since 1972, providing revision books and intensive study courses for doctors preparing for their professional examinations. Books and courses are available for the following specialties:

MRCP Part 1 and Part 2, MRCPCH Part 1 and Part 2, MRCOG, DRCOG, MRCGP, MRCPsych, DCH, FRCA, MRCS and PLAB.

For further details contact:

PasTest Ltd, Freepost, Knutsford, Cheshire, WA16 7BR
**Tel: 01565 752000   Fax: 01565 650264
Email: enquiries@pastest.co.uk   Web site: www.pastest.co.uk**

Typeset by Vision Typesetting Ltd, Manchester
Printed by Page Bros (Norwich) Ltd
Cover design by OldTinDog.com

Contents

To my family,
my friends
and my teachers

About the author

Dr Nicholas Taylor MB ChB MRCPsych
Specialist Registrar in Forensic Psychiatry, Reaside Clinic,
Birmingham

Nicholas Taylor graduated from Medical School in Bristol and subsequently worked in several clinical specialities in the south of England. Serving briefly in the Royal Naval Reserve, he became a qualified submariner, gaining his 'Dolphins' on board HMS Turbulent. His experience in psychiatry was gained as a Senior House Officer on the Birmingham training rotation. On passing the MRCPsych exam, he took up a post as Specialist Registrar in Forensic Psychiatry at Reaside Clinic. He is married and lives in the Midlands.

Foreword

To students of psychopathology, there is something familiar about the mental states one experiences as an exam candidate. Depression as the day approaches and the information does not appear to be going in. Paranoia, with ideas of persecution at the hands of unseen and unknown examiners who are going to find questions to defeat you, specifically. Bewilderment and functional cognitive impairment with a failure to remember even simple bits of information read from giant tomes, whose content seems to extend as the exam approaches. The ubiquitous background anxiety, increasing to near panic as the day approaches and you know you can't possibly cover the whole syllabus. Then there is the brief sense of relief when you spot a question you can answer, followed by hypomanic flight of ideas and pressure of thought as you try to organise and get down on paper all you can. Finally, there are the obsessional behaviours, superstitions, rituals and list-making.

I like lists. I have always found them an efficient way of organising and committing large numbers of facts to memory, a skill that is essential to success in both parts of the examination for membership of the Royal College of Psychiatrists. Most candidates will find the clinical part of the examination testing but will complete it without too much trouble having worked diligently at their clinical jobs: It is aimed to test day-to-day clinical competence and the ability to communicate information effectively to colleagues, patients and their carers. To qualify for the opportunity to prove their clinical worth, however, it is necessary to be able to regurgitate learned facts, comprising the theoretical basis for the clinical skills, in a series of written tests.

Where do you start? I remember my unsuccessful first attempt at the part two when I was faced with a multiple choice paper on basic sciences in which I didn't even know where to look up the answers, let alone how to respond. I followed this experience by investing in an address book in which I intended to keep notes, alphabetically, of any definitions or concepts that I encountered during my reading. It soon fell by the wayside amid pressured work and family life when the time taken to write, and revise from, the lists extended revision into a two-stage process that halved the amount of work completed in a given time period! This book is the work of someone who has succeeded where I failed.

Nicholas Taylor has turned obsessionality into a virtue by combining it with remarkable clarity of thought and organisation. His obsessional traits are categorised in his own definition (page 231). I've no idea whether he is punctual, but his *A-Z of the MRCPsych* has been constructed to high standards with consistency, determination, persistence, dependability and precision. In addition to the alphabetical treatment of topics, there are ten appendices covering an eclectic selection of topics including neuroscience, psychopathology, ICD–10 and the various psychological stages of child development. The definitions are clear and unambiguous and they cover, often in surprising detail for a gazetteer, the essential facts required for the individual statement questions (ISQs) and extended matching items (EMIs) for both parts of the MRCPsych. The book has the advantage of brevity combined with detail. It does not pretend to be comprehensive but nevertheless covers a huge range of essential information in a very easy format. This is a book to be dipped into for a concise account of concepts, aetiologies and names, an invaluable revision resource and complementary volume to the PasTest portfolio.

Like all examinations, the topics covered in membership are not static, but change over time. They reflect current practice and the current emphasis on continuing professional development, appraisal and revalidation for consultants is a reminder that our knowledge can quickly become dated in a rapidly-changing specialty such as psychiatry. This book comprises the revision notes developed by a psychiatrist who has recently passed the membership examination and is therefore, by definition, an up-to-date response to the requirements of the MRCPsych syllabus.

Having gained experience in developing revision aids across a variety of membership and fellowship examinations, PasTest has an unrivalled reputation for accuracy and detail combined with brevity, qualities essential to the lives of hard-working junior doctors. Their position as the leading providers of revision books and courses in these areas has been well-earned and many senior doctors owe their examination success, in part, to these books. PasTest have now turned their attention to the MRCPsych parts I and II, with their *Essential Revision Notes for the MRCPsych* providing a detailed treatment of the syllabus, complemented by this volume.

Dr Taylor is to be congratulated on providing an invaluable resource to trainee psychiatrists facing the daunting hurdle of membership. A copy of his book will also be of use to those of us who have vaulted (or climbed painfully over) this hurdle and who need to dip into it to refresh our memories. While membership candidates will still experience depression, paranoia and anxiety, their obsessionality is now managed by this volume, with the therapy for other symptoms available in the rest of the PasTest MRCPsych series.

Christopher Fear MBChB, MD, MRCPsych
Consultant General Adult Psychiatrist,
Gloucester.

Review

The A to Z of the MRCPsych is a new revision text for the MRCPsych examination. What immediately distinguishes this book from all the other available texts is its approach. Rather than providing chapters organised by subject, the book provides a dictionary approach with all entries arranged after their initial letter. This makes it simple to quickly obtain information without having to consult an index or search through more general reference works. The MRCPsych exam is famed for its devotion to obscure facts and this book features many of the favourite topics. The author has tried to provide more information concerning topics frequently asked in exams, and this is very welcome.

The scope of the book is very broad, encompassing all the subject areas required for both parts of the exam. This ranges from basic sciences through to principles of psychology and psychotherapy. The very scope of the exam can make it difficult to revise for and often requires a number of weighty reference texts for each subject. The MCQ papers in both parts of the exam require specific knowledge of individual facts, and when practising such papers these can often be difficult to locate in general texts. The dictionary approach makes it easy to locate answers rapidly, although in most cases further reading in a dedicated text would be needed to gain a thorough understanding of the topic.

There are several appendices which cover certain areas in more detail (including culture-bound syndromes, neuroanatomy, development theory, etc). These are welcome, but the selection of subjects covered seems rather random. Also, they are not always adequately referenced from the corresponding areas of the main text.

Given the broad range of subject matter covered by the book, the amount of information contained in each entry is necessarily brief but is usually sufficient to provide an overview of the subject in question.

Overall, I think that this is a well-executed and genuinely innovative book which will be extremely helpful for anyone sitting either part of the exam. It excels in that it gathers the relevant areas together into one volume, providing a single point of reference which can then be used to inform further reading. This is the first exam-related text I have seen which has succeeded in doing this.

It should definitely help candidates to make more efficient use of their revision time and allow them to quickly grasp the facts needed to pass the exam. Clearly, it cannot replace the standard reference texts but it will be an excellent companion for them.

Dr James D Reed MB ChB BMedSc

Introduction

Every aspect of this book has been designed to help you to make the most of your time in revising for the MRCPsych exams.

I passed Part II of the exam as recently as autumn 2003, with the help of the notes that have been developed into this book. Many of my colleagues used the notes and early drafts in their exams and found them invaluable. On the basis of comments from them, and my own experience, I have refined the text.

The syllabus is extremely wide ranging. An attempt to cover the entire syllabus would lead to a book with large sections covering esoteric areas that are rarely tested in the exam. To maximise *your* productivity in revising and to help you to cover as much ground as possible in the limited time you have for revision, in putting together my notes and preparing this book, I have given more space to topics (and specific questions) that are tested more often, or in more detail, in the exams. Some ideas (which are commonly tested and difficult to learn) are repeated frequently.

A–Z of the MRCPsych should be used alongside your existing books. Keep it open and refer to it when you see something you are not sure about. Use it alongside an MCQ practice book and you'll find that most of the answers can be found in seconds, rather than spending valuable time ploughing through a bigger and more 'comprehensive' book, which covers areas in excessive, sometimes unnecessary detail.

This book covers the range of subjects needed for Parts I and II of the MRCPsych exam. It will also be of interest to the many healthcare professionals who have no interest in that exam but who need to understand the concepts and language of psychiatry and related disciplines.

Nicholas Taylor

Disclaimer

The information presented in this book is intended for educational use only. The reader is strongly encouraged to consult the *British National Formulary* or the pharmaceutical industry's printed instructions before administering any of the drugs recommended in it.

AAI – Adult Attachment Interview.

Abducens (VI) – Nucleus is in the pons.

Abreaction – Is the bringing of repressed events into consciousness, leading to a resolution of dissociative symptoms (**psychic pus**) associated with their repression.

Absenteeism – Is a form of primary resistance in the large group setting.

Absorption, drug – Rate is dependent on:
- the form of the drug
- the solubility of the drug
- pKa
- particle size
- ambient pH
- rate of blood flow through tissues containing the drug.

Abuse, child – Features of children associated with child abuse include:
- low birth weight
- physical unattractiveness
- being the product of an unwanted pregnancy
- neonatal maternal separation
- habitual restlessness
- poor sleep pattern
- incessant crying
- mental/physical disability.

The father is usually the perpetrator.

Abuse, child physical – *aka* non-accidental injury.
Occurs when an adult inflicts a physical injury on a child more severe than that which is culturally acceptable.

Can lead to:
- anxiety states and anxiety-related symptoms
- re-enactments of the victimisation
- PTSD
- depression
- dissociation
- paranoid reactions and mistrust
- reliance on primitive defence mechanisms (eg denial, projection, dissociation and splitting)
- borderline personality disorder
- aggressive and destructive behaviour at home and at school
- cognitive and developmental impairment
- delayed language development
- neurological impairment
- abusive behaviour with their own children.

Risk factors include:
- social isolation
- adverse living conditions
- current stresses such as ill health
- unrealistic expectations of the child
- inconsistent parenting
- single parents
- unemployment
- history of abuse of the parent when they were young.

Typical injuries include:
- multiple bruising
- burns
- subperiosteal bleeding
- ruptured abdominal viscera.

Abuse, child sexual – The involvement of dependent, developmentally immature children and adolescents in sexual activities that they do not fully comprehend, are unable to give informed consent to and that violate the social taboos of family roles.

Can lead to:
- anxiety states and anxiety-related symptoms
- re-enactments of the victimisation
- PTSD
- depression
- dissociation
- paranoid reactions and mistrust

- reliance on primitive defence mechanisms (eg denial, projection, dissociation and splitting)
- borderline personality disorder
- inability to control sexual impulses (ie precocious sexual play with high arousal)
- weakened sexual identity
- homosexuality
- sexual abuse by the former victim of abuse
- substance misuse
- eating disorders.

Abuse, solvent – Is as common in females as males.
Is most common in the children and adolescents associated with the poorest sectors of society.

Accommodation – Is reduced by:
- TCAs (including maprotiline, mianserin, trazodone) – due to peripheral anti-muscarinic cholinergic effects
- antimuscarinics.

Is not affected by:
- benzodiazepines.

Acetylcholine – Is made from acetyl co-enzyme A and choline by choline acetyltransferase acting as a catalyst.
Is inactivated by cholinesterases.
Is the principal neurotransmitter at:
- presynaptic sympathetic ganglions
- presynaptic parasympathetic ganglions
- neuromuscular junction.

Achromatopsia – A form of colour agnosia with profound loss of colour sense, with abolition of the concept of colour.
Colours cannot even be imagined, but shapes of the same colour can be matched.
Cause is bilateral lesions of the lingual gyri.

ACTH – Adrenocorticotrophic hormone (*aka* corticotrophin).

Acting out – Has several meanings:
- it is used to describe certain behavioural phenomena that arise during the course of psychoanalysis and which are a consequence of that treatment
- it is also used to describe habitual modes of action and behaviour that are related to the individual rather than the treatment process.

Has unconscious determinants.

Freud described it as a way of remembering (the patient produces actions as substitutes for forgotten and repressed memories).

Is a possible first source of new material emerging from unconscious drives.

Is a term extensively applied outside the psychoanalytic process.

Acute stress reaction – Immediate and brief response to a sudden and intense stressor in a person free from other psychiatric disorders. The response lasts from a few hours to about three days. The patient typically appears dazed and may appear disoriented, with limited response to surroundings. They may lapse into a stupor.

Core symptoms are:
* anxiety (as response to threatening circumstances)
* depression (as response to loss).

Other symptoms:
* feelings of being numb/dazed
* insomnia
* restlessness
* poor concentration
* physical symptoms of severe anxiety (especially sweating, palpitations and tremor)
* anger
* histrionic behaviour
* flight reaction (eg when a driver flees from scene of an accident)
* purposeless activity and agitation
* fugue
* stupor.

Initial coping mechanisms include avoidance and denial, but these recede as anxiety lessens and the situation can be worked through.

Delusions and catatonia are *not* seen.

Adjustment disorder – Is the result of a psychological reaction to new circumstances, usually a major life change.

Clinical features include:
* anxiety
* worry
* poor concentration
* depression
* irritability

- autonomic arousal
- outbursts of dramatic/aggressive behaviour
- self-harm
- alcohol/drug abuse.

Gradual onset and prolonged course with impaired social function are the norm. Diagnosis depends on failure to meet diagnostic criteria for another psychiatric disorder (usually anxiety and depressive disorders). The disorder starts soon after a change in circumstances, usually within one month and always within three months. The reaction must be in proportion to and related to the stressful event.

There are five types of (ICD-10) adjustment disorder:
- Depressive.
- Mixed anxiety and depressive.
- Adjustment disorder with disturbance of conduct.
- Adjustment disorder with disturbance of emotions and conduct.
- Adjustment disorder with predominant disturbance of other emotion (ie adjustment disorder with anxiety *or* adjustment disorder with anger).

Defining characteristics:
- They arise as a direct consequence of either acute stress or continued unpleasant circumstances.
- It is judged that the disorder would not have arisen without these factors.

Adler –
- Was a psychoanalyst.
- Developed **individual psychology**.
- Was initially a follower of Freud. He saw people as being driven not by sexual influences but by the **will to power**, superiority and affirmation of their personality.
- As a result of the child's initial dependence on and inevitable feelings of **inferiority** to others, a drive for superiority develops – the **will to power**.

Inferiority is increased by:
- physical deformity
- males' failure to live up to the masculine stereotype
- females' failure to have been male
- being later in the birth order
- being part of a poor or low class family
- failure to live up to parental (over) expectations

- being a neglected, spoilt or hated child.

There are three techniques used to overcome inferiority:

- **Successful compensation** – eg superior intellectual ability compensates for physical inferiority/deformity.
- **Overcompensation** – trying too hard (and ineffectively) when the motive becomes obvious – eg the small man with the enormous car.
- **Escape from combat** – adoption of the sick role to avoid having to attempt (and fail) to live up to one's own impossibly high standards (**fictive goals**), or never fully applying oneself to a task, so that you have an excuse for having failed.

'Every neurosis can be understood as an attempt to free oneself from a feeling of inferiority to gain a feeling of superiority.' Psychoses are the result of a complete failure to conquer inferiority, to the extent that the person 'refuses to play' at the game of life.

Therapy is aimed at revealing the person's psychological processes and helping them understand them. They must also be given the courage and self-confidence that allows them to exist in a normal way, discard their fictive goals and adopt a more sensible future lifestyle.

Adler is associated with:
- aggression
- aggressive strivings
- the drive to power
- individual psychology
- inferiority complex
- masculine protest in women (as a reaction to women's inferior position in society).

He regarded the need for power and superiority as the primary drive. He put greater emphasis on the conscious. He saw birth order as important.

Admissions, psychiatric – Are highest in the summer.

Adolescence – Theories of conflicts with authority figures:
Cognitive theories hold that newly gained powers of hypothetical reasoning challenge the *status quo*.
Erikson's theory is cognitive and is seen in terms of a struggle between **identity and role confusion**. The developing person develops a sense of personal autonomy that challenges authority figures. Erikson

A

felt that adolescence is characterised by **adolescent turmoil** and a temporary, maladaptive state of **identity diffusion**, an inability to formulate clear, consistent goals and commitments, through which all adolescents pass.

There are also ethological and sociobiological models – pubertal change is adaptive and causes individual to spend more time with peers, leading to changes in outlook and an altered sense of self.

Anna Freud saw adolescence as a period of oscillation between excess and asceticism.

Affective instability and behaviour swings are caused by:
* drives stimulated by sexual maturity
* endocrine changes
* instability of newly stressed ego against these drives.

Offer and Offer conducted a seminal study:
* adolescence is less turmoil-filled than previously believed
* study carried out on 14-year-olds in 1962, from intact families with no major delinquency
* 74% went to college from school
* their views were similar to those of their parents.

Three adolescent routes were proposed:
* Continuous growth – 23% – Eriksonian intimacy is achieved, shame and guilt can be displayed. Experiences of major separation, death and severe illness are less frequent. Parents encourage independence.
* Surgent growth – 35% – 'Late developers' – there are more frequent depressive and anxious moments than with the first group and more disagreements with parents. The adolescent is less introspective and less action-oriented.
* Tumultuous growth – 21% – the adolescent experiences recurrent self-doubt and conflict within the family unit. Generally coming from less stable backgrounds, these adolescents (if good achievers) go on to careers in the arts, humanities and social sciences, rather than business.

Block and Haan used factor analysis to identify types of male adolescents:
* **ego-resilient**
* **belated adjusters**
* **vulnerable over-controllers**
* **anomic extroverts**
* **unsettled under-controllers**

and female adolescents:
- **female prototype**
- **cognitive type**
- **hyperfeminine repressors**
- **dominating narcissists**
- **vulnerable under-controllers**
- **lonely independents**.

It is generally accepted that:
- absence of turmoil is not pathological
- identity for closure involves premature acceptance of an ascribed identity.

Adrenergic receptors – β-Adrenergic receptors are blockaded by antipsychotics, causing hypotension and sedation.

Affect – A specific feeling directed toward a specific object or person. Is more specific and more time-limited than an emotion.

Affect, blunting of – Lack of emotional sensitivity.

Affect, flattening of – Restriction in the range of emotion/affect.

Affective disorder – *Bipolar disorder affective disorder* (*aka* BPAD)
- has an onset in the mid-20s
- is equally common in men and women
- is more common in higher social classes
- relatives of bipolar probands have higher rates of bipolar and unipolar illness
- bipolar disorder is more genetic than unipolar disorder
- relatives of bipolar probands have higher rates of affective illness than relatives of unipolar probands
- the morbid risk in the general population of bipolar disorder is < 1%
- the first episode is often after childbirth
- manic relapses are more common in the summer
- L-dopa can activate it (but not cause it)
- earlier onset carries poorer prognosis
- life events can precipitate relapse
- has the same presentation as unipolar depression in the depressive phase
- lithium works as well for bipolar as for unipolar
- rapid-cycling BPAD is more common in women than men.

Epidemiology:
- point prevalence is 0.4–1.2%
- lifetime risk is 0.6–1.1%.

Unipolar depression
- has an onset in the mid-30s
- is twice as common in women than in men
- has no evidence of major differences in symptomatology between cultures, but somatic symptoms may predominate in Africa and Asia
- breeds true, meaning that relatives of people with unipolar depression are more likely to suffer unipolar depression, but are not more likely to suffer bipolar depression
- is more likely to become chronic than BPAD, with adverse factors including:
  - being female
  - high familial loading
  - ill health/disability (in the elderly)
- is less genetic that bipolar disorder
- has a morbid risk in the general population for severe depression of 3%
- involves loss of circadian rhythm
- is similar to the depressive position
- is due to introjection of a loss object (according to ego psychology)
- is similar to mourning
- may see the patient regress to the oral stage
- has the highest comorbidity with panic disorder.

Clinical features include:
- turning down of corners of the mouth
- central vertical furrowing of the brow
- raised medial aspect of the eyebrows
- limited vocabulary
- hunched posture
- staring at the floor
- psychomotor retardation (including decreased rate of blinking)
- irritability
- guilt
- suicidal ideation
- nihilistic delusions
- *no* erotic delusions
- overeating.

May present as:
- hysterical conversion
- anxiety state
- shop-lifting
- hypochondriasis.

Biochemical changes include:
- reduced prolactin response to infusion of L-tryptophan (L-tryptophan is a 5HT precursor and increases 5HT concentrations)
- reduced CSF 5HIAA concentrations
- reduced growth hormone response to clonidine
- disorders of cortisol metabolism which may precipitate episodes
- disorders of thyroxine metabolism which may precipitate episodes
- blunted prolactin response to apomorphine
- hypercortisolaemia
- blunted ACTH response to corticotrophin.

Epidemiology:
- 20% lifetime risk (5–12% men, 9–26% women)
- point prevalence is between 4 and 7% (1.8–3.2% for men, 2.0–9.3% for women)
- incidence 80–200/100, 000/year (men), 250–780/100, 000/year (women)
- point prevalence of depressive symptoms is 10–30%
- higher incidence in unmarried people.

Risk factors:
- living in an urban area
- being unemployed
- being working class.

Physical illnesses particularly associated with depression include:
- Parkinson's disease
- Cushing's syndrome
- influenza
- infectious mononucleosis
- head injury
- cerebral tumours
- CVA (but depression is largely determined by social factors rather than the site of the lesion)
- subarachnoid haemorrhage, especially with posterior communicating artery aneurysms.

Immunological changes include:
- increased interleukin-2 activity
- reduced natural killer cells
- increased T-cell replication.

Immunological changes are possibly mediated by:
- hypothalamic–pituitary–adrenal axis dysfunction modulated by the Type II glucocorticoid receptor.

Biological symptoms include:
- weight loss
- diurnal variation of mood
- constipation
- loss of libido
- amenorrhoea
- sleep disturbance (with early morning waking)
- loss of appetite.

In the elderly, depression:
- may present with somatic complaints (a finding from both inpatient and outpatient studies)
- may present as:
  - food refusal
  - incontinence
  - screaming
  - aggressive behaviour
  - anxiety
- is frequently precipitated by bereavement
- is associated with cognitive impairment in 10–20%
- is *not* associated with deficits in higher cortical function.

After recovery from depressive stupor, patients can remember what was happening.

Relapses are increased by:
- a highly critical attitude of the spouse (Hooley & Teasdale).

Can be differentiated from anorexia nervosa by the presence of:
- bradycardia (in anorexia nervosa)
- psychomotor retardation
- poor appetite (in depression).

Risk factors for persistent mood abnormalities in people with affective disorder:
- female gender
- past medical history of thyroid disease
- length of time between onset of depressive symptoms and introduction of treatment (most important)
- alcohol abuse
- inadequate treatment
- non-compliance with treatment.

Affective disorder, aetiology – Family studies
- First-degree relatives of people with unipolar depression have more chance of getting depression, but their chance of getting BPAD is unchanged.
- Relatives of BPAD patients have a greater chance of both BPAD and depression.

Twin studies
- Concordance rate for monozygous twins is 67%, for dizygous is 20%.
- Monozygous and dizygous concordance rates for bipolar affective disorder are 79% and 19% respectively. For unipolar depression, the monozygous and dizygous concordance rates are 54% and 24% respectively.

Molecular genetics
- BPAD has been found as an X-linked disorder linked to colour blindness and glucose-6-phosphatase deficiency
- It has *not* been linked to chromosome 11 in Amish families.

Personality
- Cyclothymic personality disorder is a persistent instability of mood with numerous periods of mild depression and mild elation. It may predispose to BPAD.
- Depressive personality disorder overlaps with affective disorders and often co-exists.

Psychosocial stressors
- High expressed emotion (Vaughn & Leff) increases relapses in depressed patients.
- Depressed people are more sensitive to critical remarks than people with schizophrenia.
- Excess life events occur in the six months before a depressive episode starts.

- Brown & Harris identified **vulnerability factors** – these increase the risk of depression if a **provoking agent** is present:
  - having more than two children (under 14 years of age) at home
  - not working outside the home
  - lack of a confiding relationship
  - loss of mother before the age of 11 years.

Physical illness – *see* Depression, secondary.

Psychological factors
- Learned helplessness.
- Beck's **cognitive triad** (a negative view of self, present situation and future).
- Beck's **schemata** – stable cognitive patterns forming the basis for situational interpretation.
- Beck's **cognitive errors** – systematic errors in thinking that maintain depressed peoples' beliefs in negative concepts:
  - arbitrary inference
  - selective abstraction
  - overgeneralisation
  - magnification/minimisation
  - dichotomous thinking
  - personalisation.

Cognitive-behavioural factors
- learned helplessness
- impaired social skills.

Neurotransmitters
- Schildkraut's monoamine hypothesis (1965):
  - depression = central monoamine depletion
  - mania = central monoamine excess.
- evidence for the monoamine hypothesis:
  - TCAs inhibit presynaptic noradrenaline and 5HT reuptake
  - MAOIs prevent breakdown
  - SSRIs increase 5HT
  - antidepressants can cause mania (in BPAD)
  - amfetamine causes catecholamine release and lifts mood
  - reserpine (extracted from *Rauwolfia*) depletes central monoamine stores of catecholamines and 5HT and can cause severe depression and suicide
  - CSF 5HIAA (a 5HT metabolite) is low in depressed patients.

- evidence against the monoamine hypothesis:
  - antidepressants have effects immediately but take weeks to work
  - not all monoamine reuptake inhibitors are antidepressants (eg cocaine).
- evidence for abnormal 5HT function in affective disorder:
  - there is low CSF 5HIAA in depressed patients
  - low brain and platelet 5HT transporter sites are found in depressed patients
  - high brain and platelet 5HT binding sites are found in depressed patients
  - previously depressed SSRI responders who restrict dietary tryptophan have prompt relapses
  - low plasma tryptophan concentrations are seen in depression
  - all SSRIs are effective antidepressants
  - 5HT function is reduced in depression and recovers with treatment.
- adaptive changes in receptors:
  - at the same time that treatment starts to work, central receptors change (α- and β-adrenergic and 5HT receptors).

Neuroendocrine factors
- Hypothalamic–pituitary–adrenal axis
  - the normal circadian rhythm of cortisol secretion is altered, the normal morning peak is increased for longer and may be earlier
- the secretion of other substances is increased:
  - ACTH (should increase in CRH stimulation test but doesn't)
  - cortisol (should decrease in dexamethasone suppression test but doesn't in 60%)
  - β-endorphin
  - prolactin.

Affiliation – Humans have a desire to affiliate with others. Schachter suggests reasons why:
- Lessening of anxiety – we feel more secure in a group.
- Lessening the importance of our own concerns relative to those of others – which reduces anxiety again.
- Cognitive clarity – associating with others brings more information.
- Self-evaluation – we can form opinions of ourselves more clearly on the basis of our experiences of others' reactions to us. This reduces anxiety again.

Affiliation/friendship is chosen according to six factors (described by Deaux):

- **Propinquity factor** (= proximity)
  We like people we live nearer to or see more often (even people we have little to do with). This is because there is a feeling of familiarity. If someone is more available, there is less social cost in interaction. The expectation that continued interaction is inevitable gives motivation to get on with them.
- **Similarity**
  People with similar attitudes get on better than people with different attitudes.
- **Complementarity of needs**
  People choose relationships so that their needs can be gratified mutually. This is a long-term factor (eg one partner is dominant and the other submissive, in a marriage).
- **Pleasantness**
  We assess people to determine what sort of behaviour we are likely to be on the receiving end of if we interact with them. If they are kind, we will receive kindness and are more likely to like them.
- **Physical attractiveness**
  We judge physically attractive people more favourably. They are more likely to be offered jobs, more likely to get higher marks and more likely to be treated favourably.
- **Reciprocity**
  We reciprocate attraction. We like those who like us and dislike those who dislike us. People with high self-esteem are less swayed by this, however.

After-images – Are a type of visual hallucination perceived in the field of vision when one has looked at a bright light and then looked away. They are hallucinations because they occur after looking away from a bright object. This object is not in the field of vision at the time that the after-image is seen, so it must be a hallucination.
They are short lived.

Ageing –
Physical
- most elderly people are well
- brains are similar to younger people in the clinically well elderly
- there may be neurofibrillary tangles in a few cells of the hippocampus and entorhinal cortex
- senile plaques are also seen in the hippocampus, superficial layers of the entorhinal cortex, amygdala and neocortex

- there is neuronal degeneration in certain areas
- some Lewy bodies may be seen
- amyloid is present
- granulovacuolar degeneration occurs.

Psychological
- capabilities change but are not generally diminished:
  - processing speed (fluid intelligence) is lost
  - experienced-based judgement (crystallised intelligence) is increased. This is based on tasks learned over a lifetime, relying on overlearned abilities, and is most resistant to age-related decline
  - psychomotor slowing is seen
  - short-term memory is normal
  - working memory reduces slightly
  - long-term memory is impaired by poor retrieval, with semantic memory relatively spared
  - memory of source is impaired, due to frontal lobe decline
  - multi-tasking is impaired
  - cautiousness and rigidity increase
  - capacity for abstract thought decreases
  - personality is preserved
- adjustment is described by the:
  - activity theory – continuing full engagement with life, interests, social contact
  - disengagement theory- diminished family and social roles cause increasing introversion
- chronic neuroses improve with old age
- dysthymic personalities persist
- good copers with old age have **integrated** personalities
- poor copers have **passive-dependent** or **disintegrated** personalities
- ethnicity and old age:
  - **Age as leveller hypothesis** – everyone is disadvantaged in old age, so previous disadvantages based on ethnicity are masked
  - **Double jeopardy hypothesis** – if you're in a minority *and* old, you're doubly disadvantaged.

Factors affecting pharmacokinetics include:
- decrease in total body mass
- decrease in proportion of body mass made of water
- increase in proportion of body mass made of adipose tissue – so volume of distribution for benzodiazepines increases

- decrease in proportion of body mass made of muscle
- increase in gastric pH
- decreased gastric emptying
- decreased splanchnic circulation
- decreased gastrointestinal absorptive surface
- changes in plasma protein concentration (due to illness)
- reduced hepatic biotransformation
- reduced metabolically active tissue
- reduced glomerular filtration rate
- reduced renal tubular function.

Aggression – Children imitate observed aggression. Some studies suggest a link between exposure to televised violence and aggression in boys. Mechanisms for this include:
- teaching aggressive styles of conduct
- increasing arousal
- desensitisation to violence and presentation of violent person as 'goodie'
- distortion of views about conflict resolution.

Social learning theory rejects the concept of aggression having drive-like properties.
Aggression diminishes with age.

Agitation – Is *not* a feeling of increased energy (that's characteristic of mania).
Is seen in thyrotoxicosis and in depression (especially in the elderly).

Agnosia – The inability to interpret, recognise the significance of and understand sensory stimuli, even though the sensory pathways and sensorium are intact (ie it doesn't result from impairment of the sensory pathways, mental deterioration, disorders of consciousness/attention or lack of familiarity with the sensory stimulus).
Caused by lesions of the association cortex around primary sensory receptive areas.
May occur in any modality:
- visual agnosia = cortical blindness
- object recognition/knowledge of object = associative agnosia
- analysis of shape/size/colour = apperceptive agnosia.

Agnosia, apperceptive – Inability to recognise shape/size/colour.
Causes inability to copy objects or drawings.
Caused by bilateral lesions of parieto-occipital cortex.

Agnosia, associative – Able to produce reasonable copies of objects/drawings but unable to identify them.
Results from bilateral damage to the parieto-occipital areas.

Agnosia, auditory – Occurs when a patient has no deafness but cannot recognise familiar sounds.

Agnosia, finger – Is the loss of ability to recognise, name, identify or select individual fingers, of their own or someone else's body:
- results in the patient not knowing which of their fingers has been touched
- is a form of autotopagnosia confined to the fingers
- is a feature of Gerstmann's syndrome.

Agnosia, topographical – Is caused by lesions of the non-dominant parietal lobe.

Agnosia, visual – Causes a patient to be unable to recognise an object when looking at it (despite adequate eyesight), but be able to recognise it when allowed to touch it.

Anosognosia – Failure to identify functional defects caused by disease. Usually seen as unawareness of left hemiplegia or sensory inattention following lesion in right parietal lobe.

Agoraphobia – Was described by Westphal.

Recognised features include:
- panic attacks (which are more common than in other phobic disorders)
- anxious cognitions
- anticipatory anxiety (defining feature of phobia)
- occurrence mainly in women (male : female ratio = 2–3 : 1)
- usual onset in early- to mid-20s, with a second peak in the mid-30s
- sufferers are introverted and neurotic
- depressive symptoms occur
- depression, depersonalisation and obsessional thoughts are more common than in other panic disorders
- MAOIs help
- course may be chronic
- treatment of choice is behaviour therapy
- clinical features can include depersonalisation
- is associated with *mitral* valve prolapse
- is associated with fear of:
  - open spaces

- fear of leaving home
- fear of places where help is difficult to access
- has normal class distribution
- is associated with decreased libido
- is the most common phobia seen by psychiatrists (accounting for 60% of phobias seen by psychiatrists)
- course is chronic and debilitating rather than fluctuating
- serious marital problems are more common in people with agoraphobia than in controls.

Has been explained in young housewives in terms of 'role rejection', when women are unable to reject their role overtly but effectively reject their role covertly (and unconsciously), by producing symptoms.

Agraphognosia – *aka* agraphaesthesia
Failure to identify letters or numbers traced on the skin.

AIDS – Acquired immunodeficiency syndrome.

Ainsworth – Described the 'strange situation experiment'.

Akathisia – Subjective feeling of restlessness or uneasiness. Can be part of tardive dyskinesia, but this is not usual. Characterised by:
- motor restlessness
- subjective feeling of tension
- inability to tolerate inactivity,
together giving rise to restless movement.
- Acute akathisia is seen in 20% of people receiving antipsychotics, within the first few days or two weeks of treatment. There is also a late onset form.
- The cause is thought to be blockade of dopamine receptors in the mesolimbic and mesocortical dopamine pathways.
- Anticholinergics are little use but propranolol may help.
- Relatives complain of this more frequently than the patients themselves.
- Akathisia is a risk factor for suicide in people with schizophrenia.

Albert, Little – Experimented on by Watson & Rayner, 1920.
Little Albert was presented with a white rat (the conditioned stimulus, CS) and then subject to a loud noise (unconditioned stimulus, UCS) which induced fear (unconditioned response, UCR/conditioned response, CR) of the white rat initially, and then of all white furry things (as a result of generalisation).

Alcohol abuse – Is associated with:
- hepatic fatty infiltration
- hepatitis

- cirrhosis
- palmar erythema
- oesophageal varices
- gastritis
- pancreatitis
- peptic ulcer disease
- lung cancer (because most heavy drinkers also smoke)
- TB (due to malnutrition and poor hygiene)
- pathological jealousy
- 60% have a high MCV.

Alcohol dependence – Nearly 50% have another psychiatric diagnosis.
- Odds ratios of comorbid diagnoses:
    - antisocial personality disorder   21
    - mania   6
    - schizophrenia   4
    - depression   2
- Mania is a more common comorbid diagnosis than schizophrenia.
- Onset is late teens for males, later for females.
- Risk factors:
    - high social class
    - low social class
    - urban areas
    - being separated
    - ready access with little social restraint (eg publicans, entertainers and journalists)
    - male gender (male : female ratio is 4 : 1).

Clinical features include:
- anxiety in the early morning (as feature of withdrawal)
- tremor
- convulsions
- ocular palsies
- nystagmus
- central pontine myelinosis
- peripheral neuropathy (causing paraesthesiae, extremity pain and weak limbs)
- osteoporosis
- reduced erythrocyte transketolase activity
- abnormal pyruvate tolerance test.

Problems occurring with clouding of consciousness include:
- Wernicke's encephalopathy

- delirium tremens.

Problems occurring in clear consciousness include:
- alcoholic hallucinosis
- Korsakoff's syndrome.

Alcoholism – Vulnerability factors include:
- enhanced response to thyrotropin-releasing hormone
- reduced α activity on EEG
- increased static ataxia
- hyper-reactive autonomic nervous system
- increased latency and reduced amplitude of the P300 event-related potential
- possibly hyperactivity in childhood
- borderline personality disorder.

Aldehyde dehydrogenase – Is deficient in 50% of Chinese people. Activity is reduced in alcoholism.

Alertness, phasic – Reflects temporary variations in arousal in response to novel stimuli.

Alertness, tonic – Reflects intrinsic changes in the level of arousal (eg diurnal rhythm).

Alexithymia – Was described by Sifneos.
Individuals with alexithymia have difficulties recognising and describing their own feelings. They also have a diminished capacity for fantasy.

Allport – Described **discrimination**.

Alogia – Poverty of thought.

Alprazolam – Is associated with inter-dose rebound anxiety.

Altruism – Giving or sharing with no obvious self-gain. Caring for and helping others in need.

One of Yalom's therapeutic factors in group therapy.

Altruism as defence mechanism
Altruism is a higher defence mechanism acting when the individual dedicates himself to meeting the needs of others and thereby deals with emotional conflict or stressors. There is gratification from the responses of others or vicarious gratification.

Biosocial explanation

Altruism is a behaviour that helps close relatives and therefore makes one's genes (as shared by close relatives) more likely to survive, so is encouraged by evolution.

Reciprocal altruism
Gives the members of the 'herd' a better chance of survival. Based on the assumption that altruism is reciprocated, thereby benefiting a group.

Learning theory approach
- Basic learning – classical conditioning/operant conditioning
- Social learning – differs from conditioning in that:
  - modelling (observational learning) is more prominent
  - cognitive factors play a part in stimulus–response.

Telling, reinforcement (praise) and modelling (seeing others doing it) have parts to play in making children helpful, but telling them is of limited value unless the instructor is seen to be helpful themself.

Social exchange theory
We have an unwritten contract with society which dictates how we behave in certain situations. An example is given of an elderly person who retires. They stop being an economically active member of society but receive more leisure time as a result.

The 'Just world' hypothesis
This is based on the idea that you will get what you deserve. It isn't true.

Attribution process
If one of your self-attributes is 'helpfulness', you're much more likely to help someone in a given situation.

Social norm theory
Two social norms are important in helpful behaviour:
- The principle of reciprocity – if someone helps you, you will help them in return.
- The social responsibility norm – you have a duty to help others in need.
- Social norms are dependent on cultural factors. It is widely accepted that children in Japan are more helpful than children in the USA.

Ambitendence – A form of ambivalence. The patient starts to make a movement but, before completing it, starts the opposite movement. Seen in schizophrenia and learning difficulties.

Amine, secondary – Secondary amine TCAs include:

A

- trimipramine
- desipramine
- nortriptyline
- protriptyline
- maprotiline.

Secondary amines are more potent noradrenaline reuptake inhibitors than tertiary amines.

Amine, tertiary – Tertiary amine TCAs include:

- imipramine
- amitriptyline
- clomipramine
- amoxapine
- doxepin.

Tertiary amine TCAs

- have more effect as serotonin reuptake inhibitors than secondary amines
- are much more active at muscarinic acetylcholinergic receptors, α-adrenoceptors and histamine receptors than secondary amines, and so have more side-effects.

Amino acids, excitatory – Include:

- glutamic acid
- aspartic acid.

Amino acids, inhibitory – Include:

- glycine – increases calcium flux at NMDA receptors
- taurine
- adenosine
- GABA.

Amitriptyline – Has sedative properties.
Is excreted in very small quantities in breast milk.
Is metabolised to nortriptyline.
Predictors of good clinical response include:

- middle insomnia
- late insomnia
- anorexia.

Amnesia, diencephalic – Is characterised by loss of insight.

Amnesia, hippocampal – Is characterised by retention of insight.

Amnesia, catathymic – Repression of information that cannot therefore be remembered because of associated painful affect.

Amnesia, post-traumatic – Is the time between an injury and the resumption of normal continuous memory.

Correlates with:
- psychiatric disability
- change of personality after head injury
- generalised intellectual impairment
- dysphasia
- persistent deficits in memory.

Amnesia, psychogenic – Is global for specific events.
Is associated with criminal behaviour, relationship traumas and loss of personal identity.

Amnesia, retrograde – Is the time between the injury and the last memory recalled before the injury.
Is not a good predictor of outcome.

Amnesia, transient global –
- Seen in 60–70-year-olds.
- Sudden onset.
- Lasts a few hours.
- Related to migraine.

Amnesic syndrome – *aka* Korsakoff syndrome, dysmnesic syndrome *see* Appendix 1.

Amok –
- Occurs in Malay men.
- Often follows an argument, insult or personal loss and social drinking.
- Consists of a period of social withdrawal followed by a sudden outburst of homicidal aggression in which the sufferer will attack anyone. This period lasts for several hours until the sufferer is overwhelmed or killed, and is followed by deep sleep or stupor for several days, followed by amnesia for the episode.
- Is connected with cultural ideas about loss of self-esteem or 'face' and warfare.
- It was very common in Malaya at the start of the 19th century but has almost disappeared today.
- Most people running amok have no mental illness, but the most common diagnosis is schizophrenia.

Amphetamines – Chronic use causes schizophreniform psychosis.

Amygdala – Lesions cause memory loss.

Anaclitic – Means depending on others.

Anaemia, pernicious – Is an autoimmune condition causing destruction of cells secreting intrinsic factor (a carrier for absorption of vitamin B_{12}) and therefore anaemia.
Is not a feature of Wernicke's encephalopathy.

Analgesia, psychological – Is the use of psychological means (including hypnosis and explanation) to provide pain relief.
When used for labour, gives 5–10% of women complete or almost complete relief of pain.

Analysis, functional – A type of assessment similar to behavioural assessment but which looks at stimuli that seem to cause specific behaviours, rather than just the behaviours themselves.

Analysis through the group – Is associated only with Foulkes.

Anankastic personality disorder – Is the ICD-10 version of the DSM-IV obsessive–compulsive personality disorder.

Features include:
- lack of adaptability to new situations
- rigidity of view and inflexibility in approaching problems
- stubbornness
- being easily upset by change
- preference for safe and familiar routine
- lack of imagination
- failure to take advantage of opportunities
- an inhibiting perfectionism/scrupulousness/preoccupation with details, which makes ordinary work difficult
- excessive pedantry
- undue preoccupation with productivity to the exclusion of pleasure and interpersonal relationships
- excessive doubt and caution
- painfully guilty preoccupation with wrongdoing, which stifles enjoyment
- lack of humour, coupled with moralism and judgemental behaviour
- miserliness, not giving or enjoying receiving gifts (also known as parsimony)
- indecision
- sensitivity to criticism and an expectation of being judged harshly

- little expression of emotion but underlying smouldering anger and resentment, especially towards those who've interfered with normal routines.

Associated with secondary depression and a relatively high incidence of psychosis (usually reactive affective or paranoid, and most often transient) and is not rare (but was once thought to be so).

Andresen – Described positive and negative symptoms of schizophrenia.

Anhedonia – Inability to experience pleasure.
Is more than flattened affect, because patients describe it as being unpleasant *in itself*.
Is a feature of both depression and schizophrenia.
Associated with long-term use of phenobarbitone.
Detected by depression rating scales.
Supposedly diagnostic of major depression.

Anomia – *aka* nominal dysphasia/nominal aphasia
Inability to name things.

Anorexia nervosa – Is deliberate weight loss resulting in undernutrition with secondary endocrine and metabolic disturbance.

In ICD-10, it requires:
- body weight at least 15% less than expected
- BMI < 17.5 kg/m^2
- self-induced weight loss by:
  - avoidance of fattening foods
  - *and any one of*:
    - self-induced vomiting
    - self-induced purging
    - excessive exercise
    - use of appetite suppressants and/or diuretics
- body-image distortion (a dread of fatness persisting as an intrusive, over-valued idea)
- amenorrhoea in women/loss of libido and potency in men with endocrine disorder. Increased growth hormone and cortisol, low FSH and LH, abnormal peripheral thyroid metabolism and abnormalities of insulin secretion
- if onset is prepubertal, pubertal events are delayed or arrested. Puberty may only be completed on recovery from anorexia nervosa.

A

Diagnostic features include:
- amenorrhoea
- body weight maintained at 15% below that expected
- weight loss induced by an avoidance of fattening foods and at least one of:
  - self-induced vomiting
  - self-induced purging
  - excessive exercise
  - use of appetite suppressants and/or diuretics
  - body image distortion
  - delay in the sequence of pubertal events (if onset is prepubertal).

Clinical features:
- morbid fear of fatness/excessive pursuit of thinness
- denial of problem
- distorted body image
- fear of losing control of eating
- problems with separation and independence
- depressive feelings (eg insomnia, lack of concentration, irritability)
- suicidal ideas
- obsessional thoughts and rituals (may improve with weight gain)
- preoccupation with thoughts of food, enjoyment of cooking for others, dislike of eating in public
- social withdrawal.

Physical signs:
- emaciation
- slowed basal metabolic rate, low blood pressure, bradycardia
- cardiac arrhythmias/failure
- bradycardia is usual but tachycardia can result from electrolyte disturbance
- peripheral oedema
- amenorrhoea and loss of libido
- reproductive atrophy (of uterus and ovaries and cystic, multifollicular ovarian changes) as a result of hypothalamic hypogonadism (low gonadotrophins causing low oestrogen)
- osteoporosis – low calcium intake and absorption resulting in pathological fractures after 10 years
- reduced oestrogen and increased cortisol levels
- bone pain and deformity
- hypoglycaemia
- dehydration

- hypothermia, cold intolerance
- seizures
- delayed gastric emptying
- acute gastric dilation
- pancreatitis
- tetany
- degeneration of myenteric plexus of bowel – cathartic colon, constipation
- reduced growth
- muscle wasting (cardiac and skeletal)
- mitral valve prolapse
- proximal myopathy
- impaired liver function
- impaired renal function (due to chronic dehydration and hypokalaemia)
- EEG abnormalities as a result of metabolic encephalopathy
- increased ventricle size with respect to brain size, due to starvation.

Skin changes:
- lanugo hair
- purpura (due to reduced skin collagen and bone marrow suppression)
- carotenodermia
- calluses on the hands (Russell's sign)
- bruising
- dry skin.

Features caused by self-induced vomiting:
- erosion of tooth enamel
- dental caries
- parotid gland enlargement.

Haematological abnormalities:
- hypokalaemia (causing arrhythmias, cardiac arrest, renal damage)
- hypoglycaemia
- metabolic alkalosis
- hypomagnesaemia
- low zinc concentrations
- hypophosphataemia
- increased serum amylase
- hypercholesterolaemia
- hypercarotenaemia
- leukopenia with (relative) lymphocytosis

- normochromic normocytic anaemia
- low tri-iodothyronine
- low oestrogen (in women)/testosterone (in men)
- diurnal LH secretion is essentially prepubertal
- thrombocytopenia
- low erythrocyte sedimentation rate
- if severe can cause pancytopenia and bone marrow hypoplasia.

Other features:
- overeating – 50% binge-eat
- suicide relative risk is 200
- onset is typically at 16–17 years of age
- males have a better prognosis.

It is rare in Africa.

There is *NOT*:
- loss of appetite
- alcohol abuse.

Denial is commonly seen.

Anticholinergics – Are used to treat iatrogenic Parkinson's and include:
- orphenadrine
- procyclidine
- benzhexol
- biperiden
- methixene.

When given concomitantly with chlorpromazine they *reduce* the plasma concentration of that drug.

Anticholinesterases – Include physostigmine.

Antidepressant combinations – The following are valid combinations:

- Lithium + TCA/mianserin
- Lithium + SSRI
  - risk of 5HT neurotoxicity
  - aim for prophylactic lithium concentration (0.5–0.8 mmol/l)
- TCA + SSRI
  - but SSRIs increase plasma TCA levels, so use small TCA dose with monitoring of level
- Tri-iodothyronine + TCA

- beware cardiovascular disease
- MAOI + lithium
- MAOI + TCA
  - use *cautiously* because of risk of serotonin syndrome
  - MAOIs must be added to the TCA
  - *BUT* don't use
    - clomipramine
    - imipramine
  - generally consider the MAOI and TCA combination unsuitable for exam purposes
- MAOI + SSRI
- TCA + thyroxine
- TCA + thyroxine + lithium.

Antidepressants – Increase δ waves on EEG (ie slow waves).

Antidepressants, MAOIs – *see* Monoamine oxidase inhibitors.

Antidepressants, SSRIs – Important side-effects are:
- dose-related gastrointestinal:
  - nausea
  - vomiting
  - diarrhoea
- headache   } Common
- drowsiness
- dry mouth
- restlessness
- sleep disturbance
- anxiety
- delayed orgasm.

Levels are increased by administration of enzyme inhibitors and reduced by enzyme inducers.
Don't have major sedative effects at therapeutic doses (unlike TCAs, which do).

Can be used in hepatic failure, unlike TCAs.

Include:
- citalopram
- fluvoxamine   } no active metabolites
- paroxetine
- fluoxetine   } active metabolites with
- sertraline   long half-lives

Antidepressants, tetracyclic – Are sedating and reduce accommodation.

Include:
- maprotiline
  - cautioned in epilepsy
- mianserin
  - causes arthritis
  - is non-cardiotoxic and safe in overdose
  - stimulates α_1-adrenoceptor on 5HT cell bodies
  - is an α_2-adrenoceptor antagonist on 5HT nerve
  - terminals
  - is a 5HT2 and 5HT3 antagonist.

Antidepressants, tricyclic – *aka* TCAs

History
- TCAs – 1955
- TCAs – Kuhn found imipramine to have antidepressant effects.

Include:
- amitriptyline ▼
- amoxapine
- clomipramine ▼
- dothiepin ▼
- doxepin ▼
- imipramine
- lofepramine
- nortriptyline
- trimipramine ▼

and related drugs:
- maprotiline ▼
- mianserin ▼
- trazodone ▼

(▼ = sedating)

Side-effects include:
- Antimuscarinic (by blockade of muscarinic acetylcholine receptors):
- central:
  - convulsions
  - pyrexia
- peripheral:

31

- dry mouth
- blurred vision and reduced accommodation
- urinary retention
- constipation
- nasal congestion
- Antihistaminergic (by blockade of H1 receptors):
  - weight gain
  - drowsiness – major sedative effects at therapeutic doses
- Antiadrenergic (by blockade of α_1-adrenoceptors):
  - drowsiness
  - postural hypotension
  - sexual dysfunction
  - cognitive impairment
- Antiserotoninergic (by blockade of 5HT2 and 5HT1c receptors):
  - weight gain
  - membrane stabilisation effects:
    - cardiotoxicity
    - inhibition of intraventricular conduction (causing ECG changes of QT prolongation)
    - reduced seizure threshold (a paradoxical effect)
- Other effects:
  - Cardiovascular – ECG changes:
    - arrhythmias (*not* bradycardia)
    - postural hypotension
    - tachycardia
    - syncope
    - QT prolongation
    - *not* ST-segment elevation
  - Allergic/haematological:
    - agranulocytosis
    - leukopenia
    - eosinophilia
    - thrombocytopenia
    - skin rash (common)
    - photosensitisation
    - facial oedema
    - allergic cholestatic jaundice
    - *not* haemolytic anaemia
  - Endocrine:
    - testicular enlargement
    - gynaecomastia
    - galactorrhoea

- Sundry other:
  - fine tremor (common)
  - black tongue
  - paralytic ileus
  - sweating
  - hyponatraemia (especially in elderly)
  - neuroleptic malignant syndrome (NMS) – very rare
  - abnormal liver function tests
  - movement disorders
  - pyrexia
  - hypomania/mania
  - blood glucose changes.

Withdrawal effects:
- nausea
- anxiety
- sweating
- gastrointestinal symptoms
- insomnia.

TCAs:
- are lipophilic
- are strongly bound to plasma proteins
- are metabolised more slowly with age
- those that are tertiary amines preferentially block uptake of 5HT
- are sedative compared with SSRIs
- have some affinity for dopamine D2 receptors.

TCAs act at:
- muscarinic acetylcholine receptors – blockade
- H1 receptors – blockade
- α_1-adrenoceptors – blockade
- 5HT2/5HT1c receptors – blockade
- membranes – stabilise.

The following interact with TCAs:
- oral contraceptive pill – antagonises antidepressant action
- phenytoin – reduces plasma concentration of TCAs (and TCAs antagonise action of phenytoin)
- disulfiram – inhibits the metabolism of TCAs
- fluoxetine – increases blood concentrations of TCAs.

In the elderly, TCAs have:
- increased plasma half-life
- increased steady-state concentrations
- increased volume of distribution
- increased effects on postural hypotension
- increased anticholinergic side-effects (delirium, retention, glaucoma).

Contraindications
- Hepatic failure.

Types of TCA

Sedating
amitriptyline❸
clomipramine❸   used in OCD
dothiepin
doxepin❸
trimipramine

Non-sedating
amoxapine❸
imipramine❸
lofepramine
nortriptyline

❸ = Tertiary amines: are more selective than other selective serotonin reuptake inhibitors;
compared with secondary amines, they:
have more effects at muscarinic acetylcholine receptors, α-adrenoceptors, and histamine receptors, and therefore have more side-effects.

Antiepileptics – Are generally enzyme inducers and lower the levels of TCAs.

Antimuscarinics – = anticholinergics.

Antipsychotics – *aka* neuroleptics, major tranquillisers
- Reduce psychomotor excitement and control some symptoms of psychosis.
- Act by blocking dopamine receptors (especially D2 receptors – except clozapine, which acts at D1, D2 and D4). Therapeutic strength correlates with dopamine receptor blocking potency, with antipsychosis at 65–85% receptor occupancy.
- Extrapyramidal side-effects are caused by dopamine receptor

blocking in basal ganglia.
- They also block noradrenaline receptors and acetylcholine receptors, causing side-effects.
- Reduce β waves (fast waves) and increase δ and θ (theta) waves (slow waves) on the EEG.
- *Increase* dopamine production and turnover, with an increase in dopamine metabolites.
- Are absorbed in the jejunum as a result of the high pH there.

History
- Reserpine was discovered in 1931 and first used as treatment for schizophrenia in 1953 (Kline).
- Chlorpromazine was synthesised by Charpentier in 1950.
- Laborit later reported that chlorpromazine could induce an artificial hibernation.
- Paraire & Sigwald and Delay & Deniker reported that chlorpromazine was efficacious in the treatment of psychosis.
- Haloperidol was synthesised by Janssen in 1958.

Typical antipsychotics
Different classes vary more in side-effect profile than in therapeutic effects:
- antagonise:
  - dopamine
  - muscarinic acetylcholine receptors
  - adrenaline
  - noradrenaline
  - histamine
- anti-dopaminergic action:
  - occurs postsynaptically at D2 receptors
  - correlates with potency
  - has important effects on the mesolimbic–mesocortical pathway
  - has effects on the tuberoinfundibular pathway that cause hormonal side-effects (hyperprolactinaemia)
  - causes extrapyramidal side-effects by antidopaminergic action on the nigrostriatal pathway (the nigrostriatal tract connects the substantia nigra in the midbrain with the striatum in the basal ganglia)
- central antimuscarinic acetylcholine effects cause:
  - convulsions
  - pyrexia (dose-related)
- peripheral antimuscarinic acetylcholine effects cause:
  - dry mouth

- blurred vision
- urinary retention
- constipation
- nasal congestion
- anti-α_1-adrenergic action causes:
  - postural hypotension
  - ejaculatory failure
- antihistaminergic action causes:
  - drowsiness
- other side-effects include:
  - photosensitisation – especially chlorpromazine
  - hypothermia/pyrexia – dose-related
  - sensitivity reactions
  - neuroleptic malignant syndrome.

Chronic high-dose use causes:
- lens opacity
- corneal opacity
- purple skin
- purple conjunctivae
- purple corneae/retinae
- decrease in growth hormone
- akathisia.

Types of typical antipsychotic
- phenothiazines (3-ring structure with one long side-chain)
  - prominent weight gain
  - increase in appetite
  - decreased absorption with colloidal antacids
  - reduce the seizure threshold
- aliphatic/aminoalkyl – less potent, most sedative
  - chlorpromazine
  - methotrimeprazine
  - promazine
- piperazine – least sedating, most extrapyramidal side-effects, most potent
  - trifluoperazine
  - fluphenazine
  - prochlorperazine
  - perphenazine
- piperidine – less potent, more sedating, fewer extrapyramidal side-effects
  - pipothiazine (palmitate)

- pericyazine
- butyrophenones – different structure, powerful, extrapyramidal side-effects common, not sedating
  - the -peridols
- thioxanthenes – structure and effects similar to phenothiazines
  - flupenthixol
  - zuclopenthixol
- diphenylbutylpiperidines – similar to butyrophenones – but with longer half-life, so daily dosage possible
  - pimozide
  - fluspirilene.

Atypical antipsychotics

Include:
- substituted benzamides – highly selective D2 receptor antagonists, few extrapyramidal side-effects, non-sedating, not antiacetylcholinergic
  - sulpiride
  - remoxipride
- benzisoxamole – potent dopamine D2 receptor and 5HT2 antagonists
  - risperidone
- dibenzazepines
  - clozapine
  - loxapine
- thioridazine
- olanzapine
- sertindole
- zotepine.

Other drugs with antipsychotic actions include:
- tetrabenazine
- oxypertine.

Dose equivalents:

Chlorpromazine	100 mg
Clozapine	50 mg
Droperidol	4 mg
Haloperidol	2–3 mg
Loxapine	10–20 mg
Pimozide	2 mg
Risperidone	0.5–1 mg
Sulpiride	200 mg

| Thioridazine | 100 mg |
| Trifluoperazine | 5 mg. |

Antisocial personality disorder – Is the DSM-IV version of the ICD-10 Dissocial personality disorder

Anxiety – Somatic symptoms of *severe* anxiety include:
- amoxapine
- impotence
- diarrhoea
- hyperventilation
- sighing
- constipation.

- **Psychological**
  - fearful anticipation
  - irritability
  - sensitivity to noise
  - restlessness
  - poor concentration
  - worrying thoughts
  - reduced appetite
  - subjective sense of constriction.
- **Physical**
  - Gastrointestinal
    - dry mouth
    - difficulty swallowing
    - epigastric discomfort
    - excess wind
    - frequent/loose motions
  - Ventilatory
    - constriction in the chest
    - difficulty inhaling
    - hyperventilation
  - Cardiovascular
    - palpitations
    - discomfort in chest
    - awareness of missed beats
    - tachycardia
  - Genitourinary
    - frequent/urgent micturition
    - failure of erection (as distinct from loss of libido, which suggests depression)

- menstrual discomfort
- amenorrhoea
- Central and peripheral nervous systems
  - tremor (especially fine finger tremor)
  - prickling sensations
  - tinnitus
  - dizziness (*not* rotational)
  - headache
  - aching muscles
  - blurred vision
  - hyperreflexia.
- **Sleep**
  - insomnia
  - night terrors.
- **Other**
  - depression
  - obsessions
  - depersonalisation.

Anxiety can be a feature in depression of any severity and its severity does not necessarily correlate with the severity of the depression. A subjective sense of constriction is characteristic of the mood of anxiety.

Psychoanalytic theory regards the following as important aetiological factors:
- birth trauma
- fear of castration
- separation.

In psychoanalytic terms, anxiety:
- leads to repression
- can be a threat to the super-ego
- can be a warning to the ego
- is due to unresolved psychic conflicts.

Differential diagnoses for anxiety states include:
- temporal lobe epilepsy
- depression
- borderline personality disorder
- mild learning difficulties.

Anxiety, anticipatory – Occurs in:
- obsessions
- phobias
- PTSD.

Anxiety, morbid – Can be reduced by:
- implosion
- modelling
- flooding.

Anxiety, separation – Is the fear an infant shows when being separated from an attachment figure.

The rate of disappearance of separation anxiety depends upon:
- experience of previous separations (real or threatened)
- handling by mother
- perception of whether mother will die or depart
- temperament.

Occurs at eight months – when separated from an attachment figure. Proceeds from 'protest stage' of distress and anger to 'despair stage' of depression and dejection to 'detachment stage' of becoming responsive again = **acute separation reaction, syndrome of distress**.
The stages of protest and despair are harmless, but the stage of detachment can last for weeks and is harmful.

Anxiety disorder, phobic – Fear is out of proportion to the situation, cannot be reasoned away and is beyond voluntary control.
- There is anticipatory anxiety.
- Phobic anxiety is subjectively and physiologically indistinguishable from other types of anxiety.
- The individual avoids circumstances that provoke anxiety.

Anxiolytics – Increase β waves (fast waves) on EEG.

Anxious personality disorder – (Is the ICD-10 version of the DSM-IV avoidant personality disorder).
People with anxious personality disorder are:
- persistently anxious
- ill at ease in company
- fearful of rejection/criticism
- worried of embarrassment or ridicule
- cautious of new experiences
- timid

- lacking in self-esteem, believing themselves inferior to others
- lacking in close friends.

They are *NOT* emotionally cold (unlike people with schizoid personality disorder); in fact they crave social relationships which they cannot attain.

Apathy – Absence of feelings, often associated with loss of energy and volition.

Aphasia – *see* Appendix 8.

Aphasia, anomic – *aka* nominal aphasia
Difficulty with word-finding and list generation. Leads to circumlocutions.
Seen in early Alzheimer's disease and when recovering from more severe aphasias.
Is an organic problem that can be used to differentiate depression from dementia.

Aphasia, Broca's – *aka* non-fluent aphasia, motor aphasia, expressive aphasia
see Appendix 8.

Disorder of language production.
Phoneme errors occur despite great effort (ie 'I try hard but get my worms mixed up'). Grammar is severely distorted and simplified.
Language comprehension is normal.

Aphasia, nominal – *aka* anomic aphasia

Aphasia, receptive – *aka* jargon aphasia
Speech is incoherent and irrelevant.

Aphasia, transcortical motor – Similar to Broca's aphasia but the ability to repeat sentences is well preserved.
Caused by:
- anterior cerebral artery infarction
- Pick's disease.

Aphasia, transcortical sensory – Similar to Wernicke's aphasia but with fluent, error-filled speech. Comprehension is severely affected. Ability to repeat sentences is preserved because phoneme processing is maintained.

Aphasia, Wernicke's – *aka* Wernicke's fluent aphasia, receptive aphasia, sensory aphasia *see* Appendix 8.

Difficulty comprehending the meanings of words.
Speech is fluent but speech content is abnormal with many errors and meaningless words. Structure (intonations, rate, etc) is well preserved. There is impaired auditory comprehension.

Types include:

- Agnosic alexia – words can be seen but not read.
- Pure word deafness – inability to understand spoken words.
- Visual asymbolia – words can be transcribed but not read.

Aphonia – Loss of ability to vocalise, due to neurological disorders or dissociation.

Apophany – Is an autochthonous delusion.

Approximate answers – *aka* passing by the point, *vorbeigehen*
Answers to questions that are wrong but suggest that the correct answer is known (eg 'How many legs does a dog have?' '5')
Often part of Ganser syndrome, also associated with hysterical pseudodementia and organic states.

Apraxia – Inability to perform purposeful volitional acts, not resulting from paresis, inco-ordination, sensory loss or involuntary movements.

Apraxia, constructional – Inability to construct drawings (eg of a clock face).
Is caused by lesions of the parietal lobe (especially the non-dominant side).
Is an organic disorder that can be used to differentiate dementia from depression.

Apraxia, dressing – Inability to put on clothes appropriately.

Apraxia, ideational – Inability to carry out co-ordinated sequences of actions, such as taking a match from a box and striking it.

Apraxia, ideomotor – Inability to perform increasingly complicated tasks to command (eg touching right ear with left middle finger while placing right thumb on left elbow).

Aptitude – Is the raw potential ability of an individual.

ARAS – Ascending reticular activating system.

Arbitrary inference – Drawing a conclusion when there is no evidence for it.

Arcuate fasciculus – Is the pathway between Broca's and Wernicke's areas.
Damage leads to a conduction dysphasia when people cannot repeat back what is said to them. Comprehension and verbal fluency are normal.

Area, Broca's – The motor speech area. It co-ordinates the organs of speech to produce coherent sounds.
Located in inferior frontal gyrus.

Controls:
- speech intonation
- speech rhythm.

Damage results in:
- expressive dysphasia
- no effects on speech comprehension.

Area, motor – Located in the precentral area of the frontal lobe.
Posterior precentral area is the primary motor area.
Anterior precentral area is the secondary motor area (premotor area).
This is why frontal lobe lesions can lead to Jacksonian epilepsy.

Area, somaesthetic – Located in parietal lobes.
Primary somaesthetic area – postcentral gyrus.
Secondary somaesthetic area – lateral sulcus (superior lip of posterior ramus).

Area, Wernicke's – *see* Appendix 8.
Sensory speech and language area – it mainly handles reception of speech, but has an important role in production of speech, coming earlier in the pathway than Broca's area.
Occupies posterior auditory association cortex of superior temporal gyrus.

Damage results in:
- inability to comprehend written/spoken language
- abnormal speech content (but normal speech structure – intonation, etc)
- empty words (thing, it) and paraphrasias becoming common
- fluent receptive dysphasia.

Argyll Robertson pupil – Is small, irregular, fixed and responds to accommodation but not to light.
It is caused by syphilis affecting the oculomotor nerve bilaterally, with sparing of the parasympathetic connections.

Arousal – The degree of the individual's alertness.
Increased arousal improves the performance of older and less neurotic people; it decreases the performance of younger and more neurotic people.

It is influenced by several factors:
- endogenous factors
- personality – neuroticism
- circadian rhythm
- exogenous factors
- drives (hunger, thirst, pain)
- incentives (anticipation of pleasure or pain)
- environmental circumstances (eg noise/bright lights)
- surprising/novel events
- drugs – amfetamines/caffeine and alcohol/barbiturates
- difficulty of task – the harder the task, the greater the arousal
- tonic alertness reflects the circadian rhythm.

Artefactual illness – Illness or complaints produced by the patient.
Includes:
- Factitious disorder – symptoms deliberately simulated or produced by the patient to maintain a sick role but not for external incentives.
- Munchausen's syndrome – chronic factitious disorder with physical symptoms.
- Malingering – symptoms deliberately simulated or produced by the individual for recognisable external motives (eg compensation).

Artery, posterior communicating – Aneurysms here causing subarachnoid haemorrhage are strongly associated with depression, as they interfere with the fine perforating vessels to the hypothalamus.

Arthritis, rheumatoid – Has a negative association with schizophrenia.

Assessment, behavioural – Is what an operant therapist will carry out.
Aims to answer three questions:
- What undesirable behaviour/maladaptive response does the patient engage in?
- What reinforcers maintain these maladaptive responses?
- What environmental changes can be made to alter the maladaptive behaviour?

Involves:
- narrowing down and defining the problem

- providing a record of what needs to be changed
- recording a very full record of the behaviours you want to change and their incidence, duration and intensity as well as what progress is being made.

- It is part of treatment.
- It is shared by client and therapist.
- When the assessment involves examining the stimuli presumed to increase or decrease the behaviour, it becomes a **functional analysis**.

Assessment, initial, of a psychotic patient –
- Avoid implying expectations in questions.
- It is sensible to enquire about psychotic symptomatology first before asking screening questions in other areas.
- Mental state examination may reveal useful information before a full history is taken.

Astereognosia – Failure to identify 3-dimensional form by touch.

Astrocytes – Fibrous astrocytes have longer and thinner processes than protoplasmic astrocytes.

Asyndesis – A disorder of thought/abnormality of association in which speech and thought become fragmentary, resulting in speech incoherence.
Seen in:
- schizophrenia
- dementia
- confusion.

Ataxia – Can be caused by:
- Drugs:
  - benzodiazepines
  - lithium (as an acute toxicity reaction)
  - phenytoin (a dose-related side-effect)
- Lesions of the:
  - dorsal spinal column
  - cerebellum
  - brainstem
  - frontal lobe
- Conditions:
  - delirium tremens
  - Creutzfeldt–Jakob disease
  - Ganser syndrome (where it's psychogenic)

- inherited cerebellar ataxias
- Friedreich's ataxia
- Huntington's (also, in early onset Huntington's, cerebellar ataxia can be seen).

Ataxia, Friedreich's – Clinical features:

- progressive gait ataxia
- ataxia of all 4 limbs
- hypertrophic obstructive cardiomyopathy
- diabetes mellitus/impaired glucose tolerance (30%)
- dysarthria
- areflexia
- optic atrophy/sensorineural deafness (occasional)
- epilepsy (rare)
- onset – typically pubertal, usually before 25 years
- progress to being-wheelchair bound by late 20s
- cardiac failure usually causes death.

Pathology
- Effects on nervous system and heart.
- Dorsal root ganglia then spinal cord are affected.
- Medulla, cerebellum and pons are affected (it's *not* a cerebellar ataxia).
- Gene identified on chromosome 9.
- Triplet repeat: 7–22 repeats are normal, 200–900 are in Friedreich's ataxia, with a mean of 700–800.
- The gene has been identified as involved in mitochondrial function.

Athetosis – Slow, writhing, semi-rotatory movements.

Atmosphere, delusional – *aka wahnstimmung*

Atopognosia – Failure to know the position of an object on the skin.

Attachment – The tendency of infants to remain close to certain people (attachment figures) with whom they share strong positive emotional ties.
or
The bond of affection directed towards a specific individual.
or
A relatively enduring emotional tie to a specific other person.

Behaviours suggestive of attachment were thought by Bowlby to have survival value and include:
- **Seeking proximity** – Moving towards and staying close to the

parent or main care giver, especially when distressed/afraid.
- **Separation distress** – protest on separation from the adult.
- **Secure base effect** – clinging to the adult, who is used as a 'secure base' from which to explore.
- Also mentioned:
  - clinging hard when distressed
  - being more playful and talkative when the adult is present
  - joy/relief on reunion with an attachment figure
  - being generally oriented to attachment figures.
- These behaviours are most marked between 6 months and 3 years.
- Mother's attachment behaviour is reinforced by:
  - smiling
  - movement
  - crying.
- It takes 6 months for attachment behaviour to become fully established.
- Rejection enhances clinginess and this enhances rejection in a positive feedback cycle.
- There is a 'sensitive period' from 6 to 18 months for the development of attachment but this is not absolute.
- It is quality of attachment time, not quantity, that is important.
- Attachment persists throughout life and is exacerbated by distress or illness.
- Attachment is not eradicated by persistent negligence and abuse from the attachment figure.
- Attachment is different from:
  - the feeding relationship (as demonstrated by Harlow)
  - learned behaviour (children attach to abusing parents)
  - imprinting.
- Weaknesses of attachment theory:
  - Cultural variations are not fully understood.
  - There are no standard definitions for 'angry behaviour', 'distress', etc.
  - There is no set format for the Strange Situation Procedure (SSP).
  - The setting for the SSP provides an ecological setting that influences results.
  - The original attachment typing was based on only 26 babies in the USA.
  - The typing is too simple.
  - The SSP measures a specific relationship rather than characteristics of the child, and results are different if the father is used instead.

Attachment, adult – Is assessed according to the Adult Attachment Interview (AAI). There are three categories:

- Adult AAI category
  - Secure/autonomous
  - Preoccupied
  - Unresolved
- Associated infant SSP pattern
  - Secure
  - Resistant
  - Disorganised

There is **social transmission of attachment** from parents to children.

Attachment, monotropic – Described by Bowlby.
Attachment to one individual, usually the mother.
- The first strong attachment to one individual occurs at 8 months.
- Almost every infant has a range of attachment figures.
- 'Mothers' can be male or female.

Attachment, polytropic –
- Develops after monotropic attachment – by 18 months.
- Is *less* common.

Attachment theorists – Include:
- Main
- Waters
- Sroufe
- Klaus
- Grossman
- Bowlby.

Attachment theory – Is highly compatible with general systems theory.

Attacks, drop – May be caused by vertebrobasilar ischaemia.

Attacks, panic –
- Usually last about 20 minutes.
- Rarely last longer than 1 hour.
- Hyperventilation is common.
- Have a 90% overlap with agoraphobia.
- The highest co-morbidity with panic disorder is with depression.

The cognitive theory states:
- the initial attack is *not* de novo
- avoidance is a maintaining factor
- attacks be precipitated by internal stimuli.

But *not*:
- that bodily sensations are misinterpreted as being the result of an underlying physical illness (that, rather, is hypochondriasis).

Attention – Is the focusing of consciousness upon an experience. It can be active or passive.
Maintenance of attention is concentration.

There are different types of attention:
- *Selective/focused attention* – one type of stimulus is attended to while others are disregarded. However, there is still processing of other stimuli and attention can be given to these as appropriate (ie the cocktail party effect – when involved in one conversation, attention can still be diverted by other stimuli, such as someone else mentioning your name).
- *Divided attention* – when two stimuli/tasks are attended to at once and performance suffers. Dual-task interference causes loss of performance.
- *Sustained attention* – is concentration. Performance degrades over time.
- *Controlled attention* – effort is required to maintain concentration. This is defective in schizophrenia.
- *Stroop effect* – occurs when an automatic process is so ingrained that it interferes with controlled processing (eg performing the Stroop Test – reading out words such as red, blue, green, etc which are written in different colours).

    Attention may be reduced:
- normally – sleep, hypnosis, tiredness, boredom
- abnormally – organic states (brain injury, drugs, alcohol, metabolic disturbance), mania, dissociation
- by being *narrowed* in depression.

Attitude – 'A mental and neural state of readiness, organised through experience, exerting a directive and dynamic influence upon the individual's response to all objects and situations with which it is linked.' (Allport, 1935).
Attitudes are mutually consistent and internally consistent.

There are three components:
- Cognitive – includes perceptions of objects and events and reports or beliefs about them (eg 'living by a main road is noisy and dangerous').

- Affective – feelings about and emotional responses to objects (eg 'I worry about living near the main road, it makes me unhappy').
- Behavioural/conative – concerns intentions – 'I'm going to sell my house because it's near the main road' (but there is doubt about this because behaviour isn't always consistent with attitude).

Measurement of attitudes
- Likert scales – list of statements with five choices next to them, from 'strongly disagree' to 'strongly agree'. Some statements are in the negative, to avoid someone agreeing all the way through (the **acquiescence response set**).
- Thurstone's scale of attitude measurement:
  - Thurstone wrote 130 statements representing a wide variety of attitudes. Judges ranked them as favourable, unfavourable and neutral on an 11-point scale. The most consistently agreed upon were then presented to the participants whose attitudes were to be measured, and they were asked to indicate which they agreed with. Numerical scores were attached to each participant's responses and used to measure attitudes.
  - Weaknesses include ambiguity – different response patterns give same score, unwieldy, prone to bias.
- Semantic differential scales (Osgood): a 7-point bipolar scale between pairs of opposite adjectives (eg bad - - - good, fair - - - unfair, etc) looking at three dimensions (evaluation: good/bad; potency: strong/weak; activity: fast/slow). They are reliable and do not demand the construction of a scale but need careful analysis to avoid bias.

Changing attitudes
- A change in one of the three components of attitudes results in changes in the other two components.
- Attitudes are partly learnt by:
  - direct experience of the object of the attitude (eg changing opinion about France, having been there on a visit)
  - the **mere exposure effect** – the more exposure you have to something, the more strongly you feel about it
  - classical conditioning (eg you love your father, and he smokes cigars, so you generally feel well-disposed to cigar smokers)
  - operant conditioning (eg children might quite like stealing sweets, but having been told off by their parents for stealing sweets, they like stealing sweets less)
  - observational learning (eg your mother stayed at home to look after you as a child, so you like it when mothers stay at home to

look after their children)
- and partly formed by other cognitive processes:
  - cognitive appraisal (Lazarus)
  - by modification in the light of new information
  - new information that modifies attitudes can come from two sources:
    - central pathways, when new information is considered
    - peripheral pathways, when cues are presented.
- Heider's balance theory – each individual attempts to organise his/her attitudes, perceptions and beliefs so that they are in harmony/balance with one another.

Attitudes and behaviour – Attitudes and behaviour are inconsistent. La Piere toured the USA with a Chinese couple (the Fangs) in the 1930s. Having contacted hotels in advance, he was told that very few of them would serve the Fangs. On arriving at the same hotels, La Piere and the Fangs were served without objection by the vast majority of hotels. This demonstrated the difference between attitudes and behaviour.

There is a **Theory of Reasoned Action**:

subjective norm = what is expected of one in a given situation
- attitude = one's personal impression of the situation/proposal, etc
- behavioural intention = internal decision taken about a general situation
- behaviour = what actually happens.

A specific action will be performed if:
- the attitude is favourable
- the subjective norm is favourable
- there is high perceived behavioural control.

Attraction, interpersonal – Theories include:
- Balance theory
  - Shared attitudes/beliefs between people who like each other cause agreement and this strengthens bonds between them.
  - If you don't like someone or don't know someone and you have different attitudes and beliefs, there is no incentive to change.
- Reinforcement/affect theory
  - If someone is nice to you, you will like them. If they are unpleasant to you, you will dislike them. There is an element of positive feedback here.
- Social exchange theory

- Each person assigns costs and benefits to the peoples' involvements in a relationship. In friendship, there must be reciprocity – a balance between what is given and received. In business dealings there may be a **minimax** strategy (the idea that input will be minimised and returns maximised).
- Interdependence theory
  - Is like social exchange theory but with added cognitive elements – people have an expectation of what the rewards of a relationship will be. If it doesn't deliver these rewards, they leave the relationship, if the **evaluation of alternatives** suggests that this is a good idea.
- Equity theory
  - Modifies social exchange according to various principles:
    - **Minimax** principle – maximisation of reward and minimisation of cost.
    - Consensus – there must be agreement on a system to share reward.
    - Avoidance of distress – equitable systems avoid distress.
    - Need to restore equity – the losing partner in an inequitable relationship will do whatever it takes to restore equity.

Relationships proceed at increasing depth, with progressive and mutual disclosure.

Attribution, situational – *aka* external attribution
The inference that the cause of the behaviour is outside the person.

Attribution error, primary – *aka* fundamental attribution error.
Is the mistake made when you think that a behaviour is due to a person rather than the situation they are in. This means assuming that something happened because of someone's behaviour rather than simply as a result of circumstance. For example, if a friend has an accident while driving, you might assume that this was due to your friend's poor driving rather than the fact that his car's brakes did not work.

Attribution theory – Was described by Heider.
Is a description of the way in which we observe other people in an attempt to gain understanding about (and possibly influence over) their behaviour. There are several principles:
- Internal and external bases of behaviour are identified as **internal/dispositional attribution** and **external/situational attribution** respectively.
- **Primary/fundamental attribution error** = a bias towards

A

dispositional rather than situational attribution when inferring the cause of other people's behaviour. This means assuming that something happened because of someone's behaviour rather than simply as a result of circumstance. For example, if a friend has an accident while driving, you might assume that this was due to your friend's poor driving rather than the fact that the car's brakes did not work.

Other things are looked for in observing and trying to predict behaviour:
- motivation – underlies behaviour and will help us predict behaviour if understood
- causation – people tend to look for a reason behind events
- prediction – attempts to increase accuracy of predictions about behaviour lead to the search for stable, enduring causes that are consistent in many situations.

People tend to attribute negative things to external forces/agencies and positive things to themselves.

Autism, infantile – Features:
- abnormalities of language and social interaction (marked and early)
- routine and consistency are preferred
- unusual preoccupation
- self-injury
- overactivity
- pronominal reversal
- poor speech comprehension
- compulsions
- lack of attachment behaviour.

Autochthonous delusions –
- Synonymous with primary delusions.
- Rarely preceded by a delusional atmosphere (*wahnstimmung*).
- Just appear.
- Can be a source of secondary delusions.
- Are *not* pathognomonic of schizophrenia.
- Are 'brain waves'.

Automatisms – *see* Epileptic automatisms.

Autoscopy – The experience of seeing one's whole body as though from a vantage point some distance away or projected into external space.
It is a hallucination *or* a special form of delusion.

It can be a symptom of epilepsy.

It is not common.

Features include:

- visual hallucinations
- phantom mirror image

Autotopagnosia – Condition in which one is unable to recognise part/s of one's own body.

Associated with parietal lobe lesions.

Avoidant personality disorder – Is the DSM IV version of the ICD-10 anxious personality disorder.

Axons –

- Are neurites.
- There is one axon per neurone.
- If myelinated, the myelin is interrupted at **nodes of Ranvier**, with the (myelinated) area between these being called the **internode**.
- The proximal part of the axon (which arises from the perikaryon or from a large dendrite) is unmyelinated and is known as the **axon hillock** – this is usually where the action potential starts.
- There are **terminal boutons** distally, beyond where the axon's myelin sheath ends.
- They do *not* contain Nissl substance.

Babbling –
- Is independent of learning or culture.
- Begins at 6–9 months.
- Coincides with a phonetic expansion.
- Is secondary to developmental maturation.
- Occurs in deaf babies.
- Occurs in babies born to deaf/mute parents.

Balance theory – Was described by Heider.
Holds that each individual attempts to organise their attitudes, perceptions and beliefs so that they are in harmony or balance with each other.

Balloon cells – Are seen in Pick's disease.

Bandura – **Triadic reciprocal determinism** is the 3-way, tri-directional influence of:
- behaviour
- environment
- personal variables.

Barbiturates – Were first synthesised in 1864 as malonylurea, or barbituric acid.
Were introduced to clinical practice in 1903.

Basal ganglia – Structures include:
- claustrum
- caudate nucleus (putamen)
- lentiform/lenticular nucleus (globus pallidus).

Atrophy of the basal ganglia occurs in Pick's disease.

Basic assumption theory – Bion believes that groups operate at a number of levels simultaneously:

Work Group

This is how the group is seen from outside; it's their level of performance. Members of the group are consciously aware of their functioning at this level.

A Work Group is defined as an organisation of individuals using conscious tools (such as social customs, hierarchical organisation, a constitution or code of practice) or any other conscious agenda to manage in spite of unconscious impulses.

Basic assumption

This is a more primitive level of functioning, of which the group are unaware. If the group acted *only* at this level, they would act according to one of the following three assumptions:

* That the group had come together to fight or flee from something. This is known as **Basic Assumption Fight/Flight** or simply **baF**.
* That the group had come together to pair or mate. *aka* **Basic Assumption Pairing (baP)**.
* That members of the group had come together to depend on someone or something outside themselves (either within or outside the group). *aka* **Basic Assumption Dependence (baD)**.

If the group acted only at this level, they wouldn't be very productive (eg a group of soldiers would only fight; they wouldn't organise themselves, maintain their equipment or eat). Groups act more constructively by talking about things and coming to a consensus as to how to behave, then proceed with this in mind. They are then acting at the level of a Work Group.

Proto-mental system

This is a lower level of functioning still. Soldiers have come together with baF, but they need a little baD so that they will depend upon, trust and follow their leader.

Bion gave several examples of large, institutionalised Work Groups:

The military – operates at Work Group level to control baF (the disorganised, emotional use of force). First described in a similar way by Freud.

The church – operates at Work Group level to control the chaotic impulses of dependency and spirituality. First described in a similar way by Freud.

The aristocracy – historically operated at Work Group level to control chaotic sexual and breeding impulses (ie baP) by a strict code of conduct, with punishment for those who transgress (ie being unacceptable in 'Society' after indiscretion).
- Basic assumption theory is *not* associated with:
  - common group tension
  - analysis through the group
  - cohesiveness.

Basic encounter – Is facilitated in encounter therapy.

Bateson – Described double-bind communication.

Batson's empathy/altruism hypothesis – Suggests that there may be a genuinely altruistic reason (**empathy**) why we help others in distress. When we see others in distress, we share their distress and genuinely want to help them relieve it. *But* it may be that there are other egoistically based motives for wanting to help, such as the desire to feel 'good' or to appear more desirable to others by demonstrating our helpfulness.

Baumeister & Levy – The theory of **belongingness as a fundamental need** states that the wish to have affiliations diminishes after a few close affiliations have been established.

Beck's cognitive distortions –
  Arbitrary inference – drawing a conclusion when there is no evidence for it.
  Overgeneralisation – drawing a general conclusion on the basis of a single incident.
  Selective abstraction – focusing on a detail and ignoring more important features of the situation.
  Personalisation – relating external events to oneself in an unwarranted way.
  Minimisation – underestimation of the individual's performance, achievement or ability.
  Magnification – inflation of the magnitude of the individual's problems.
  Dichotomous thinking – seeing the world in simplistic terms as 'good' and 'bad', in an all-or-nothing way.

Beck's cognitive triad –
- Negative view of oneself.

- Negative view of current experience.
- Negative view of the future.

Behaviour, maternal – Is determined by the characteristics of the neonate and the early experiences of the mother, but *not* by sex hormones.

Behaviourism – Sees humans as mechanistic systems controlled by the effects of the environment, in contrast to psychoanalysis.
It developed from empiricism. Locke described the state of the mind at birth as a *tabula rasa* (blank slate) and maintained that humans were driven and informed solely by experience, rather than by innate drives.

Is based on four assumptions:

- **Environmentalism**
  All organisms are shaped by the environment and learn from experience.

- **Experimentalism**
  Science can tell us which environmental variables caused certain behaviours and how we can change the behaviours.

- **Optimism**
  The organism can be changed if we alter its environment.

- **Anti-mentalism**
  Mental feelings, thoughts and events are not valid objects of scientific enquiry.

Clinically, abnormality is caused by learning of maladaptive habits. Therapy alters behaviour to encourage good habits.

According to behaviourism, there are two basic learning principles:

- classical conditioning (involuntary)
- operant conditioning (voluntary).

Benzodiazepines –
- Potentiate the action of GABA (both pre- and postsynaptically) and act as anxiolytics.
- Most benzodiazepine receptors are coupled to the GABA receptor and the chloride channel in one complex.
- Benzodiazepine antagonists (eg imidazodiazepine, flumazenil) antagonise the actions of anxiolytic and anxiogenic compounds.
- Benzodiazepine receptors are found centrally and peripherally (ie inside and outside the CNS) and are therefore heterogeneous.

- Clonazepam has a high affinity for the CNS benzodiazepine receptor.
- Benzodiazepine receptors are found throughout the brain.
- *Can* cause excessive weight gain.
- Withdrawal is distinct from opiate withdrawal, being more like alcohol withdrawal. It is closest to barbiturate withdrawal.
- Readily cross the blood-placental barrier.
- Increase the risk of cleft palate in 1st trimester.

Recognised effects include:
- anterograde amnesia
- sedation
- hypnosis
- muscle relaxation
- anticonvulsant activity
- decrease in amount of REM sleep
- ataxia.

With chronic use:
- there is reduced hypnotic effect
- there is reduced anticonvulsant effect
- physical dependence may occur at 1 month
- they cause a decrease in alpha activity and an increase in beta activity.

They do not:
- induce liver enzymes.

Dependence can occur after four weeks, is more likely with shorter-acting agents, and withdrawal can cause:
- anxiety symptoms
- low mood
- abnormal experiences:
- depersonalisation
- derealisation
- hypersensitivity to sensation in all modalities
- distorted perception of space
- tinnitus
- formication
- a strange taste
- influenza-like symptoms
- psychiatric/neurological symptoms:
  - seizures
  - confusional state

- psychotic episodes
- insomnia
- loss of appetite
- weight loss
- symptoms of withdrawal present 2–3 days after stopping the drug
- withdrawal symptoms reach a maximum in 7–8 days and reduce in 14 days
- higher doses cause more withdrawal phenomena and cause them in a shorter time
- time to withdrawal features is shorter in short-acting benzodiazepines
- there is a greater risk of withdrawal features in people with chronic dysphoria
- people with obsessional personalities are less likely to show dependence symptoms on withdrawal.

Half-lives:
- lorazepam 7–35 h
- diazepam 100 h.

Bereavement – Any loss event, from the death of a relative to unemployment, divorce or the loss of a pet. It places us in a state of mourning.

Parkes described five stages of bereavement:

- alarm
- numbness
- pining – with illusions or hallucinations
- depression
- recovery and reorganisation.

When a child's parent dies, there is an initial bereavement reaction that includes:
- prolonged sadness
- crying
- irritability.

and also:
- in young children:
  - functional enuresis
  - temper tantrums
- in older children:
  - sleep disturbance
  - depressive reactions

- impaired school performance.

Berne, Eric – Founded **Transactional Analysis**.

Biological symptoms of depression – Can include:
- weight loss
- diurnal variation in mood
- constipation
- loss of libido
- amenorrhoea
- sleep disturbance with early morning waking
- anorexia.

Biorhythms – Include:
- circadian rhythm
- infradian rhythm = less common, governing, eg seasonal affective disorder
- ultradian rhythm = hunger cycle (4 hours) or stages of sleep (90 min).

Bizarre – A word describing patients' actions or thoughts that should be used when they are really very extraordinary, to the point of virtual impossibility.
For example, a patient stating that he is getting a flying saucer to Mars this afternoon with Jesus, as arranged by the ants in his garden, is bizarre. A patient saying that he is going to be a prominent charity worker or build hospitals to help the poor is *not* bizarre, merely (over) ambitious.

Black patch disease – Is a psychosis resulting from an understimulated state, originally described fter cataract surgery.

Blatz, William – Developed **security theory**.
This stated that secured independence is impossible to achieve.

Bleuler, Eugen – Described:
- schizophrenia (in 1908)
- the **4 As** (Associative disturbance, Affective changes, Ambivalence, Autism) as fundamental symptoms, and hallucinations, delusions and catatonia as accessory symptoms.

There were two Bleulers – father (Eugen) and son (Manfred).

Blindness, psychogenic – Characteristic features include:
- normal pupillary reflexes
- normal visual evoked responses

- tunnel vision
- absence of visual hallucinations
- no significant worsening at night.

B$_{max}$ – Measures density of receptors per unit of tissue.

BMI – Body mass index.

Bonding – The feelings of warmth and affection from mother to child. This is strengthened by tactile contact as soon as possible after birth.

Bonnet's syndrome – Visual hallucinations in a blind or partially sighted person, of an elementary or complex type (often of people or animals) that are vividly coloured. They occur in the blind field.

Borderline personality disorder – Is characterised by:
- unstable relationships
- poor impulse control which is harmful to the person
- variable moods
- lack of control of anger
- recurrent suicidal threats/behaviour   } diagnostic
- uncertainty about personal identity
- chronic feelings of emptiness
- efforts to avoid abandonment (real or imagined)
- transient stress-related paranoid or severe dissociative symptoms
- splitting
- primitive idealisation   } also present
- saddened affect
- chronic feelings of emptiness.

There is overlap with histrionic, narcissistic and dissocial personality disorder. It is thought to result from disturbances in the earliest phase of development (0–1 year).

It is more common in the first-degree relatives of people with borderline personality disorder.
Only a few patients with borderline personality disorder go on to develop schizophrenia.

Is associated with:
- affective disorders
- eating disorders
- substance abuse.

Borderline syndrome – *aka* Borderline personality disorder.

B

Bowlby – Attachment theorist. Considered attachment to be an important primary drive in higher primates.
He considered the period from 9 months to 3 years to be the time of maximal attachment behaviour.
He:

- was influenced by psychoanalysis and believed that the attachment a child formed with its mother was the basis for all subsequent attachments (ie he believed in monotropy)
- noticed that children who grew up in institutions frequently displayed listless and troubled behaviour and were poor social interactors
- explained the child's attachment to the mother as a 'secondary drive' – the 'primary drive' was towards satisfaction of basic needs (such as food and water) and the mother was a source of satisfaction
- believed that the aim of attachment behaviour was a feeling of security
- believed there was a 'critical period' for mothering
- believed that a child was capable of goal-corrected partnership at 3–4 years.

BPAD – Bipolar disorder affective disorder.

Brain fag syndrome – Is a culture-bound syndrome seen in many parts of Africa and New Guinea.

- It is a widespread, low-grade stress syndrome.
- Often seen among students at exam time, it consists of:
  - head symptoms (aching, burning, crawling sensations)
  - eye symptoms (blurring, watering, aching)
  - difficulty in grasping the meaning of spoken or written words
  - poor retentivity
  - sleepiness on studying
  - resistance to psychological interpretation of symptoms
- More common in peasant areas, rare in upper class areas.
- May be a form of depression with depressive features not being articulated in Western terms.

Brain waves – Are evidence of cortical activity and can be measured with an EEG.
see Appendix 7.

Breast feeding – Drugs that are present in harmful concentrations:

- sulpiride
- diazepam.

Drugs that are minimally present or absent:
- amitriptyline
- carbamazepine
- sertraline – present but not harmful.

Avoid:
- TCAs (also mianserin and trazodone) – although transmission is probably too small to be harmful
- doxepin – a metabolite causes sedation and respiratory depression in the child
- antipsychotics – only a small amount present in breast milk, but potential for neurotoxicity
- lithium.

Breast milk – Is more acidic than plasma.

Briquet's syndrome – *aka* multiple somatisation disorder, St Louis hysteria
It is a form of hysteria and was named after Briquet by the St Louis group.
Briquet wrote a monograph on hysteria in 1859.

Epidemiology
- female to male ratio is 5–20 : 1 (although the St Louis group reported it as only occurring in women)
- there is a 0.1–0.2% prevalence in women
- begins before the age of 30 years
- depending on the definition used, the prevalence is 0.38–4.4% of the total population
- conversion symptoms are not essential to the diagnosis
- there is a familial component:
  - 20% of first-degree female relatives of cases have it
  - male relatives of cases have increased rates of alcoholism and psychopathic personality disorder
- sufferers have three times as many surgical procedures as physically well or physically unwell controls
- psychiatric symptoms of anxiety and depression are seen.
- frequently has associated sexual symptoms
- no organic basis
- somatic complaints *usually multiple*, often of long duration, especially:
  - dyspnoea
  - palpitations
  - chest pain

- also back pain, arthralgia and menstrual symptoms
- conversion syndromes may be seen
- poor prognosis
- recurrence is common
- depression and anxiety
- sexual symptoms are frequent.

Also:
- Patients often have co-morbid depression.
- The chronicity required for a diagnosis of somatisation disorder has led to the suggestion of it best being conceived as a personality disorder.
- Continuing care by one doctor with minimal investigation can reduce use of health resources and improve the functional state.
- In managing the disorder, negotiate a simplified pattern of care, agree aims of treatment with patient, and review these often. Cure is not realistic, but aim for progression with reduction of impact of symptoms on daily life.
- Menstrual symptoms, sexual indifference and frigidity are so common that their absence casts doubt on the diagnosis.

Broadcasting, thought – Was described by Kurt Schneider.
Is a Schneiderian first-rank symptom causing the patient to believe that others can experience their thoughts.

Bromism – Results from excessive (usually chronic) intake of bromides, causing:
- confusion
- psychosis
- cognitive impairment
- slowed movement
- affective lability
- depressed mood
- hypomania
- auditory/visual hallucinations
- delusions
- halitosis.

Brown-Sequard syndrome – *see* Appendix 2.

Bruner – Proposed a cognitive developmental theory.
- influenced by Piaget
- believed in schemata that mature
- didn't like stages and preferred **modes of development**:

- **enactive** – representation of the world through motor responses
- **iconic** – mental image of past experiences
- **symbolic** – language influences thought.

Also proposed a language development theory:
- **Topic-comment** structure of language – the mother waits until she and the child are attending to an object before she talks about it.

Bulimia nervosa – Is repeated bouts of overeating and excessive preoccupation with the control of body weight, leading to extreme measures to mitigate against the fattening effects of food.
There is the same fear of fatness as seen in anorexia nervosa.
- Persistent preoccupation with eating and an irresistible craving for food.
- Episodes of overeating in which large amounts of food are consumed in short periods of time.
- Attempts to counteract the fattening effects of food by one or more of:
  - self-induced vomiting
  - purgative abuse
  - alternating periods of starvation
  - use of drugs (such as appetite suppressants, thyroid drugs, diuretics) – or neglect of insulin treatment in diabetics
  - morbid fear of fatness, with weight threshold set by patient well below healthy weight.
- Previous history of anorexia nervosa is common.

Subtypes of bulimia nervosa:
- **Purging type** – regularly self-induced vomiting or misuse of laxatives, diuretics or enemas during current episode.
- **Non-purging type** – no regular use of self-induced vomiting/laxatives/diuretics/enemata during current episode, but other inappropriate compensatory behaviours used (eg fasting/excess exercise).

Related disorder:
Binge-eating disorder – recurrent episodes of binge eating in the absence of the regular use of inappropriate compensatory behaviours characteristic of bulimia nervosa.

Clinical features:
- morbid fear of fatness

- distorted body image, with over concern with weight and shape
- irresistible urge to overeat, with subsequent guilt and disgust
- self-induced vomiting (90%), induced by fingers initially, then reflex vomiting later, which causes relief from physical discomfort and reduction in anxiety about weight gain
- laxative abuse (in 30%), excessive exercise and food restriction
- depression, irritability, poor concentration and suicidal ideas
- patients can be underweight, normal weight or overweight
- menstrual abnormalities are present in fewer than 50%
- most have:
  - depressive symptoms
  - self-mutilation
  - attempted suicide
  - substance abuse
  - low self-esteem
  - anxiety
  - impulsive or compulsive behaviours
  - problems with interpersonal relationships
- stealing and substance dependence are common
- acute gastric dilation (due to binging) is a medical emergency
- abdominal striae.

Compared with anorectics, patients
- are older
- are more socially competent
- are more sexually experienced
- have more insight (and often seek help).

Related to vomiting:
- toothache/dental erosion
- parotid gland enlargement
- Russell's sign (= calluses on back of hand)
- oedema
- conjunctival haemorrhages caused by increased intrathoracic pressure
- Mallory–Weiss tears
- ipecacuanha intoxication (usually fatal with cardiomyopathy and cardiac failure).

Related to purgative abuse:
- rectal prolapse
- constipation/diarrhoea
- damaged myenteric plexus (causing cathartic colon).

Buspirone – Is similar to, but not one of, the benzodiazepines. It acts at the specific serotonin (5HT1A) receptors as a partial agonist and has anxiolytic properties, which have a delay in onset of two weeks. It does not alleviate benzodiazepine withdrawal. Dependence and abuse potential are low, but it is licensed for short-term use only. It is *not* a sedative (unlike benzodiazepines, zopiclone, zolpidem, etc) as it does not act as a hypnotic. It has no anticonvulsant or muscle relaxant properties.

Bystander intervention – Is explained by Piliavin's bystander calculus model, which has 5 stages:
- **Awareness** – becoming aware that someone needs help.
- **Emotional arousal** – caused by (cognitive) awareness.
- **Interpretation** – one's aroused physiological state has to be interpreted in the context of the environment. If you perceive that you are aroused because of an emergency happening in the vicinity, you will help, whereas if you attribute your arousal to another stimulus, you won't be as inclined to help.
- **Cost-benefit analysis**:
  - Costs – effort, time, loss of resources (including opportunity cost), risks
  - Rewards – financial, self-esteem, social approval.
- **Decision** – to help or not to help?

Other points:
- men are more likely to help in an emergency
- women are more empathic than men
- agentic helping (heroism and chivalry) is more common in men
- personality differences have *not* been consistently reported.

Cade – Helped to introduce lithium.

Caffeinism
- Withdrawal syndrome starts at 12–24 hours and lasts up to 1 week.
- Half-life is 3–6 hours.
- Can precipitate panic attacks.
- Clinical features include muscle tension.

CAH – Congenital adrenal hyperplasia.

Camberwell study – carried out by Brown & Harris.

- looked at vulnerability factors for depression in women
- identified four factors:
  - not working outside the home
  - loss of mother by death or separation before the age of 11 years
  - having no one to confide in
  - caring for three or more children under the age of 14 years
- these increase the risk depression if a **provoking agent** is present.

Cannabis –
- Has anticholinergic effects.
- Can cause an acute toxic psychosis.
- Exacerbates schizophrenia with chronic use.
- Main active ingredient is 9-tetrahydrocannabinol.
- Reduces spermatogenesis.
- Produces tachycardia.
- Is associated with gynaecomastia.
- Use is associated with relative risk of 2.5 for schizophrenia.

Cannon–Bard theory (of emotion) – States that, following the perception of an emotionally important event, the somatic responses and experience of emotion occur together.
The stimulus is processed in the thalamus and signals passed to the cerebral cortex (causing emotion) and to other systems (eg the

autonomic nervous system), causing the associated somatic response. Cannon criticised the James–Lange theory of emotion, saying that similar physiological responses can accompany different emotions and that artificial stimulation of physiological states does not induce a similar emotion. The James–Lange theory of emotion therefore cannot explain our ability to *differentiate* between emotional states purely in terms of the physiological quality of their experience.

Canon – Described **homeostasis**.

Capgras' syndrome – *aka* the illusion of doubles, *l'illusion des sosies*, delusion of doubles
Not an illusion, but a delusional perception, it is more common in women and is usually associated with schizophrenia (or affective disorder), but may have an organic component. Any associated cerebral dysfunction is always located in the non-dominant hemisphere.

- *not* frequent
- often implicates the spouse
- may *not* be based on a real impostor
- involves splitting
- is rarely associated with organic disorder.

Carbamazepine –
- Is an effective treatment in:
  - acute mania
  - prophylaxis of BPAD
- is not excreted in breast milk
- can cause spina bifida if used in pregnancy
- decreases blood levels of oral contraceptive pills and warfarin because it's an enzyme inducer (like other antiepileptics).

Carebaria – Means subjective feelings of discomfort in the head.

Catalepsy – *aka* posturing
A condition associated with certain abnormal mental states, including schizophrenia, catatonia and hysteria, in which the patient, usually female, remains motionless, often with the limbs in fixed positions, for a variable period of time.

Cataplexy – Consists of episodes of sudden weakness that can be precipitated by heightened emotional states. It is a flaccid paresis and accompanies narcolepsy.

Catatonia – Described by Kahlbaum in 1863.

Symptoms include:
- stupor
- excitement
- catalepsy (aka *flexibilitas cerea*)
- mitgehen
- mutism
- nonsensical talking
- verbigeration
- vorbeireden
- palilalia
- logoclonia
- posturing
- negativism
- command automatism.

Catecholamines – Consist of a catechol nucleus with an attached amine group.
Synthesised from phenylalanine.
Include:
- dopamine
- noradrenaline
- adrenaline.

They're monoamines.

Cattell – Was a nomothetic personality theorist who used **oblique factor analysis**.

Caudate nucleus – Major part of basal ganglia, along with lentiform/lenticular nucleus.
Marked atrophy occurs in Huntington's chorea.

CBT – Cognitive Behavioural Therapy.

CCK – Cholecystokinin.

Ceiling effect – A problem with scales which makes them unreliable above a certain level, because either few people got marks that high or several people got the top mark. Whichever, it is difficult to discriminate between these top people.

Central pontine myelinosis – Has a nutritional aetiology and consists of demyelination, especially of the pyramidal tracts within the pons.

Clinical features include:
- quadriplegia

- pseudobulbar palsy
- loss of pain sensation in the limbs and trunk.

Cerebellum –
- contains the dentate nucleus
- receives afferents from proprioceptors
- it has three layers:
  - molecular
  - Purkinje (contains Purkinje cells)
  - granular (contains Golgi type II cells)
- lesions produce:
  - ipsilateral effects
  - impaired ipsilateral co-ordination
  - ipsilateral intention tremor
  - ipsilateral dysdiadochokinesia
  - truncal ataxia
  - scanning speech.

Chaining – The teaching of a difficult task by breaking it up into smaller pieces, teaching these separately and then stringing them together. Used in learning difficulties.

Charcot – Concerned himself with hysteria and hypnosis.

Charpentier – Synthesised chlorpromazine.

Child minding – Is not damaging for children (as long as the quality of care is high). Children do not need the 24 hour/day, 7 days/week presence of their mother as Bowlby believed, *but* placing children younger than 1 year into day care for more than 20 hours each week may be damaging.

Chloral hydrate – Has a very low safety index.

Chlordiazepoxide – Was synthesised by Sternbach in the late 1950s and introduced in 1960.

Chlorpromazine – Was first synthesised by Charpentier.
Was reported on by:
- Paraire & Sigwald
- Delay & Deniker

Is an aliphatic phenothiazine.
It blocks postsynaptic dopamine receptors, causing increased production and turnover of dopamine and an increase in the metabolites of dopamine.

Plasma half-life is 6 hours, *but* it remains bound for much longer and metabolites are excreted for 6 months.
Plasma concentration is increased by concomitant TCA.
Peak concentration occurs 3 hours after oral dose.
Therapeutic effect is directly proportional to the plasma concentration.
Concomitant anticholinergic *reduces* plasma concentration.

C

Recognised side-effects include:
* photosensitisation
* cholestatic jaundice (a hypersensitivity reaction, usually in first few weeks)
* direct negative inotropic action
* quinidine-like antiarrhythmic effect
* ECG changes (QT and PR prolongation, ST-segment depression, T-wave blunting)
* impaired glucose tolerance and insulin release (not seen with other antipsychotics)
* amenorrhoea (via decreased urinary gonadotrophins, oestrogen and progesterone)
* weight gain and increased appetite.

Cholecystokinin – *aka* CCK
* is a neurotransmitter that is structurally the same as the gastrointestinal hormone called cholecystokinin
* is found in high concentrations in the CNS, especially:
  * cerebral cortex
  * hypothalamus
  * limbic system
* CCK-like neuropeptides include CCK–4 and CCK–8.

Chomsky, Noam – Put forward ideas about language development:
* People have an **innate language acquisition device** – independent of other (non-linguistic) cognitive factors.
* Environmental influences allow a child to develop cognitively in relation to language acquisition.
* Pre-verbal patterns develop to respond to mother (so there is an element of learning theory).

Chorea, Sydenham's – *aka* St Vitus' dance
* rare in adults
* more common in females than males
* associated with:
  * rheumatic fever in children

- obsessive-compulsive behaviour.

Clinical features:
- sudden involuntary jerking movements (which rarely cause injury)
- frequent association with:
  - emotional instability
  - muscle weakness
- gradual onset may be seen.

Patients present with:
- nervousness
- tumbling
- dropping things
- clumsiness
- grimacing
- speech disturbances
- chorea is increased by emotion and reduced in sleep
- 10–30% of children with rheumatic fever develop it.

Chronic fatigue syndrome – Usually shows hypocortisolaemia
- Is best treated with graded exercise
- Co-morbid depression is common and responds to antidepressants.

Cialdini's negative state relief model – Proposes that children learn that:
- it is gratifying to help
- this gratification can help them to overcome sadness (at seeing others suffering) and guilt (that others are suffering but that they are not).

Cingulate gyrus – Part of limbic lobe.

Circumstantiality – *aka* circumstantial thinking
Thinking is slow, with unnecessary trivial details. It remains goal directed and the goal is eventually reached.
- results from difficulties in figure–ground differentiation
- logical connection between thoughts is maintained
- is seen in:
  - epilepsy
  - organic disorders

- mental retardation
- hypomania.

CJD – Creutzfeldt–Jakob disease.

Clang associations – *aka* clanging
An association in a verbal task in which two words or other stimulus items become linked because of acoustic similarity.
Occurs more often in mania than in schizophrenia.

Client-centred therapy – *see* Psychotherapy, client centred.

Clomipramine – Inhibits the reuptake of both noradrenaline and 5HT.

Clozapine – Synthesised in 1958.
- First trial in schizophrenia – 1961–2 (low doses, poor results).
- Good results – 1966.
- Withdrawn – mid 1970s.
- Was reported on by Kane in 1988 in treatment-resistant schizophrenia. Social functioning improved.

Atypical antipsychotic with weak affinity for dopamine D2 receptors. Has effects on other receptors, including:
- 5HT2 – main action
- D4
- D1
- muscarinic acetylcholine
- α-adrenergic.

Side-effects include:
- neutropenia
- agranulocytosis (<0.8%)
- sialorrhoea
- other typical antipsychotic side-effects, such as extrapyramidal side-effects (EPSEs) – but it tends not to cause EPSEs, even at high doses
- it causes seizures within the recommended dose range
- urinary incontinence
- myocarditis
- weight gain – plateaus at 6 months
- delirium
- neuroleptic malignant syndrome (NMS)
- hyperglycaemia.

5% of a dose is excreted unchanged in the urine.
- is effective in <60% of treatment-resistant schizophrenics

- is the prototypic atypical antipsychotic.

CNS – Central nervous system.

Cocaine – Inhibits presynaptic dopamine reuptake.
- Causes psychosis with paranoia and hallucinations (auditory, visual and tactile).
- Acute effects include:
  - euphoria
  - reduced hunger
  - tirelessness
  - agitation
  - tachycardia
  - hypertension
  - sweating
  - nausea
  - vomiting
  - mydriasis
  - impairment of judgement and social functioning
- chronic effects include:
  - tolerance
  - dependence
  - chronic anxiety.

Coenestopathic state – Deep and constant awareness we have of our bodies and the general tone of functional activity.

Cognition – The use or handling of knowledge.
Functions controlled from the higher brain centres of the cortex, generally conscious and able to override lower functions.
Including:
- selective attention
- perception
- memory
- language
- thought.

Cohesiveness – Is one of several therapeutic factors specific to groups described by Yalom.

Coma – A state of altered consciousness when the patient shows:
- no external evidence of mental activity
- little motor activity other than breathing
- no response (ie unrousability) to strong stimuli.

Combat neurosis – Symptoms include:
- anger
- poor interpersonal relationships
- guilt
- flashbacks.

Common group tension – Is an expression coined by Ezriel to describe the group conflict resulting from a shared, wished for, but avoided relationship with the therapist.

Communication, double-bind – (Bateson)
Communication occurs on several levels simultaneously (verbal, facial, posture, tone of voice, etc) and double-bind communication is the giving of simultaneous messages on more than one level that contradict each other.
This:
- leads to the generation of internal conflict
- occurs in states of emotional arousal
- is usually received from a familiar figure
- (usually) involves an adult and a child involved in communication.

Exam questions will try to confuse it with 'double-blind'.

Communication, persuasive – Is the means of causing another to change behaviour or attitudes.
There are 4 factors that affect the 'persuasiveness' of communication:

Communicator variables
- superficial characteristics of the communicator
- credibility
- personal characteristics (eg attractiveness, expertise, trustworthiness, prestige).

Message variables
- **fear arousal** – must couple concern in audience with achievable means to allay concerns (eg in STD-awareness campaign, fear is of HIV, achievable strategy of allaying fear is to practise safe sex)
- **one-sided messages** – if people are in agreement with a message then telling them it again strengthens their belief
- **two-sided messages** – if people disagree with a message, then presenting two arguments (for and against, with the 'for' argument being stronger) is more persuasive than a one-sided message (but because groups are made of people who do believe and don't believe, there is no difference between one- and two-sided messages in practice)

- **repetition** – works if people are not paying too much attention, if they are, then repetition with variation is the key.

Channel variables –
- audio/visual messages – have immediate superficial impact, the extent determined by communicator's credibility
- written messages – the quality of argument is important, as it can be checked against other sources.

Audience variables
- intelligence – clever people are more persuadable if the message is complex and argument sound
- self-esteem – moderate self-esteem correlates with greater persuasibility
- mood – good mood is more receptive to simple messages
- understanding – people who try harder to understand messages are only persuaded by high quality messages.

Compulsions – *aka* obsessive rituals
Repetitive and seemingly purposeful behaviours performed in a stereotyped way, accompanied by a subjective sense that they must be carried out and usually by an urge to resist. They are recognised as senseless and are often associated with obsessions as if they have the function of reducing the distress caused by that obsession, eg obsessional thoughts that one's hands are contaminated can lead to compulsive hand washing. It may be the case that the extent of the associated obsession is simply the urge to carry out the compulsive act.

- Often repeated because of doubts that they were carried out correctly at first.
- They are *not* antisocial, as social convictions are maintained.
- *May* increase anxiety levels.

Three types are common:
- Checking rituals – concerned with safety (equal sex distribution).
- Cleaning rituals (more common in women).
- Counting rituals – often counting in a special way (eg in threes).

Also described:
- dipsomania
- nymphomania/satyriasis
- dressing rituals
- kleptomania
- polydipsia

- trichotillomania.

Compulsive rituals – *aka* compulsions

COMT – Catechol-*O*-methyltransferase.

Concentration – Is the maintenance of voluntary or involuntary focusing of consciousness (ie attention) on a task.
May be reduced (like attention) in organic states, in mania (due to high distractibility), or in psychosis (due to distracting – hallucinations).

Concepts – Conceptual impressions of the essential characteristics of objects of a perception.
They allow rapid and effective processing and appropriate behaviour in response to a stimulus.
Concepts are made of **attributes**; eg the concept of a London bus is defined by the attributes of being red, double-decked, having wheels and carrying people. **Salient attributes** are those most easily noticed.

Conditioning – The establishment of new behaviour by modifying stimulus–response associations.
Conditioning is an example of associative learning.

Conditioning, classical – *aka* respondent learning
Is the association of a reflex/involuntary response with a stimulus not normally associated with that response.

In **classical conditioning** (in dogs, by Pavlov, 1927), a stimulus not normally associated with a particular response is presented together with the stimulus that evokes the response automatically. This is repeated until the first stimulus evokes the response by itself (*see* Conditioned reflex).

Food = **unconditioned stimulus (UCS)**
Salivation = **unconditioned response (UCR)**
Bell = **conditioned stimulus (CS)**
Salivation (to bell) = **conditioned response (CR)**

- **Acquisition** stage of conditioning is when the association is being acquired between the conditioned stimulus and the unconditioned stimulus.
- **Extinction** is the gradual disappearance of the CR when the CS occurs without the UCS.
- After extinction, the CR may reappear when the CS is presented but it is much weaker. This is called **spontaneous recovery** or **partial recovery**.

- **(Stimulus) generalisation** can only occur after the CS and CR are established. It occurs when the CR is produced in response to stimuli similar to the CS.
- The opposite of **generalisation** is **discrimination** – if two similar stimuli (including the CS) were produced but UCS only presented after one of them, the dog would learn to **discriminate** between the two stimuli.
- This process of **conditioned discrimination** has been used to investigate the perceptual abilities of animals (eg colour vision in bees).
- **Incubation** is the increase in strength of the CR resulting from repeated brief exposure to the CS.
- **Stimulus preparedness** states that some stimuli are more likely to become CS than others. It has a role in phobias (which more commonly involve spiders than cats).
- **Delayed conditioning** is present when the CS occurs just before the UCS. The CS *continues* until the response occurs. Optimal delay is 0.5 s.
- **Simultaneous conditioning** is less successful than delayed conditioning. In simultaneous conditioning, both the UCS and CS occur together *and the CS continues* until the response occurs.
- **Trace conditioning** – the CS stops before the UCS starts. Conditioning decreases, the greater the time between the two.

Conditioning, escape – A variety of negative reinforcement in which the response learnt provides complete escape from the aversive stimulus.

Conditioning, higher order – Is the development of a CS from a neutral stimulus as the result of pairing with an established CS.
- Isn't an aetiological factor in simple symptom phobias.

Conditioning, – *aka* instrumental learning
(Thorndike, 1911; Skinner, 1938)
A voluntary response leads to a positive or negative event each time it occurs, so that in time it comes to occur more (or less) frequently. It is independent of stimuli. **Respondent behaviour** is similar, but based on known stimuli.

Trial and error learning can lead to operant conditioning. Thorndike's **law of effect** states that voluntary behaviour followed by positive consequences will tend to be repeated and voluntary behaviour followed by negative consequences will tend not to be repeated.

Again, there is a CR: hunger (UCS) affects rats in a box which press a lever (CR) to get food (**positive reinforcer**). Discrimination and extinction can occur, with partial recovery. **Negative reinforcers** are also seen.

Learning to press a lever to avoid a negative reinforcer is **avoidance conditioning**. An example of both negative reinforcement and avoidance conditioning is **escape conditioning**, in which a CR provides complete escape from the negative reinforcer (UCS). This is very resistant to extinction.

Punishment occurs when an aversive stimulus is presented every time a certain behaviour is carried out. It occurs *after* the behaviour.

Primary reinforcement occurs via reduction of basic drives (eg food/drink). **Secondary reinforcement** derives from association with primary reinforcers (eg money, tokens).

There are **schedules of reinforcement**:
- **continuous reinforcement** – every CR leads to reinforcement – this is maximally effective
- **partial/intermittent reinforcement** – only some of the individual's responses count towards the reinforcement – has the advantage that, once established, the CR is very resistant to extinction (they keep wondering if they'll get the reward next time)
- **fixed interval** – only reinforced after specific time period – poor
- **variable interval** – variable time – very good
- **fixed ratio** – after a certain number of CRs – very good
- **variable ratio** – after a variable number of CRs – good.

Negative reinforcement is not punishment – a negative reinforcer is an aversive stimulus which, although present initially, can be removed by good behaviour, so the behaviour occurs and the negative reinforcer is removed. An example would be passing an electric current through the floor of a rat's cage until the rat pressed a lever. That's negative reinforcement. The punishment version of the same situation would be the passing of an electric current through the rat's cage if it *didn't* press the lever. Punishment occurs *after* the behaviour which is to be influenced.

Confabulation – Is a 'falsification of memory occurring in clear consciousness in association with an organically derived amnesia'. The patient's account is generally coherent but false. Two forms have been described in Korsakoff's syndrome:
- momentary

- occurs mainly in the later stages
- fantastic
  - occurs mainly in the initial stages

It occurs *early* in Korsakoff's syndrome, becoming less marked as intellect deteriorates.
It is an organic problem that can be used to differentiate depression from dementia.
It is also seen in dementia.

Conformity – There are two types:

Informational social influence – an individual conforms to the consensual opinion and behaviour of the group both publically and in their own thoughts. This occurs when there is an ambiguous situation and the individual could easily decide in favour of or against the group, if they were not present.

Normative social influence – the individual conforms in public but not in private. The aim is to avoid social rejection. This occurs where there is an unambiguous situation and the group has a clear preference for an opinion or behaviour.

Characteristics making people less vulnerable to group pressure are:
- self-reliance
- intelligence
- expressiveness
- social effectiveness
- disagreement within the group.

Confusion – A poorly defined term relating to a state of lack of capacity for clear and coherent thought.
- Characteristic of organic states (but may be functional).

Consciousness – A state of awareness of the self and the environment.

An altered state of consciousness is any that differs from that normally experienced and can include highly focused attention, coma, dreaming and intoxication.

Levels of consciousness are not on a continuum from full consciousness to unconsciousness (consider trance or sleep-walking) and include three dimensions:

- Vigilance ↔ Drowsiness – ability to stay alert deliberately.
- Lucidity ↔ Clouding – level of awareness of internal and external stimuli.
- Consciousness of self – ability to experience and an awareness of

self.

Consciousness, clouding of – Occurs when the patient is drowsy and does not react completely to stimuli.
There is disturbance of attention, concentration, memory, orientation and thinking (which is slow and muddled) and slight drowsiness. Events may be misinterpreted.

Exists on a continuum:

Normal ↔ Clouding ↔ Drowsiness ↔ Sopor ↔ Coma ↔ Death

Consciousness, heightened – Subjective sense of richer perception, exhilarated mood, synaesthesiae – caused by:
- special events (eg falling in love, religious/noumenal experience)
- drugs (eg LSD, amfetamines)
- psychosis.

Consent – To give *informed consent*, the patient must have **a clear and full understanding of the nature of a treatment procedure and its probable side-effects** and must **freely agree to receive the treatment**. Competent adults have a right to refuse medical treatment, even if this results in death or permanent disablement.

Situations in which consent is not needed:
- **Implied consent** – when a patient is unconscious and a reasonable person would consent.
- **Necessity** – where grave harm or death are likely to occur without intervention and there is doubt about the patient's competence.
- **Emergency** – to prevent *immediate* serious harm to the patient or to others, or to prevent a crime.

If a patient is to refuse treatment, the doctor has to ask:
- Is the patient *competent* to refuse?
- Has the patient been *influenced by others* to the extent that the refusal cannot be relied upon?

To be *competent* a patient must be able to:
- comprehend information about the treatment,
and • retain,
- believe ⎫
⎬ it to make an informed choice
and • use ⎭

Under common law, doctors can give treatment without consent if the treatment is essential to safeguard the health or preserve the life of the patient.

Under the Mental Health Act (MHA), any treatment (for a mental disorder) that is not irreversible or hazardous can be given to a detained patient if it is immediately necessary to save the patient's life, to prevent a serious deterioration in his condition, to alleviate serious suffering or to prevent violence or danger to the patient or to others.

No treatment can be given to a patient for a mental illness (under the Mental Health Act) without consent if the patient is detained under Sections 4, 5, 135 or 136, or if they have been remanded to hospital for a report or if they are subject to a Section 41 order but conditionally discharged by the Home Secretary.

In terms of treatments, there are three groups:

- **Treatments giving rise to special concern**
  Includes psychosurgery. Applies to voluntary and detained patients. The patient *must* consent and there *must* be a second opinion from an independent doctor, who will be required to consult two people (one a nurse, one neither a doctor or a nurse) who have been professionally concerned with a patient's treatment. Two independent people must certify the patient's ability to give consent.
- **Other treatments listed in Regulations**
  Applies only to detained patients. Includes some medications and ECT. A second opinion must be obtained if a patient refuses consent, cannot give consent or withdraws consent.
- **Other forms of treatment**
  Other treatments can be given to detained patients without their consent. According to the Mental Health Act, medical treatment 'includes nursing and also includes care, habilitation and rehabilitation under medical supervision.'

Context, influence of on development – *aka* The Ecology of Development
Studied by Urie Bronfenbrenner (1979).
- The environment within which an individual develops is more than just 'the immediate, concrete setting containing the living creature' (although this may be appropriate for animals).
- There are four nested systems to the ecological environment:
  - **microsystem** – an individual's experiences in an individual setting (eg the home for an infant, the school for an older child)
  - **mesosystem** – the relationships between microsystems (eg between home and school)
  - **exosystem** – settings which the child does not participate in but

which affect the child (eg parents' workplaces/social activities)
- **macrosystem** – the organisation of the social institutions and ideologies which exist in the individual's society (eg government policy on childcare, age of starting school or maternity leave/flexible working).

Context of development – The environmental conditions that a person experiences or is affected by, directly or indirectly.

Conversion – Physical illness with no organic pathology produced by subconscious mechanisms with secondary gain for the patient. These symptoms are mediated by the *voluntary* nervous system.

Conversion symptoms include:
- convulsions
- aphonia
- blindness.
- There are no EEG changes.

- Up to 1/3 of those affected have symptoms secondary to organic disease.
- They are not seen frequently in general practice, but somatisation disorders are.
- There's no evidence of twin concordance.

Convulsions, febrile –
- May cause temporal lobe damage (ie mesial temporal sclerosis).

Cooper – Compared patients admitted to psychiatric hospitals in New York and London in 1972.
Symptoms were identical, but schizophrenia was diagnosed twice as often in New York.

Coprolalia – Was described by Gilles de la Tourette.
The obsessive use of obscene language, either for sexual gratification or due to a psychiatric disorder.

Coprophagia – Ingestion of faeces.
Exam questions may try to confuse this with coprolalia.

Core – Part of a concept that is essential for determining membership of that concept (eg with regard to the **concept** of a car, wheels are a core).

Corpus callosum – Broad band of neuronal tissue connecting the two cerebral hemispheres.
With acquired division of the corpus callosum, there is difficulty in

feeling an object with the left hand and describing it verbally.
This is not found with congenital division of the corpus callosum.

Corpus striatum – The part of the basal ganglia in the cerebral
hemispheres of the brain consisting of the caudate and the
lentiform/lenticular nucleus (part of which is the putamen).
Major sources of afferents include:
- cerebral cortex (corticostriatal projections)
- substantia nigra – in midbrain (nigrostriatal)
- thalamus (thalamostriatal)
- raphe nuclei.

Cortex, auditory association – Is found in the temporal lobe.

Cortex, cerebral –
- Is 90% neocortex.
- Has 6 cellular layers.
- Contains Martinotti cells.

Cortex, frontal –
- Houses short-term memory.

Cortex, orbital – Functions include:
- social behaviour
- personality.

Cortex, prefrontal – Is part of the frontal lobe.
Functions include:
- problem solving
- perceptual judgement
- memory
- programming and planning sequences of behaviour
- verbal regulation
- level of response emission
- adaptability of response pattern
- tertiary motor control.

Corticotrophin releasing hormone – *aka* corticotrophin releasing
factor (= CRH/CRF)
- is found in many areas of the brain (including the cerebral cortex)
- increases blood pressure and pulse
- inhibits feeding and sexual behaviour
- increases plasma glucose concentrations
- is probably involved in anorexia nervosa and depression
- is secreted by the hypothalamic paraventricular nucleus to the

hypothalamic–hypopituitary portal system, where it controls release of pro-opiomelanocortin-derived peptides, including corticotrophin (= ACTH).

Cotard's syndrome – Characteristic features include:
- delusion of negation (*aka délire de negation*)
- more common in women
- acute onset
- onset in later life
- association with depressive illness (can occur in schizophrenia and organic syndromes).

Countercathexis – Is a psychotherapeutic term that describes resistance to remembering.

Countertransference – Displacement onto the patient of ideas and feelings related to others (eg parents).

Refers to the specific emotional response aroused in the analyst by the specific qualities of the patient.
It has 2 elements:
- the analyst's own unresolved conflicts and problems transferred on to the patient
- the specific emotional response giving information about the patient's unconscious processes.

- was originally seen (by Freud) as an obstacle to treatment
- can be a useful therapeutic tool (enabling the therapist to engage with the patient more deeply and effectively)
- is applicable to any professional-patient relationship, even outside psychoanalysis
- an example would be a young psychiatrist being excessively deferential to an older patient who reminded them of their father.

CPK – creatine phosphokinase.

CR – Conditioned response.

Crack – Is a stable form of freebase cocaine.

CRH – Corticotrophin releasing hormone.

Criminality –
- Peak is 15–17 years.
- Female offenders account for 1 in 5 offences and reach their highest level of criminality 2–3 years earlier than male offenders.
- Monozygous concordance rate for criminality is 6 times the

dizygous concordance rate.
- Level of criminality is closer to that of biological parents than of adoptive parents.

Criteria, operational –
For schizophrenia include:
- DSM-IV
- ICD-10
- Research Diagnostic Criteria.

Cryptamnesia – Failure to realise/remember that one is remembering (eg believing that an argument you are putting forward is your own, original idea when, in fact, you have heard it before and are really just repeating it).

Cryptographia – Use of written word with private meaning.

Cryptolalia – Use of spoken word with private meaning.

CS – Conditioned stimulus.

CSF – Cerebrospinal fluid.

CT – Computed tomography.

Culture – A system of meanings and customs, including values, attitudes, goals, laws, beliefs, morals and physical artefacts (eg tools, dwellings, etc.) that is shared by an identifiable group and passed from one generation to the next.
or
The learned way of life of a group of people bound together by a common social heritage. People of the same cultural group behave, think and give meaning to life in a similar way and share a set of values and beliefs.

Cumming & Henry – Argued that the elderly relinquish social roles as preparation for death.
This sort of **disengagement theory** has been replaced by **activity theories**, stressing the benefits of continued activity.

Culture-bound syndromes – Disorders that are unique to a given culture (the **cultural determinist** view).
Universal phenomena influenced by culture (the **universalist** view).
see Appendix 6 for details of individual syndromes.
Include:
- amok
- koro

- dhat
- windigo
- latah
- piblokto
- brain fag syndrome.

Cupboard love theory – States that a baby will become attached to its mother who feeds it. It's wrong – babies become attached to people who spend time with them and play with them.

CVA – Cardiovascular accident.

Da Costa's syndrome – Type of panic disorder described in the American Civil War/World War I when soldiers developed panic attacks and concern about heart disease.

Data, types of – Include:
- Nominal – they have names (eg male/female).
- Ordinal – they are in order (eg depression/euthymia/hypomania/mania).
- Interval – ordinals with *constant* intervals between them (eg 1, 2, 3, 4, 5).

De Clerambault's syndrome – *aka* erotomania
The delusion that someone (usually of high status) is in love with you.
- extremely rare
- usually associated with paranoid schizophrenia
- usually seen in single women (more commonly in women than men)
- a 'pure' form of the syndrome was originally described
- the patient desires a sexual relationship.

Features include:
- a paranoid state
- a manic state.

Death – Sudden infant death syndrome is more grief-inducing than perinatal death.

Timely death – one approximately achieves one's life expectancy.

Untimely death – the length of time lived is significantly shorter than one's life expectancy, due to:
- premature death
- sudden unexpected death
- violent/accidental death.

Subintended death – when one acts in such a way as to hasten death by, eg substance misuse, but stops short of actually taking one's own life more directly.

Impending death is experienced through 5 stages:
- Shock and denial
- Anger
- Bargaining (eg with God)
- Depression
- Acceptance.

Defence mechanisms – Techniques used to cope with conflicts between the conscious and unconscious.
- **Acting out** = expressing unconscious emotional conflicts or feelings directly in actions without being aware that this is what you are doing.
- **Denial** = refusing to accept a painful aspect of reality. Denial is the defence mechanism characteristic of hysteria.
- **Displacement** = one's feelings are taken out on something else instead of the real target.(eg your boss shouts at you and you kick the cat, rather than your boss).
- **Idealisation** = a defence mechanism that splits something you are ambivalent about into two representations, one good and one bad.
- **Identification** = the incorporation or *introjection* of an object/person into oneself.
- **Introjection** = is related to *identification*. It's the defence mechanism characteristic of bereavement.
- **Incorporation** = *introjection*/*identification*.
- **Isolation** = thoughts/affects/behaviour are isolated so that their links with other thoughts or memories are broken. For example, talking very calmly about a recent and extremely traumatic experience. (It's a form of dissociation.)
- **Projection** = unacceptable qualities, feelings, thoughts or wishes are projected onto another person or thing. The opposite of identification. For example, 'I hate you' becomes 'You hate me'. This is the basis of paranoia/persecutory ideation in personality disorder, but does not form the basis of 'primary' persecutory delusions.
- **Projective identification** = projection occurs then the patient acts in such a way as to force the other person into behaving in such a way as to reinforce the patient's own belief in the projection. For example, the patient hates the doctor but projects the hate into him, going on to behave in such a way that the doctor

really does come to hate the patient.

- **Rationalisation** = making up an acceptable 'cover story' for something really unacceptable – 'I only did it for you!'
  or
  Basic urges being given a more acceptable explanation.
- **Reaction formation** = the adoption of an attitude in direct opposition to a repressed wish, eg being polite to someone you dislike or developing a compulsion about cleanliness when your real (but repressed) wish is for dirt.
  or
  Acceptance of an opposite ideal.
  This defence mechanism is characteristic of obsessions.
- **Regression** = behaving in a way characteristic of an earlier stage of development, eg going to bed to be looked after when ill.
- **Repression** = suppression of inappropriate ideas, affects, emotions, memories and drives by relegating them to the unconscious. It's a primitive defence.
- **Reversal into the opposite**.
- **Splitting** = dividing things (such as clinical teams) into good and bad, eg when a patient with borderline personality disorder regards the Community Practice Nurse as marvellous and the Consultant as her worse enemy. This is a primitive defence mechanism.
- **Sublimation** = a form of displacement in which one's real desire to act in an unacceptable way is allowed out by a more acceptable form of activity. For example, one's desire to commit acts of violence is resolved in the gym. This is a sophisticated defence mechanism.
  or
  Urge changes into praiseworthy actions.
- **Turning against the self**.
- **Undoing**.

Deindividuation – Occurs when an identity is lost among a mass of people. Someone blends in to a group.

Déjà vu – 'Never' involves misidentification.

Delinquency, juvenile – Is law-breaking behaviour by 10–21-year-olds.

Risk factors:
- unsatisfactory child rearing
- low IQ

- childhood conduct disorder
- parent criminality
- large family size.

Good prognostic indicators:
- counselling
- establishment of a good relationship with a parent or counsellor
- improvement in the home environment
- a good school experience
- a good peer group
- successful employment
- a good relationship or marriage.

Approximately 50% of juvenile delinquents stop being delinquent by the age of 19 years.

Delirium – An abnormal, quantitative change in consciousness. Impaired attention, distractibility and disorientation in time, place and person with the individual appearing fearful, confused and often experiencing illusions and hallucinations, leading to misidentification and unusual behaviour.

Defined in ICD-10 as occurring when symptoms are present in *each* of the following areas for less than 6 months:
- impairment of consciousness and attention
- global disturbance of cognition (eg illusions, hallucinations, perceptual distortions)
- psychomotor disturbance (eg hypo- or hyperactivity, including unpredictable changes from one to the other)
- sleep disturbance (eg insomnia, worsening of symptoms at night, disturbing dreams or nightmares)
- emotional disturbance (eg depression, anxiety, irritability).
- visual hallucinations are common and often have a fantastic content
- other hallucinations can be tactile or auditory
- persecutory delusions
- delirium involves true hypoacusis
- is worse at night.

Delirium, occupational – Refers to the performing of actions when delirious which are normally seen performed during one's job.

Delirium tremens – A dramatic and rapidly changing picture of disordered mental activity seen in people who have been drinking

excessively for several years and then stop. Features include:
- clouding of consciousness
- disorientation in time and place
- impairment of recent memory
- severe agitation with restlessness, shouting and fearfulness
- insomnia
- marked tremor
- truncal ataxia
- sweating, pyrexia, tachycardia, hypertensions, mydriasis
- dehydration, electrolyte disturbance.

It lasts 3–4 days and is worse at night, often ending with a period of prolonged sleep from which the patient may wake with no symptoms and little or no memory of he period of delirium.
Is *characterised* by:
- Lilliputian hallucinations
- clouding of consciousness
- auditory or visual illusions
- auditory or visual hallucinations.

Alcohol withdrawal can cause a choking feeling.

Delusion – A belief or idea, held with absolute conviction based (illogically) on inadequate evidence, that is not culturally bound and persists despite evidence to the contrary, and is manifestly absurd or wrong to others.

The term refers to the *form* rather than the content of the thought.

Factors in formation of delusions
Brain functioning disorders
Sensitive personality
Need to maintain self-esteem
Mood
Reaction to perceptual disturbance
Reaction to depersonalisation
Cognitive overload

Factors in maintenance of delusions
Need for consistency
Communication difficulties (eg social isolation,
lack of social/language skills, deafness)
Persecutory delusions leading to hostility
Delusional interpretation secondary to the effects of loss of respect
from others

Cognitive explanations for delusions
- Tendency to jump to conclusions based on a single piece of evidence.
- Social attribution theory – you attribute negative things to external causes and positive things to yourself.
- Delusions are an adaptive response to factors triggering psychosis.

Delusion, autochthonous – *aka* delusional intuition, primary delusion, apophany
- Arises 'out of the blue' in a single step.
- Is usually self-referent and of interest to the patient.

Delusion, hypochondriacal – A term used to describe a range of delusions including those occurring in:
- organically determined disorders of body image
- states of clouded consciousness
- schizophrenia
- depression.

Delusion, nihilistic – A term used to describe a sensation in which an individual denies that he or she exists or is alive.

This is seen more commonly in schizophrenia than in affective disorder.

Delusional work – Is the incorporating of delusions into a more systematised series of beliefs.

Delusions, paranoid – Occur in:
- schizophrenia
- organic psychosis
- depressive psychosis.

Include delusions of:
- persecution
- reference
- eroticism
- jealousy
- grandiosity
- litigious delusions.

Delusions, partial – Sometimes used to describe beliefs that are held with delusional intensity while the patient is unwell, but which are doubted on recovery.

Delusions, persecutory – the most common paranoid delusions

- occur in schizophrenia, depression, mania and organic states.

Delusions, primary – Occur without being caused by other psychopathological features such as delusional mood.
Are reported as being pathognomonic of schizophrenia
Are *not* a characteristic of depressive psychosis.

Delusions, psychotic – The psychotic delusion is an absolute conviction of the truth of a proposition which is idiosyncratic, ego-involved, incorrigible and often preoccupying.

Delusions, secondary – Are understandable in the light of other psychopathological features such as delusional mood.

Delusion of reference – The absolute conviction that events, objects or people in one's environment have a special significance for oneself.

Demence precoce – Was described by Morel.
Means early onset dementia and was originally used to describe severe intellectual deterioration in an adolescent who might today be diagnosed as suffering from schizophrenia. The term was later translated into Latin as dementia praecox by Kraepelin, who refined its use and identified subtypes of this disorder.

Dementia – Global impairment of intellectual functioning without impairment of consciousness.
Features include:
- perseveration
- initial amnesia for recent events
- catastrophic reactions
- personality deterioration.

Dementia, cortical – Impairment in functioning as a result of damage to the cortex, *BUT* it's usually subcortical too, in that cholinergic neurones are affected. An example of a subcortical dementia is Alzheimer's disease.

Dementia, Lewy body – Clinical features
Spontaneous features of parkinsonism:
- tremor
- rigidity
- postural change
- bradykinesia
- gait disturbance

Fluctuating impairment of memory and higher functions

Deficits in:
- attention
- visuo-spatial ability
- frontal subcortical skills

Visual hallucinations – usually detailed and recurring
Hallucinations in other modalities
Systematised delusions
Repeated falls
Sensitivity to neuroleptics.

Pathology
Large number of Lewy bodies, especially subcortical
Higher concentration of Lewy bodies (unlike Parkinson's disease) in the:
- cingulate gyrus
- parahippocampal gyrus
- temporal cortex.

Neurochemistry
Reduced:
- dopamine
- choline acetyl transferase.

Notes
Lewy bodies contain:
- protein neurofilaments
- granular material
- dense core vesicles
- microtubule assembly protein
- ubiquitin
- tau protein.

Dementia, subcortical – Impairment in psychological functioning due to an impairment in brainstem nuclei.
For example, cerebrovascular disease, Huntington's disease.
Patients do very well on the Folstein Mini-Mental State Examination, but function very badly in reality.

Subcortical dementias include:
- Parkinson's disease
- Huntington's disease
- vascular dementia
- AIDS dementia complex
- progressive supranuclear palsy.

Dementia, vascular – Clinical features:
- relatively sudden onset
- stepwise progression
- preservation of personality
- prone to falls
- affective symptoms are common (especially depression, anxiety and lability)
- nocturnal confusion
- focal cognitive deficits
- insight is maintained
- physical signs:
  - hypertension
  - signs related to atherosclerosis
  - transient ischaemic attacks
  - neurological signs (hyperreflexia, pseudobulbar palsy, sensory deficits).

Aetiology
Caused by brain infarction.

Risk factors:
- age
- hypertension
- smoking
- hypercholesterolaemia
- alcohol
- cardiovascular disease.

Dementia praecox – Proposed by Kraepelin.

Dementia pugilistica
- Neurofibrillary tangles are seen.
- There are *no* senile plaques.

Dementias, prion – Include:
- CJD
- kuru.

Dendrites – Are neurites (ie projections from neurones) which conduct information to the perikaryon, contain Nissl substance and are branched and studded with dendritic spines, which are sites of synaptic contact.
- there is usually more than one dendrite on a neurone
- they contain mitochondria
- may be myelinated or unmyelinated

- are found outside the brain
- 'act as synaptic plates'
- 'bear spikes which act as sites for synaptic contact'.

Denial – Is characteristic of:
- dissocial personality disorder
- dissociative states
- terminal illness
- anorexia nervosa
- hysteria.

Dentate gyrus – Found in the hippocampus.

Dentate nucleus – Found in the cerebellum.

Dependence psychoactive substance – In ICD-10, criteria include: Three or more of these seven experienced or exhibited at some time during the previous 12 months:
- strong desire or sense of compulsion to take the substance
- difficulties in controlling substance-taking behaviour in terms of its onset, termination or levels of use
- a physiological withdrawal state when substance use has ceased or been reduced
- evidence of tolerance
- progressive neglect of alternative pleasures or interests because of psychoactive substance use
- persisting with substance use despite clear evidence of overtly harmful consequences
- narrowing of the personal repertoire of patterns of psychoactive substance misuse.

DSM-IV adds:
- recurrent use in situations in which it is physically hazardous.

Dependent personality disorder – People with dependent personality disorder appear/have:
- weak willed
- unduly compliant with the wishes of others
- lacking in vigour and capacity for enjoyment
- not to take responsibility or be self-reliant
- often to achieve their aims by protesting helplessness and having others act for them
- limited capacity to make normal decisions without excess advice and reassurance.

If married, their spouse will often 'wear the trousers' but if unmarried, they may end up long-term unemployed or homeless.

Depersonalisation – An emotional disorder in which there is a loss of contact with one's own personal reality, a *derealisation* accompanied by feelings of strangeness and an unreality of experience.
or
A term used to describe a peculiar change in the awareness of self in which the individual feels as if he or she is unreal (Sedman).
or
The subjective unpleasant experience *as if* the individual were unreal.

BUT reality testing remains intact.

In severe cases, parts of one's body feel alien or altered in size and one may have the experience of perceiving oneself from a distance. It is unpleasant and can be very distressing. There is (by definition) good insight.

Seen in:
- gradual onset may be seen.
- depression
- schizophrenia
- hysteria
- phobic anxiety
- panic attacks
- dissociation
- alcohol/drug misuse
- PTSD
- normal people (briefly)
- temporal lobe epilepsy (as an aura).

It is associated with:
- derealisation (almost always)
- prolonged sleep deprivation
- sensory deprivation
- temporal lobe epilepsy
- obsessional personality.

An example would be the loss of capacity to feel emotions, despite the ability to express them.
- there is associated affect
- it usually occurs with derealisation
- equally common in males and females
- anxiety is *increased*
- time perception is altered

- it's an 'as if' phenomenon.

Depersonalisation/derealisation syndrome –
- Rare.
- Features:
  - feeling of unreality of
    - mental activity,
      body,
      or surroundings
    - loss of emotions.
- Associated with:
  - 'near death experiences'
  - phobic disorders
  - sensory deprivation
  - depression.

Depression, agitated – Is seen more commonly in middle-aged and elderly patients.

Depression, anaclitic – Is seen in infants who lose their mother and do not get a suitable replacement.
Is characterised by:
- initial vigorous protest
- severe despair
- 1st stage – protest
- 2nd stage – depression and withdrawal
- 3rd stage – recovery (2–3 months)
- it is *not* a predisposition to manic-depressive psychosis.

Depression, cognitive behavioural model of – Was influenced by and uses **schemata**.

Depression, cognitive triad of – Described by Beck.
Is:
- negative views of self
- negative views of current experience
- negative views of the future.

Depression, post-CVA
- Is more related to social than neurological factors.
- *But* is associated with posterior communicating artery aneurysms, as these affect the fine perforating vessels to the hypothalamus when they rupture.

Depression, psychotic – Typical delusions include:

- guilt
- deserved punishment
- persecution.

Depression, secondary – Can be caused by:
- influenza (when depression may be refractory)
- infectious mononucleosis
- Parkinson's disease
- Cushing's syndrome (83%)
- Addison's disease
- CVA
- carcinoma
- Alzheimer's dementia
- hepatitis A
- brucellosis
- hypothyroidism
- hyper/hypoparathyroidism
- drugs:
  - methyldopa
  - clonidine
  - digoxin
  - propranolol
  - reserpine
  - bromocriptine
  - phenothiazines
  - cimetidine
  - steroids (this is not dose-related).

Deprivation, maternal – Bowlby's studies on orphanages led to his hypothesis stating that the loss of the mother figure during the early years of life was permanently damaging. This work was flawed and what he should have said is that the *absence* of a mother figure can be permanently damaging and that the only consequence of the *loss* of a mother figure is distress in the short-term.

What matters is *privation* (ie initial absence) not *deprivation* (ie initial presence and subsequent loss).

Effects of maternal privation:
- developmental language delay
- indiscriminate affection-seeking
- shallow relationships
- enuresis
- aggression

- lack of empathy
- social disinhibition
- attention seeking and overactivity in school
- poor growth (leading to deprivational dwarfism).

Bowlby also mentioned **affectionless psychopathy**, which described people who had no regard for the feelings of others as a result of early maternal separation, *but* this turned out to be due to an early failure to develop bonds with anyone, not just the mother.

Derailment – Described by Carl Schneider.
Is a breakdown of the connection between one thought and another *or* the shifting from one thought to another without connection.
- Is seen in schizophrenia.

Derealisation – Includes abnormalities of perception, especially depth perception and perceptual constancy, and is usually organic.

Developmental theories, types of –
- *Stage theories* – the child progresses through a number of stages, completing one before progressing to the next in the appropriate order and at certain ages, eg Piaget, Freud, Kohlberg, Erikson.
- *Maturational task theories* – there are several tasks which must be completed for the patient to have matured. They can be completed in any order and at different rates.
- *Psychodynamic* – Freud, Erikson (who worked by systematically studying adult recollections of childhood, rather than directly with children).
- *Social learning* – a task-based theory derived from Behaviourism, incorporating modelling.
- *Cognitive* – Piaget, based on information processing and the formation of schemata to understand the world – based on observation of only a few children (his own!).

Methods of theoretical development:
- Systematic study of adult recollections – Freud – easy to carry out, but memories may be unreliable. Freud didn't study children to formulate his theories – he studied adults' recollections of their childhoods.
- Observation of one or a few children – Piaget/Kleinians – allows detailed observation, but there is limited applicability of results.
- Cross-sectional – compares two groups of children (of different ages) and assumes that one group will develop into another.
- Cohort studies – follow children's development. Expensive and

time-consuming, but proactive of high-quality results. Done for special populations (eg people affected by thalidomide), but results cannot be published for many years, because of the long period of study.

Dhat – Is a *common* culture-bound syndrome in Asia (India, Nepal, Sri Lanka, Bangladesh, Pakistan).
- Vague somatic symptoms (eg fatigue, weakness, anxiety, loss of appetite, guilt, etc).
- Sexual dysfunction (impotence, premature ejaculation).
- Is attributed by the patient to excessive masturbation/intercourse resulting in exhaustion of one's supply of semen.
- Typical patient is rural, with conservative attitudes and lower class.
- Literacy and religion seem unimportant.
- 65% of patients in some genitourinary clinics have Dhat.
- Age of onset is early 20s.
- Most have little depression or anxiety.
- Treatment is with antianxiety or antidepressant drugs.
- It really is culture bound, because of specific beliefs about semen in Indian culture.

Diagnosis, psychiatric reliability of –
- Was influenced by and uses **schemata**.
- Is improved by operational definitions.
- Does not matter if diagnostic categories have low validity.
- Is improved by semi-structured interviews.
- Is *not* improved by multiaxial classification.

Diaphoresis – Is excessive sweating.

Diazepam – Is excreted in significant quantities in breast milk, causing lethargy and weight loss in the infant.

Diencephalon – A major subdivision of the forebrain consisting of the:
- thalamus
- subthalamus
- epithalamus (containing the pineal body)
- hypothalamus (with mamillary bodies).

Disability, learning – Deliberate self-harm in patients with learning disability is most problematic between 10 and 30 years of age.

Discrimination – Is enacted prejudice.

Work by Allport describes 5 stages:
- **anti-locution** – not talking to members of the group who are

prejudiced against
- **avoidance** – avoiding them
- **discrimination** – behaving in an unfair way and negative towards them
- **physical attack**
- **extermination** – attempting to eradicate them entirely ('ethnic cleansing').

Disease, Addison's – Involves an underactive adrenal cortex causing reduced cortisol, aldosterone and androgen production.

Characteristic features include:
- depression (not often psychotic – that's Cushing's)
- apathy
- emotionally withdrawal
- loss of drive
- loss of initiative
- hypotension
- memory difficulties
- fatigue.

Disease, Alzheimer's –
Clinical features:
- marked memory disturbance from the onset
- gait disturbance
- extrapyramidal features
- abnormal EEG
- apraxia and agnosia (including topographical agnosia).

Mild
- Appearance/Behaviour
  - fatigue
  - occasional odd behaviours
  - exaggerated personality traits
  - loss of interest
- Speech
  - dysphasia
- Mood
  - anxiety/depression
  - minor forgetfulness
- Cognitive
  - impaired new learning
  - impaired concentration
  - difficulties with complicated tasks

- nominal aphasia/anomic aphasia.

Moderate
- Appearance/Behaviour
  - neglect of personal care
  - decline in social behaviour
  - restricted activities
  - motor restlessness/inactivity
  - aggression
  - waking at night
  - wandering
- Speech
  - poverty of content of speech
  - repeated asking of questions
  - dysphasia
  - dysarthria
- Mood
  - irritability
  - emotional lability
  - catastrophic reactions
- Cognitive
  - misidentifications
  - hallucinations
  - delusions
  - disorientated in time and space
  - lose ability to read/write
  - apraxias and agnosias
  - only remember very familiar material
  - familiar names/geography forgotten
  - day-to-day memory impaired
  - need help with activities of daily living

Severe
- Appearance/Behaviour
  - severe personality deterioration
- Speech
  - uncommunicative
- Cognition
  - intellectual functioning severely impaired
  - unable to recognise family
  - failure to recognise self in mirror – the 'mirror sign'
  - failure of registration
  - no intelligible ideation

- Physical
  - hypertonicity
  - primitive reflexes
  - incontinence
  - unable to carry out activities of daily living.

Pathology

Macro
- generalised cortical atrophy particularly affecting the frontotemporal lobes
- widening of sulci
- hippocampus, and other medial temporal structures, are very much involved
- relative sparing of subcortical grey matter
- ventricular enlargement
- cell loss in the:
  - nucleus basalis of Meynert (acetylcholine)
  - locus caeruleus (noradrenaline)
  - raphe nuclei (5HT).

Micro
- amyloid-containing senile plaques/neuritic plaques scattered densely throughout the cortex (which are *not* seen in dementia pugilistica) – number correlates with impairment
- neurofibrillary tangles – paired helical filaments of tau protein and ubiquitin
- amyloid protein deposits in blood vessels
- neuronal degeneration (especially of the outer 3 layers)
- glial proliferation
- not Lewy bodies – they're in Dementia with Lewy Bodies (DLB) and Parkinson's
- granulovacuolar degeneration
- Hirano bodies.

EEG
- abnormal.

Neurochemistry
Acetylcholine activity is reduced and correlates with extent of impairment.
Noradrenaline/5HT cell loss may relate to aggression/mood disorder.
Reduced intrinsic neurotransmitters:
- GABA

- Somatostatin.

Genetics

Increases rapidly with increasing age.
More common in females.
First-degree relatives have risk of dementia increased three times.
Autosomal dominant inheritance with incomplete penetrance is seen in some families.
Late-onset Alzheimer's disease is associated with homozygotes for E4 allele of apolipoprotein E (chromosome 19), which may precipitate amyloid deposition.
Chromosome 21 – amyloid precursor protein gene (therefore people with Down's syndrome get it early).

Environmental
Aluminium is found in higher concentrations in affected brains, and dialysis causes a dementia because of the high aluminium concentrations, which may increase production of amyloid peptide.
Head injuries predispose to dementia.

Epidemiology
Accounts for 50% of dementia cases.
Is (therefore) more common than multi-infarct/vascular dementia.

Notes
Apraxia and agnosia are more common in Alzheimer's than in Pick's disease.
- Is associated with:
  - cell loss in the:
    - nucleus basalis of Meynert (acetylcholine)
    - locus caeruleus (noradrenaline)
    - raphe nuclei (5HT)
  - reduced intrinsic neurotransmitters:
    - GABA
    - somatostatin.

Characteristic neuropathological features include:
- generalised cortical atrophy particularly affecting the frontotemporal lobes
- widening of sulci
- neuronal degeneration (especially of the outer 3 layers)
- amyloid-containing senile plaques/neuritic plaques scattered densely throughout the cortex (which are *not* seen in dementia pugilistica)

- relative sparing of subcortical grey matter
- neurofibrillary tangles
- glial proliferation
- *not* Lewy bodies – they're in DLB and Parkinson's.

Characteristic features include:
- marked memory disturbance from the onset
- gait disturbance
- extrapyramidal features
- abnormal EEG
- apraxia and agnosia (including topographical agnosia)
- autosomal dominant inheritance with incomplete penetrance is seen in some families
- aluminium is found in higher levels in affected brains
- dialysis causes a dementia due to high aluminium levels
- late-onset Alzheimer's disease is associated with the E4 allele of apolipoprotein E.

Disease, Binswanger's – A progressive subcortical vascular encephalopathy.
CT scan reveals markedly enlarged ventricles as a result of infarction in hemispheric white matter, especially in periventricular and central areas.
- age of onset: 50–65 years
- gradual accumulation of neurological signs, dementia and disturbances in motor function
- pseudobulbar palsy
- often a history of severe hypertension, vascular disease and CVA.

Disease, Creutzfeldt–Jakob – Characteristic clinical features include:
- parietal lobe symptoms
- cortical blindness
- EEG showing triphasic sharp wave complexes superimposed on progressive suppression of cortical background activity
- myoclonic jerks
- epileptic fits
- speech disturbance such as dysphasia and dysarthria.

Characteristic pathological features include:
- relative sparing of the parietal and occipital lobes
- generalised damage elsewhere
- histological triad of:
- spongiform degeneration of grey matter
- astrocytic proliferation

- neuronal degeneration.

In CJD (*not* new variant CJD):
- there's a triad of:
  - dementia
  - ataxia
  - myoclonic jerks
- equally common in males and females
- positive family history in 15%
- *status spongiosus* of the cortex is characteristic
- early CT changes are not seen, but there is generalised atrophy
- periodic (especially biphasic) sharp waves are seen on EEG
- 90% have 14–3–3 protein in CSF
- prions are seen primarily in the cortex.

In nvCJD (new variant):
- patients are more likely to present to psychiatrists, often with non-specific symptoms (eg anxiety/depression)
- strange sensory disturbances are seen (ie with non-dermatomal distribution)
- there's a longer course of illness (ie lasts longer than 6 months)
- there is no classic EEG change; it's just abnormal
- distribution of prions is different, as they are seen in:
  - brainstem
  - cerebellum
  - cortex
- specific CT change is a high signal in the pulvinar area (ie posterior thalamus).

Disease, Cushing's – Involves excess production of cortisol, usually from a tumour. It causes psychotic depression.

Features include:
- moon face
- buffalo hump
- purple striae on thighs and abdomen
- hirsutism
- hypertension
- amenorrhoea
- impotence.

Disease, Parkinson's –

Clinical features

- resting tremor
- bradykinesia/akinesia } Classic triad
- cogwheel rigidity
- postural abnormalities
- festinant gait
- cognitive decline – on a continuum with dementia:
  - bradyphrenia
  - impaired abstract reasoning
  - poor retrieval
  - poor short-term memory, especially frontal lobe working memory
  - remote memory is relatively spared until late
- seen in 1% of over 70-year-olds
- peak incidence is 50–60 years
- depression is seen in 1/3
- dementia in 15–20% (late).

Pathology
Cellular degeneration of the substantia nigra with striatal dopamine depleted by >90%.
Presence of Lewy hyaline inclusion bodies in the striatum and cortex.

Neurochemistry
Damage to ascending monoamine systems with effects on:

- dopamine
- 5HT
- noradrenaline
- damage to the substantia innominata causes disruption of acetylcholine systems.

Notes
There is a well-established association with depression.
In treatment, avoid anticholinergics.

Disease, Wilson's – Characteristic features include:

- myoclonic jerks
- *reduced* serum copper and caeruloplasmin
- *increased* 24 hour copper excretion and *increased* urinary copper
- Kayser–Fleischer rings on ophthalmoscopy (a brown ring coincident with outer edge of iris, but seen over iris rather than sclera)

Neuropathological features include:

- neuronal loss in the caudate and putamen
- Alzheimer nuclei (astrocytic nuclei with a vesicular appearance)
- normal brain size
- pericapillary concretions staining for copper
- large phagocytic cells (Opalski cells)

- autosomal recessive inheritance
- onset usually before 20 years but may be as late as 50 years
- usually presents with hepatic or neurological involvement
- affective and other psychoses can result
- treat with penicillamine
- is a rare cause of psychosis.

Disorder, delusional, persistent –
- Is characterised by:
  - non-bizarre delusions
  - encapsulated delusions with internal consistency
  - a chronic course with preservation of social functions but poor insight.
- Is not organic or substance-related.
- May feature intermittent depressive symptoms and/or intermittent hallucinations.
- Hallucinations are only allowed to be persistent if they relate to the delusion.
- In ICD-10 lasts longer than 3 months.
- Is probably a disorder distinct from affective disorders and schizophrenia.

Risk factors:
- first-degree relatives of people with
  - paranoid personality traits
  - delusional disorder
- immigrant populations
- low social class
- low educational standards.

Precipitating factors:
- social isolation
- head injury
- imprisonment
- deafness.

Epidemiology
- onset in middle or old age

- equally common in males and females
- delusional jealousy is more frequent in males
- erotomania is more frequent in females
- prevalence is less than 10 in 100, 000.

Prognosis
- at 22–39 years of age
  - total recovery in 37%
  - mild deficit in 32%
  - moderate impairment in 10%
  - severe impairment in 22%
  - 3–22% develop schizophrenia
- is better if:
  - married
  - reactive
  - jealous-type delusional disorder (characteristically 6 years older at first admission, symptoms duration 1 year greater with more stressors, better employment history and more social contacts)
- is worse if:
  - more than six months of symptoms before treatment.

Disorder, gender dysphoric –
- Is associated with Klinefelter's syndrome.
- Is *not* associated with homosexuality.

Disorder, gender identity –
- Cross-dressing starts before the age of 4 years.

Disorder, generalised anxiety –
Characteristic features include:
- initial insomnia (lie awake worrying)
- night terrors
- waking during nightmares
- waking unrefreshed
- waking intermittently throughout the night
- digital paraesthesia
- subjective difficulty in breathing.

Unpleasant dreams are not a feature.
Is associated with:
- derealisation
- marked autonomic symptoms
- depression
- increased genetic concordance in close relatives

- prevalence of 2–5%
- amenorrhoea
- tinnitus may occur.

Disorder, neurotic –
- Symptoms are quantitatively but not qualitatively different from normal experience.
- 28% of people over 65 years of age have a neurotic disorder.
- Is often ego-defensive.
- Twice as common in females as in males.
- Has a good prognosis when mild.

Disorder, periodic limb movement – Causes periodic episodes of repetitive and stereotyped limb movements.
- seen in 1/3 of over 60-year-olds
- common cause of insomnia, leading to disrupted sleep and daytime fatigue
- also in latter half of pregnancy
- uraemia makes it worse
- associated with:
  - Pickwickian syndrome
  - narcolepsy
  - benzodiazepine withdrawal
- exacerbated by:
  - TCAs
  - phenothiazines
  - MAOIs.

Disorder, personality disorder, Cluster A –
- paranoid personality disorder
- schizoid personality disorder
- schizotypal personality disorder
  (Mad).

Disorder, personality disorder, Cluster B –
- antisocial personality disorder
- borderline personality disorder
- histrionic personality disorder
- narcissistic personality disorder
  (Bad).

Disorder, personality disorder, Cluster C –
- avoidant
- dependent

D

- obsessive-compulsive personality disorder
  (Sad).

Disorder, schizophrenic thought – Includes:
- asyndesis
- metonymy.

Disorders, anxiety – OCD is found in 3–7% of the parents of patients with anxiety disorders.

Disorders, puerperal –
- PTSD is *not* common after childbirth.
- Querulent (ie argumentative) reactions are uncommon, occurring in 1% of those affected.

Disorientation – Lack of awareness of one's setting in time, place and person.
Disorientation in time occurs first – defined as being inaccurate by more than one hour.
Disorientation in place follows, then person.

Displacement – Is the process occurring in dreams whereby something occurs in the manifest dream as a substitute for something else involved in the latent wish (eg a queen appears in the dream instead of one's wife).

Disposition – Research into dispositions in relation to personality focuses on:
- intra-individual stability
- inter-individual variability.

Dissocial personality disorder – Is a difficult disorder to define. The most constant core features are:
- failure to make loving relationships (lack of feelings for others, with self-centredness and heartlessness, callousness if severe – superficial charm may be present)
- impulsive actions
- lack of guilt
- failure to modify behaviour based on previous experiences.

Also:
- disregard for social restrictions
- lack of feeling for others
- tendency to blame others by offering plausible rationalisations for behaviour.

but *not*

116

- emotional coldness (that's schizoid personality disorder) or attention to detail (seen in anankastic personality disorder).

Dissociation – Narrowing of the field of consciousness with amnesia.
or
Unconscious psychogenic symptoms that confer advantages (ie secondary gain) on the patient..

D

Dissociative states – *aka* prison psychosis
- 20% have histrionic personality
- There is no evidence of twin concordance.

Dissociative/hysterical amnesia
Starts suddenly, with inability to recall long periods of one's own life, even one's own identity. Some patients have concurrent organic diagnoses, especially epilepsy, multiple sclerosis or head injury. If the cause is organic, they have a picture similar to psychogenic cases. Consciousness is clear, retention is normal, memory loss is selective and there are no hallucinations.

Dissociative 'pseudodementia'
Extensive abnormalities of memory, behaviour, general intellectual impairment.
Memory tests answered wrongly, even simple ones, often in a way such that we feel the correct answer is in the patient's mind. Sometimes associated with organic brain disease, epilepsy, schizophrenia.
'Pseudodementia' alone is used for apparent dementia of depressed people, but is a vague term with several meanings that should be avoided.

Dissociative stupor
Patients appear motionless and mute, failing to respond to stimulation, but remain aware of their surroundings. Dissociative stupor is rare. Schizophrenia, depressive disorder and organic brain disorder must be excluded. It has abrupt onset (often following traumatic experience) and rarely lasts more than 3 weeks.

Ganser syndrome
Described by Ganser in 1897.
Rare.
Four central features:
- give approximate answers to questions designed to test intellectual function
- psychogenic physical symptoms

- hallucinations – visual and elaborate
- apparent clouding of consciousness.

The obvious advantage to be gained from illness plus the approximate answers often points towards malingering, but it's felt to be unconsciously maintained as it is so consistent. Organic or functional psychosis must be excluded, especially if muddled thinking and visual hallucinations are prominent.
There's no specific therapy.
'Pseudohallucinations' are an occasional feature.

Dissociative identity disorder
aka*multiple personality disorder*

Sudden alterations between two patterns of behaviour, each of which is forgotten by the patient when the other is present. Only one is present at once.
Complex, integrated emotional responses, attitudes, memories and social behaviour are present, often in contrast with patient's normal state.
It is rare, although it can appear more common when doctors are interested/looking for it, 'The 3 faces of Eve', a book by Thigpen causing increased interest in the USA, led to increased cases.
May occasionally have organic cause.
Many report physical/sexual abuse during childhood, but studies are retrospective.
There is often a co-morbid diagnosis (eg antisocial personality disorder, drug and alcohol abuse, anxiety and depression).

Dissociative trance
aka trance and possession disorder in ICD-10.
Features temporary loss of personal identity, with full awareness of surroundings. Can be induced by religious ritual, when there is a sense of being taken over by a deity or spirit. The person may repeatedly perform the same movements, postures or utterances.
If induced temporarily and willingly in participants at religious ceremonies, does not indicate the presence of a disorder.
The term 'trance/dissociative disorder' is used for states that are not wanted, outside ceremonies, or exceptionally prolonged after one of these ceremonies. The cause and treatment are poorly understood.

See also latah, amok, and transcultural variations.

Dissociative trance states:
- occur in hysteria

- may be seen under hypnosis
- include fugue states
- include multiple personalities
- are not seen with epilepsy.

Dissociative fugue
Is characterised by:
- dissociative amnesia
- apparently purposeful travel beyond the usual everyday range
- maintenance of self-care
- simple interaction with strangers.

Behaviour is appropriate and the individuals appear to be in contact with his/her environment. Duration is short and onset is sudden, in response to emotional stress.
Patients lose their memory and wander, deny the whereabouts of the place they have wandered to and then regain their memory and identity. Dissociative fugue also occurs in epilepsy, severe depressive disorders and alcoholism. It may be associated with suicide attempts. Subjects often have a history of disturbed relationships as children. Others are habitual liars.
- onset of any of these states is very rare after the age of 40 years
- there is no clouding of consciousness.

Couvade syndrome
see Syndrome, Couvade.

Dissonance, cognitive – Exists when there is a conflict between thoughts, beliefs or attitudes.
Was described by Festinger.

There may be:
- **cognitive consonance** – when there is agreement
- **cognitive dissonance** – when there is disagreement
- **cognitive irrelevance** – when two thoughts/beliefs/attitudes have no relation to one another.

The size of the conflict/level of tension it creates relate to:
- importance (of the elements to a person)
- ratio (of consonant to dissonant elements)
- amount of cognitive overlap (the less two elements have in common, the greater the conflict).

When one acts in contradiction of one's internal thoughts/beliefs/attitudes, this is **attitude discrepant behaviour**.

119

Distortion, sensory – Occurs when real perceptual objects are perceived to be distorted.

Includes distortions of:
- intensity
  - heightened, often in mania
    - eg hyperacusis – normal sound is deafening; visual hyperaesthesia – normal colours appear intense
  - diminished, often in depression
    - everything appears dull
- quality
  - often in acute organic states and epilepsy, includes:
    - macropsia
    - micropsia
    - megalopsia
    - change in spatial form
- feelings associated with perception
  - derealisation
  - depersonalisation
  - ecstasy state (when ordinary objects are perceived as being extraordinary – eg drugs)
  - loss of intensity of feelings and enjoyment
- splitting of perception
  - often in schizophrenia
  - inability to link two or more different modalities of perceptions from a single source (eg can't associate the face and the voice or someone speaking to you).

Distribution of drugs – Drugs can be distributed between the components of the body:
- lipids
- protein
- water.

The extent to which this occurs depends on:
- lipid solubility
  - Increases volume of distribution.
  - Most psychotropic drugs are highly lipid soluble at ambient pH.
  - Is seen in non-polar drugs.
- plasma protein binding
  - All drugs are partly bound to plasma and partly free in plasma.
  - Is competitive and reversible.
  - Acts as a reservoir for the drug.

D

- Acid drugs bind albumin.
- Plasma binding is dependent on:
  - Plasma drug concentration
  - Plasma protein concentration – decreased in:
    - hepatic disease
    - renal disease
    - cardiac failure
    - malnutrition
    - carcinoma
    - surgery
    - burns
  - Drug interactions:
    - displacement
    - change to tertiary structure of plasma proteins
  - Physiological variables – concentrations of:
    - urea
    - bilirubin
    - free fatty acid
- volume of distribution
  - = mass of drug in body/blood or plasma concentration of the drug
  - inversely related to duration of action
  - increased by:
    - lipid solubility
    - excess adipose tissue
    - age (more adipose tissue)
    - female gender
    - related also to physical disease.
- blood–brain barrier
  - components:
    - tight junctions of capillary endothelial cells
    - cerebral capillary basement membrane
    - gliovascular membrane
  - drug lipid solubility increases penetration
  - infection increases permeability
  - brain receptors bind psychotropic drugs in the brain, creating a reservoir there (CSF has very low protein concentration, so this is not seen there)
  - active transport – eg levodopa
  - small molecules (eg lithium) diffuse well across the blood-brain barrier
  - it depends on the permeability of the capillary membrane

- it's selectively permeable
- it's guided by the 'pH partition hypothesis'.
- placenta
  - can be crossed by:
    - passive diffusion
    - active transport
    - pinocytosis.

Divorce – Affects children *more than parental bereavement*. Protective factors include:
- Amicable access arrangements
- Good parental relationship with the child
- Good relationships between the child and older siblings
- The child's temperament.

DLB – Dementia with Lewy Bodies.

Dominance, cerebral hemispheric – 99% of right handers have a dominant left cerebral hemisphere.
60% of left handers have a dominant left cerebral hemisphere.
Is plastic in early life.

DOPA – Dihydroxyphenylalanine.

DOPAC – Dihydroxyphenylacetic acid.

Dopamine – Is made:

Tyrosine
↓
DOPA
↓
Dopamine

- Is a precursor of noradrenaline (phenylalanine →tyrosine → dopa → dopamine → noradrenaline).
- Inactivation is by presynaptic reuptake and it is broken down mainly to HVA but also dihydroxyphenylacetic acid (DOPAC) in humans, but *not* in lower primates.
- It is an inhibitory neurotransmitter, acting on the **thalamic filter** via GABAergic neurones in opposition to glutamate (which is excitatory).
- Reserves are depleted by reserpine.
- Doesn't cause psychosis in normal individuals if given orally.
- Acts to *reduce* prolactin concentrations.
- When released from the hypothalamic–hypophyseal pathway, it *inhibits* prolactin release.

- Dopamine D1 and D5 receptors are similar.
- D2, D3 and D4 receptors are similar.
- It is a sympathomimetic amine, stimulating adrenergic receptors directly, along with:
  - adrenaline
  - noradrenaline
  - isoprenaline.

D

Blockade of mesolimbic and mesocortical dopamine receptors causes akathisia.

It is found particularly in the:
- ventromedial tegmental area
- nigrostriatal area (connects substantia nigra in midbrain with the striatum in the basal ganglia)
- *not* in the cerebellum.

Dopamine receptor antagonists:
- include:
  - bromocriptine
  - metoclopramide
  - phenothiazines
  - e antiemetics (act on medullary dopaminergic pathway)
  - increase prolactin concentrations
  - decrease growth hormone concentrations.

Dopamine receptor agonists:
- are emetics
- inhibit prolactin release (acting at hypothalamic-hypophyseal pathway)
- increase drive.

Important dopamine systems are:
- Mesolimbic system
  - Ventral tegmental area (VTA) → limbic system
- Mesocortical system
  - VTA → frontal cortex and septohippocampal region
- Tuberoinfundibular system
  - Hypothalamic arcuate nucleus → median eminence
- Nigrostriatal system
  - Substantia nigra pars compacta (in midbrain) → striatum (in basal ganglia)
- Mesolimbic and mesocortical systems mediate the reward effects of stimulants.

Doxepin – Has sedative properties.

Dream work – The process by which the latent dream is converted into the manifest dream, including:

- **Displacement** – the use of symbols in dreams, whereby a familiar figure involved in the repressed wish (eg one's wife) is replaced with a substitute symbol (eg a queen).
- **Condensation** – one part of the manifest dream represents several aspects of the latent wish, so, in the dream, one's father, government and authority figures may be subsumed into a king (or a devil) by condensation.
- **Symbolisation**/symbolic representation.
- **Concrete representation** – the expression of an abstract idea in tangible form, eg a king could be a concrete representation of wealth or power.
- **Secondary elaboration**/secondary revision – revising/elaborating after waking to review the dream and make it more consistent with the rules of secondary process.

Dreams – Disguise fulfilments of repressed wishes (Freud).
Described by Freud as 'the Royal Road to the unconscious' – ie signs of the conflict between the id and the ego.
Aim to give expression to repressed desires without waking the dreamer – 'dreams are the guardians of sleep'.

Composition:
- **Day residue** – emotionally charged memories of the day.
- **Nocturnal stimuli** – external and internal.
- Unconscious wishes.

Dreams, day – Are more easily understood than night dreams, because they are kept in check by consciousness, although they remain very dependent on emotion.
May be of interest in the psychotherapeutic setting.
May be escapist fantasies.
May be rehearsals for future actions or attempts to find solutions to problems.
Are of particular importance in people with sexual problems.

Dreams, latent – The meaning of the dream.

Dreams, manifest – What we are conscious of about our dreams when we wake.
Consist of:

- day residue
- the repressed wish.

Dressing rituals – A form of compulsion when the person has to lay out their clothes in a particular way or put them on in a special order.

Drivelling – Described by Carl Schneider.
The mixing of parts of a thought.
or
Results from extreme derailment and fusion, and results in completely illogical thoughts and incomprehensible speech.

Drives – Were described by Freud and include:
- **libido** – the sexual drive providing energy for the **eros**
- **eros** – the life-preservation drive
- **thanatos** – the death drive.

Drowsiness – The tendency to drift into unconsciousness while still able to be kept awake by constant stimuli. Associated with subjective sleepiness, slurred speech, slow actions and reduced muscle tone.

Drugs, illicit, classes of –
- Class A
  - phencyclidine
  - opium
  - iv amfetamines
  - cocaine
  - LSD
  - diamorphine
  - morphine
  - methadone
  - pethidine
  - dextromoramide
  - dipipanone
  - alfentanil
- Class B
  - oral amfetamines
  - barbiturates
  - some opiates
- Class C
  - most benzodiazepines
  - buprenorphine
  - cannabis (recently reclassified)

Class B drugs become Class A drugs when prepared for injection.

DSM-IV – Diagnostic and Statistical Manual of Mental Disorders-IV.
   Categorises disorders along five axes:

I   Clinical disorders.
   • Other disorders that may be a focus of clinical attention.
   • Disorders first diagnosed in infancy, childhood or adolescence
      (*not* mental retardation),
         • eg learning, communication, pervasive, autistic, Rett's,
            Attention-Deficit/Hyperactivity Disorder, tic, elimination
            disorders.
   • Delirium, dementia and amnestic and other cognitive disorders.
   • Mental disorders caused by a general medical condition.
   • Substance-related disorders.
   • Schizophrenia and other psychotic disorders.
   • Mood disorders.
   • Anxiety disorders.
   • Somatoform disorders.
   • Factitious disorders.
   • Dissociative disorders.
   • Sexual/gender identity disorders.
   • Eating disorders.
   • Sleep disorders.
   • Adjustment disorders.

II   Personality disorders.
   • Mental retardation.

III   General medical conditions.

IV   Psychosocial and environmental problems.
   • eg problems with support group, social problems, etc.

V   Global assessment of functioning.

Dysarthria – Difficulty with articulation of speech.
   Found in bulbar and pseudobulbar disorders.

Dyscalculia – Is the impairment of capacity for calculation in patients
   who have previously shown no difficulties with arithmetic.
   Secondary dyscalculia may result from:
   • short-term memory defects
   • perseveration
   • concentration impairment.

Dysfunction, sexual
- Is influenced by:
- inadequate information
- poor sex education
- depression
- poor communication
- loss of attraction.

Dysgraphia – Inability to write.

Dyslexia – Doesn't exist in Spain, as Spanish is written phonetically.

Dyslexia, neglect – Results from mistaking one word for another due to not paying attention.

Dysmorphophobia – Is a condition occurring when someone believes that some part of their body is too large, too small or misshapen, when the body part appears normal to others.

Areas of particular concern include:
- nose
- chin
- penis
- breasts
- wrinkles.

If the patient has personality disorder, they usually have overvalued ideas. If they have a psychiatric disorder, they have delusions.
Personality disorder and psychosis are the most common co-existing disorders.
Is close to obsession or overvalued idea in terms of psychopathology.
Patients often present to plastic surgery, dermatology or ENT clinics.

Dysphasia – *see* Appendix 8.

Dysphasia, conduction – Inability to repeat what has been said.
Results from damage to arcuate fasciculus (pathway between Broca's and Wernicke's areas).
Comprehension and verbal fluency are intact, but the indvidual can't repeat messages.

Dysphasia, expressive –
- Lesions of Broca's area (ie motor association area) cause loss of rhythm, intonation and grammar.
- Articulation may be impaired because Broca's area is close to motor areas.

D

- Comprehension is normal.
- The person knows that their speech is difficult for others to follow and frustration results.
- Speech is slow and hesitant.
- Is a dysfluent expressive dysphasia.
- Allows repetition of messages.

Dysphasia, receptive – Is the impaired ability to comprehend language – written or spoken.

It is caused by damage to Wernicke's area (ie auditory association area) and this leads to associated difficulties in language production, with an expressive dysphasia. The patient is unable to understand that their dysphasic language is difficult for others to understand.

Speech is normal in rhythm and intonation (ie fluent) (Broca's area is intact) but has abnormal content. The individual cannot repeat messages.

Dysphonia – Impairment of vocalisation.

Dysprosody – Speech with loss of its normal melody.

Dystrophy, myotonic –
- autosomal dominant
- trinucleotide repeat
- mutation located on chromosome 19
- Clinical features:
  - muscle weakness starts distal and moves to be proximal
  - frontal baldness
- anticipation
- may be associated with wasting of the neck muscles
- may be associated with cataracts.

Eating – Overweight people *don't* eat more than normal people in states of low anxiety, they just respond more to the usual cues that trigger increased eating in everyone (high anxiety, advertising, etc).

Echolalia – Occurs when the patient repeats another's speech, even if it is in another language and they don't understand it.
- Seen in:
  - schizophrenia
  - organic states
  - mental retardation.

Echopraxia – When the patient imitates the interviewer's every action, despite having been asked not to.
- It's an abnormal voluntary movement.

Ecstasy – An exalted state of happiness, usually self-referent with a loss of distinction of ego boundaries (eg the feeling that one is merged with the world).
Is a normal phenomenon which can also occur in:
- hysterical dissociation
- organic states (including epilepsy)
- schizophrenia
- mania
- mass hysteria
  - Is not a passivity experience.
  - May *not* occur in alexithymia.

ECT – Electroconvulsive therapy.
Has effects on:

- Noradrenaline
  - increased noradrenaline function
  - increased cerebral noradrenaline activity
  - increased plasma catecholamines

- 5HT
  - acute increase in cerebral 5HT
  - chronic ECT causes increase in 5HT2 receptors
- Dopamine
  - increased dopamine function
  - acute increase in cerebral dopamine
  - increased behavioural response to dopamine agonists
  - increased number and activity of dopamine D1 receptors (in rats)
- GABA
  - increased functional activity
- Acetylcholine
  - decreased central acetylcholine function
  - acute decrease in acetylcholine with acute increase in cholinesterase
  - increased CSF acetylcholine concentration
  - chronic ECT causes:
    - reduced muscarinic acetylcholine receptor density in cerebral cortex and hippocampus
    - reduced 2nd messenger response to muscarinic acetylcholine receptor stimulation
- Endogenous opioids
  - chronic ECT causes:
    - increased cerebral met-enkephalin concentration and synthesis
    - increased cerebral β-endorphin concentration and synthesis
    - changes in opioid ligand binding.

Side-effects include:
- memory disturbance
- headache
- musculoskeletal pains
  (these are common but short-lived).

- Is not contraindicated in the 1st trimester.
- EEG changes do not last for more than 1 week.
- Increases prolactin.
- Does not cause reduction of cortisol measurable at 1 hour.
- Causes initial bradycardia then tachycardia.
- Increases cerebral circulation.

Edwards' criteria – If met, they suggest that a possible adverse drug reaction is more likely to be attributable to the drug in question. They are:

- a close temporal relationship between the effect and taking the drug or toxic concentrations or its active metabolites in body fluids being demonstrated
- the effect differs from manifestations of the disorder being treated
- no other substances are being taken or withdrawn when the effect occurs
- the reaction disappears when the treatment is stopped
- the effect reappears with a challenge test.

EEG – Electroencephalogram.
see Appendix 7.

α (alpha) activity – decreased by benzodiazepines
β (beta) activity – increased by benzodiazepines

Is abnormal in:
- subdural haematoma
- cerebral abscess.

Effect, Law of – Is an operational conditioning concept described by Thorndike.
The Law of Effect states 'Voluntary behaviour paired with subsequent reward is strengthened'.

Effect, primacy – The tendency to remember the first item in a list.

Effect, recency – The tendency to remember the most recent item in a list.

Effect, weapon – The increased likelihood of an aggressive response in the presence of a weapon, even if the weapon itself is not used.

Ego, the – The ego operates mainly subconsciously and is concerned with:
- rational thinking
- external perception
- voluntary motor function.

There are two aspects:
- punitive (primitive) aspects
- the ego-ideal (more positive).

The ego brings the defence mechanisms into action. The ego is relaxed during sleep and fatigue, and when intoxicated or psychotic. It is at the centre of object-relations, in both the inner and outer worlds.

Egomania – Is a pathological obsession with oneself.

Ekbom's syndrome – Delusion *or* overvalued idea of infestation with a small but macroscopic organism/organisms.
- may result from or lead to tactile hallucinations
- may be a form of monosymptomatic hypochondriacal psychosis.

Elaboration – Is a factor involved in determining how memorable something is. The more elaborate, long-winded and unusual the circumstances are surrounding a fact, the easier it is to remember. Single words are used to test short-term memory in the Folstein Mini-Mental State Examination, to reduce the effect of elaboration and therefore make the test harder.

Elimination of drugs – Occurs through the:
- kidney
- gastrointestinal tract (via bile and faeces)
- lung
- saliva
- sweat
- sebum
- milk.

EMG – Electromyogram.

Emotion – A mental feeling or affection having cognitive, physiological and social concomitants.
Plutchik described 8 primary emotions:
- acceptance
- anger
- anticipation/expectancy
- disgust
- fear
- joy/happiness
- sadness
- surprise.

Any two adjacent emotions can give rise to a secondary emotion (eg joy + acceptance = love, acceptance + fear = submission, surprise + sadness = disappointment, disgust + anger = contempt).

Emotional response is made up of:
- subjective awareness – feeling happy/sad
- physiological changes – sweating, pulse rate
- cognitive/behavioural elements – includes appraisal.

The two basic theories of emotion are the James–Lange theory and

the Cannon–Bard theory. Schachter also came forward and claimed that the (conscious) experience of an emotion is dependent on a wider range of factors, including:
- the emotionally important event (ie the stimulus)
- somatic/physiological responses
- cognitive factors
- cognitive appraisal of the situation (eg cues)
- influence of long-term memory.

Schachter believed that the physiological experience of an emotion gave it its intensity (ie quantitative aspect), but that the cognitive experience determined which emotion was experienced (ie qualitative aspect) – **cognitive labelling theory**.

Emotionally unstable personality disorder – Features:
- Unstable and capricious mood.

Emotions, development of – Harris' 5 stages:
- Phase 1
  - Age 3–6
    - Single situation-based emotions recognised
- Phase 2
  - Age 6–8
    - Two consecutive emotions can be envisaged
- Phase 3
  - Age 7–8
    - Simultaneous emotions recognised as possible when of same valence (ie either both positive or both negative, but not one of each)
- Phase 4
  - Age 10
    - Simultaneous emotions of different valences possible, if from different sources
- Phase 5
  - Age 11
    - Single episode/emotional stimulus envisaged with 2 emotional aspects.

Emotions, primary – Plutchik described:
- Acceptance
- Anger
- Anticipation
- Disgust
- Fear

- Joy
- Surprise
- Sadness.

Encephalitis, pan-, subacute sclerosing (SSPE) –
- Result of chronic CNS infection with measles.
- Presents 2–12 years after the original infection.
- Clinical features:
  - cognitive decline
  - myoclonus
  - amnesia
  - irritability
  - seizures
- It is *not* a cause of increased pressure on lumbar puncture.

Encephalopathy, hepatic –
- impaired consciousness (always present, starting with hypersomnia and daytime sleepiness, progressing to marked confusion, semi-coma or coma)
- frightening visual hallucinations
- θ (theta) waves replacing α waves on EEG triphasic waves are seen later and indicate poorer prognosis
- mildly exaggerated tendon reflexes
- unobtrusive tremor
- blank/grimacing facial expression
- characteristic flapping tremor (asterixis)
- fluctuating neurological disturbance.

Encopresis – Is the involuntary passage of formed faeces after the age of 4 years
- uncommon
- much more common in males than females
- is exacerbated by coercive and obsessional toilet training.

Encounter groups – Use rocking and rolling to facilitate basic encounter.

Endogenous opioids – Are derived from pro-opiomelanocortin (with corticotropin).

Include:
- enkephalins (which are pentapeptides)
- endorphins
- dynorphins.

Endorphin, β –
- A peptide neurotransmitter.
- Found throughout the brain.
- Localised to layers 2 and 3 of the cerebral cortex.
- Released in response to stress.
- Is involved in the perception of pain.
- Released from the pituitary.

ENT – Ear, Nose and Throat.

Enteral administration – Is via the gastrointestinal tract:
- oral
- buccal
- sublingual
- rectal.

Enuresis – Involuntary passage of urine in the absence of physical abnormalities after the age of 5 years.

Risk factors:
- low IQ
- large families
- family history
- small bladder capacity.

Primary = present since birth.
Secondary = recurrence of enuresis after at least 6 months of dryness – poorer prognosis.

Treatments:
- amitriptyline
- the bell and pad method is the most effective
- TCAs – high rate of relapse is seen on withdrawal of treatment
- star charts – are good for monitoring and can help.

Enzyme inducers – Include:
- barbiturates
- phenytoin
- rifampicin.

Lead to:
- reduced TCA concentrations.

Enzyme inhibitors – Include:
- phenothiazines
- butyrophenones

- MAOIs
- SSRIs (increase levels of TCAs, antipsychotics, anticonvulsants, warfarin).

  Lead to:
- increased TCA concentrations.

Ependyma – Are a type of neuroglia that line the cavities of the central nervous system, using cilia to move CSF.

Ependymocytes
- Line the ventricles and spinal cord
  except:
- the floor of the 3rd ventricle over the median eminence (tanycytes line this area).

Epilepsy –
- Absence seizure
  - Starts without an aura and ends abruptly
- Complex partial
  - The individual loses touch with the surroundings and may show automatisms.
  - Characteristic features include
    - impaired consciousness
    - aura (typically epigastric)
    - a preceding simple partial seizure
- Personality disorder is no more common in 'organic' than idiopathic epilepsy, but it is more common in grand mal than petit mal.
- More than 75% of epilepsies are primary.
- 30% of people with learning difficulties have epilepsy.

Epilepsy, complex partial – Characteristic features include:
- impaired consciousness
- aura (typically epigastric, felt as churning spreading to the neck)
- possibility of progression to generalised seizure
- loss of touch with surroundings
- automatisms
- simple partial seizure occurring first.

N.B. Absences do not form part of this presentation.

Epilepsy, schizophrenia-like psychosis in – Differs from schizophrenia in that:
- there is a warm affect

- there is no family history
- visual hallucinations are more common, often with a mystical content
- the progression of the disorder is more benign, with less personality deterioration and social deterioration.

Epilepsy, temporal lobe – The predominant feature of a partial temporal lobe seizure can be:

E

- forced thinking (compulsion to think about particular subject, eg death)
- ecmnesic hallucinations (previous experiences are recalled by the individual and relived with great intensity)
- visual hallucinations (simple or complex)
- auditory hallucinations (simple or complex)
- gustatory hallucinations
- olfactory hallucinations
- marked depersonalisation
- marked derealisation
- dysphasia (when part of the aura suggests a focus in the dominant temporal lobe).

- Is associated with mesial temporal sclerosis (which results from hypoxic damage resulting from febrile convulsions).
- May present as a hebephrenic illness.
- May have personality changes.
- May cause automatisms (eg lip-smacking).
- May cause *déjà) vu*.
- In childhood is frequently (33%) associated with a psychiatric disorder.
- An important differential diagnosis is anxiety state.

Epileptic automatisms – A state of clouding of consciousness during or immediately after a seizure during which posture and muscle tone are maintained in which the patient performs well-organised movements or tasks while unaware of doing so. The movements may be simple and repetitive, such as hand clapping, or they may be so complex as to mimic a person's normal conscious activities.

- They are commonly associated with temporal lobe epilepsy.
- Include automatic writing.
- Characteristic features include normal amnesia for the period of the automatism and continuous diffuse slow waves on EEG.

Epileptic twilight state – Characteristic features include:

- impaired consciousness

- duration from 1 to several hours (although they may last for more than a week)
- visual hallucinations (usually very vivid and highly coloured)
- extensive paranoid delusions are common
- abnormal affective states include:
- panic
- terror
- anger
- ecstasy
- marked psychomotor retardation and perseveration.

EPSE – Extrapyramidal side-effect.

Equity theory – Holds that the preferred relationships are those in which each feels that the cost-benefit ratio of the relationship for each person is approximately equal.

Erikson – Believed that children learn a **basic trust** or **basic mistrust** from their mothers.
- Influenced by Freud, but used psychosocial rather than psychosexual ideas. He thought these were universal and transcultural.
- Each stage marks a crisis or struggle that has to be overcome to progress. This progression is **epigenesis**.
- There are 8 stages covering the whole of life:

Trust vs mistrust – 0–1 year
Consistent, stable care needed to feel secure.
Success leads to trust in the environment and hope for the future.
Failure leads to suspicion, insecurity and fear of the future.

Autonomy vs shame and doubt – 1–3 years
Sense of independence from parents sought.
Success leads to a sense of independence and self-esteem.
Failure causes shame and doubt about one's autonomy.

Initiative vs guilt – 3–6 years
Exploration of environment and sexuality.
Success leads to enjoyment of new activities.
Failure leads to fear of punishment and guilt due to one's feelings.

Industry vs inferiority – 6–11 years
Important cultural knowledge and skills acquired.
Success promotes a sense of competence, achievement and confidence.

Failure causes feelings of inadequacy.

Adolescence – 12–18 years
Identity vs confusion

Coherent personal and vocational identity sought.
Success produces sense of being consistent and integrated person with strong self-identity.
Failure causes a confused sense of self-identity.

Young adulthood – 20s–30 years
Intimacy vs isolation
Deep and lasting relationships are sought.

Middle adulthood – 40–64 years
Generativity vs stagnation
Continued growth, productivity and contribution to society sought.

Late adulthood – 65+ years
Integrity vs despair
Reviews and evaluates what's been accomplished.
Success leads to ego integrity, with an integrated view of one's life, achievements and meaning. Mortality is accepted, one is satisfied with life and feels ready to face death.
Failure causes despair, about one's own life's path and the way one has treated others. One feels that life is transient when faced with death. There is no sense of contentment and completion.

Basic trust is laid down in the first year of life.

see Appendix 5.

Esquirol – Described hallucination as perception without an object and illusions as transformations of perception.

Euphoria – A subjective feeling of unconcern and contentment.
or
A state of excessive and unreasonable cheerfulness.

Seen in:
- mania
- organic states
- frontal lobe damage
- drug misuse.

Events, life – An excess of life events (positive or negative in quality) has been demonstrated in the months before:

- depressive disorder
- suicide attempts
- neurosis
- schizophrenia.

Evoked potentials –
- Represent slow synaptic activity.
- Are obtained by averaging a series of EEG recordings in a modality to increase the signal : noise ratio.
- There are positive (P) and negative (N) components.
- Early peaks are **exogenous;** late peaks are **endogenous** and are more susceptible to internal factors (eg attention).
- Visual evoked P100 has increased latency in multiple sclerosis.
- Auditory evoked P300 is abnormal in schizophrenia.

Existential logotherapy – Was developed by Frankl.

Experts – When solving problems, tend to reason forward from a solution to find the answer to a given problem.

Exposure, cue – Used in treatment of drug abusers. They undergo prolonged and repeated exposure to a situation that causes strong desire to use the drug, in order to become desensitised.

Exposure, interoceptive – Relates to patients being allowed to experience and become accustomed to physical signs of increased anxiety (such as hyperventilation).

Exposure (treatment) – Technique aiming to reduced undesirable behaviour by supervised exposure to an aversive stimulus.
Used in OCD to reduce compulsions to carry out rituals.
Part of habituation training along with response prevention.
Uses graded hierarchies.
Exposure is repeated and prolonged.
The first task undertaken should provoke anxiety.
The interval between sessions should not be long.

Extrapyramidal effects (EPSEs) – Caused by antidopaminergic effects of antipsychotics on nigrostriatal pathway (connecting substantia nigra in midbrain with striatum in basal ganglia).
Seen in Parkinson's disease:
- parkinsonism
- dystonias
- akathisia
- tardive dyskinesia

- festinant gait
- resting tremor (especially pill-rolling)
- cogwheel rigidity (ie lead-pipe rigidity with superimposed tremor)
- hypersalivation
- micrographia
- bradykinesia/akinesia.

Extrapyramidal side-effects of antipsychotic drugs include:
- Acute dystonias
  - soon after treatment
  - especially in young men
  - especially with butyrophenones and piperazine phenothiazines
  - Clinical features:
    - torticollis
    - tongue protrusion
    - grimacing
    - opisthotonos.
- Akathisia
  - unpleasant feeling of physical restlessness and desire to move.
  - seen as inability to keep still
  - usually in first few weeks of treatment, but can present up to several months later
    o if seen early in treatment, stops if dose reduced
  - sometimes occurs much, much later and is difficult to discriminate from tardive dyskinesia.
- Parkinsonism
    - akinesia
    - blank facies
    - lack of associated movements when walking
    - rigidity
    - coarse tremor
    - stooped posture
    - festinant gait if severe
  - may not appear for months
  - may spontaneously remit
  - antiparkinsonian drugs can be used.
- Tardive dyskinesia
  - serious because does not (necessarily) remit when drugs stopped – does in 50%
  - seen in 20–40% of patients treated with long-term antipsychotics
    - chewing/sucking movements

- grimacing
- choreoathetoid movements
- akathisia
- sometimes seen in those who haven't taken antipsychotics
- more common in:
  - women
  - elderly
  - those with diffuse brain pathology
  - affective disorder.

Extroversion – Term coined by Jung.

Eysenck – Was a nomothetic personality theorist who used **orthogonal factor analysis**.

Ezriel – Described **common group tension**. Was interested in **analysis** *of* the group.

Facial expression, imitation of by infants – Occurs as early as 36 hours after birth.

Facial nerve (VII)
- Nucleus is located in the pons.
- Innervates the muscles of facial expression *only*.
- The sensory component serves the anterior 2/3 of the tongue.
- The parasympathetic fibres innervate the submaxillary and sublingual glands.

Facilitation, social – Is the way in which tasks are made easier when carried out in the presence of others, even if they are just watching (ie the **audience effect**).

Factor analysis
- Used by nomothetic personality theorists (ie Eysenck & Cattell).
- Eysenck used orthogonal factor analysis:
- second-order factor analysis to identify a small number of powerful independent factors
- Cattell used **oblique factor analysis**:
- first-order factor analysis to identify a large number of less powerful factors that correlate (ie are non-independent).

Fading – The gradual withdrawal of prompts used to guide an individual to a desired response after it has become well established.

Fairburn – Was an object relations theorist.
Described:
Internal world
- A substitute for unsatisfying external relationships.
- Peopled by **actors on a stage**.
- Derived from early relationships and associated fantasies.
- Template for present and future relationships.
- **Libidinal/antilibidinal object** – **internal saboteur**.

- The object relationship determines the libidinal attitude.

Falret – Described *folie circulaire*.

Families, dysfunctional – May exhibit:
- discord
- overprotection
- rejection
- enmeshment
- disengagement
- triangulation
- communication difficulties (eg **ambiguous, incongruous communication**)
- **myths**.

Family cycle – Divided by Carter & McGoldrick into a 6-stage schema based on emotional processes.

Family function
- Described by Olson in his **circumplex model**.
- 16 types of family systems.
- Two dimensions – **cohesion** and **adaptability**.

Family structure – The composition of the family unit making up the family home affects children's development:
- Single-parent families – more behavioural and emotional problems.
- Extended families – no problems.
- Lesbian parents – no problems.
- Large family – more educational and behavioural problems, decreased intelligence.
- Only children – slight advantage in intellectual development.
- Oldest children – slight advantage in intellectual development.
- Twins – delayed language development.

Fathers
- Play more vigorously with children.
- Do not sit as close to children.
- Talk in more adult language to their children.

Fear – An unpleasant emotional state (a feeling of apprehension, tension or uneasiness) caused by a realistic current or impending danger that is recognised at a conscious level.

Fear, development of –
- 6 months

- Fear of novel stimuli (eg strangers) – peaking at 18 months to 2 years.
- 6–8 months
  - Fear of heights – worse when walking starts.
- 3–5 years
  - Fear of animals, the dark, monsters.
- 6–11 years
  - Fear of social shame/ridicule.
- Adolescence
  - Fear of death, failure, social failure, nuclear war.

Freud also proposed theories to explain fear.
Fear has been explained in terms of learning – situations become fearsome after negative experiences in similar situations.
Lack of control – fear results from a feeling of helplessness in any situation beyond one's control.

Fear of negative evaluation – Is the principal cognitive factor in social phobia.

Feighner criteria – *aka* St Louis criteria
Are a set of criteria proposed for the diagnosis of schizophrenia.
- Are restrictive.
- Were developed in St Louis.
- Were developed for use with the Research Diagnostic Criteria.

They specify that:
- the individual should have been continuously ill for at least 6 months
- manic or depressive symptoms should not be prominent
- the only psychotic symptoms required are delusions or hallucinations of almost any type, or clear-cut thought disorder
- at least 3 of these 5 are required:
  - being single
  - poor premorbid social adjustment
  - family history of schizophrenia
  - absence of alcoholism/drug misuse for 1 year before diagnosis
  - onset of illness before the age of 40 years.

Fenfluramine –
- Is chemically similar to amfetamine.
- Has sedative properties.
- Acts mainly on the 5HT pathway.
- Has an anorectic activity solely in the D-isomer.

- Increases uptake of glucose into muscle cells.

Festinger – Cognitive dissonance.

Fetal alcohol syndrome – First described by Lemoine in France.
Clinical features:
- abnormal facies
- small stature/low birth weight
- psychological overactivity
- low IQ
- increased still-birth rate, increased congenital malformation and congenital abnormality rates
  BUT drinking mothers are also more often older, single mothers, of lower social status and greater parity who have smoked more. Even when these variables are accounted for, the effect of alcohol is still significant.

  Children, as they grow up, continue to have developmental problems, eg Attention-Deficit/Hyperactivity Disorder, but assessment is difficult as by this stage they are socially deprived as a result of their earlier problems.
  Can occur with as few as four drinks a day.
  Can cause hydronephrosis in baby and mild mental retardation.
  Causes cleft lip and palate.
  There are no associated liver abnormalities in the child.

Figure–ground differentiation – The ability to differentiate between an object and the background.
There are **ambiguous figures**, seen when the figure alternates with the ground.

Fixed role theory – Was developed by Kelly.

Flashbacks – Episodes of repeated reliving of the trauma in intrusive memories.
Vivid memories of stressful events intruding into awareness as images. If persistent, form part of PTSD.

Flexibility, waxy – *aka* flexibilitas cerea

A feeling of plastic resistance resembling the bending of a soft wax rod as the examiner moves part of the patient's body that then remains 'moulded' in the new position.

- Is commonly associated with frontal lobe tumours.

Flight of ideas – Is a formal thought disorder.

146

- is *not* a loosening of associations
- is a rapid, continuous, fragmentary stream of ideas, thoughts and images without any coherent pattern or
- ocus, as expressed in speech
- the logical sequence of ideas is maintained, so there is no loosening of associations, but the goal of thinking is not maintained for long, as the *determining tendency* is weak
- is typical of mania
- is associated with easy distractibility.

Characteristic features include:
- clang and verbal associations
- punning
- rhyming
- responding to distracting cues.

Flooding – The immersion of a phobic patient in a phobic situation (real or imagined) for several consecutive hours. Phobia diminishes as the association between the object and the fear diminishes.
If the exposure is imagined, it's called implosion rather than flooding.

Flumazenil –
- Is a benzodiazepine antagonist.
- Also reverses the effects of zopiclone.

Fluoxetine –
- Increases blood levels of TCAs.
- Most common side-effect is nausea.
- Needs to have been stopped for five weeks before an MAOI is started.

Flupenthixol – Has some antidepressant effects.

Fluphenazine – Is a phenothiazine with an aliphatic side chain.

Fluvoxamine – Increases blood concentrations of warfarin.

Folic acid deficiency – Can cause an acute or chronic organic reaction.

Folie à deux –
- Most patients are blood relatives.
- Separation leads to disappearance in fewer than 50% – more likely in the recipient.
- Brothers are *not* most commonly affected.
- Shares the same psychopathology as *folie à plusiers*.
- Delusions are usually persecutory.

Folie circulaire – Described by Falret.

Formication – The sensation of insects crawling over the body.
Seen in withdrawal from cocaine and sometimes from alcohol.

Fornix – Lesions cause memory disturbance.

Fortification spectra – Are a type of visual hallucination. They are
scintillating luminous zigzags perceived during a migraine.
They are caused by occipital ischaemia.

Foucault – Argued strongly for the **antipsychiatry school**.

Foulkes – Is associated with **analysis through the group**.

Frankl – Developed **existential logotherapy**.

Fregoli syndrome – Is the false identification of familiar people in
strangers.

Freud, Anna – Talked about resistance as a source of information about
the patient's mental state, representing the type of conflict and the
defences used.
- Is associated with these defence mechanisms (described in 1936):
  - regression
  - repression
  - reaction formation
  - isolation
  - undoing
  - projection
  - introjection
  - turning against the self
  - reversal.
- Discussed **ego psychology**.

Freud, Sigmund – Was associated with:
- prominence of a general life force or libido (along with Jung)
- infantile sexuality.

- Considered infantile sexuality to be **polymorphously perverse**,
  with several sources of sexual excitation.
- His dual theory of drives stated that sexual drives were more
  important than aggressive drives in motivating behaviour.
- His first ideas about the psychodynamic organisation of the mind
  were described in the **affect/trauma model**.

Freud's theory of development:

- The **oral phase** occurs between **birth and 15–18 months** – feeding (especially from nipple) and placing objects into the mouth leads to satisfaction.
- **15–18 months to 3 years = anal phase**:
  - the infant gets gratification from gaining control over faeces, initially by eliminating and later by withholding
  - fixation at the anal-expulsive stage causes messy, disorderly, disorganised careless and extravagant behaviour
  - fixation at the anal-retentive stage has well-known consequences.
- **3–5 years = phallic-Oedipal phase** – time of anxiety about sexual differences, when child becomes aware of his/her genitalia – pre-sexual penis-based satisfaction. Boys pass through the **Oedipal complex** (child loves parent of opposite gender, fears the same-sex parent as a rival and fears castration as retribution – resolved by identification with the same-sex parent) and girls pass through the **Electra complex**.
- The **latency period** follows the phallic-Oedipal phase and comes before puberty. It is a period of relative quiescence of sexual interest.
- **Genital phase** – adult stage of sexual satisfaction.

see Appendix 5.

Friendship – There are friendship rules (Argyle & Henderson), and friends must:
- Share news of success with a friend.
- Show emotional support.
- Volunteer help in time of need.
- Strive to make a friend happy when in one another's company.
- Trust and confide in one another.
- Stand up for a friend in their absence.
- Repay debts and favours.
- Be tolerant of other friends.
- Not nag.

During the development of a friendship, there is a lot of initial interaction that diminishes with time but becomes more intimate. Female friends are more verbally oriented and based on emotional sharing, with a lot of communication and self-disclosure. Males friends are more activity-oriented and friendships grow out of shared activities and interests.

Social exchange theory

F

Relationships are seen in terms of economics (ie mutual exchange, equity, investment).

The two motivations for friendship are:
• the need for affiliation
• the need for intimacy.

Friendships develop into networks that are:
• good insurance
• a source of growth and stimulation.

Fromm-Reichman – Expounded the idea of the **schizophrenogenic mother**.
This idea was later demonstrated to be unfounded.

Frontal lobe syndrome – *see* Appendix 4.

Frontal lobe tests – Include:
• motor sequencing
• cognitive estimates (eg how many pints in a bath, how fast do racehorses run?)
• proverb interpretation
• similarities and differences.

FSH – Follicle-stimulating hormone.

FTA – Fluorescent treponema antibody.

Fusion – Was described by Carl Schneider.
Is the illogical linking of two unrelated thoughts.
or
The joining of separate thoughts in an unclear manner.
• is seen in schizophrenia
• is associated with a weak determining tendency.

GABA – (γ-aminobutyric acid).
- Is an amino acid found widely in the CNS (as the *principal inhibitory neurotransmitter*).
- It acts as a postsynaptic inhibitory transmitter in the cerebral and cerebellar cortices.
- In the spinal cord, mediates postsynaptic inhibition of afferent pathways.
- Is not found outside the CNS.
- Decreased brain concentrations cause convulsions.
- Is made from glutamic acid by glutamic acid decarboxylase.
- It is degraded by mitochondrial GABA transaminase.
- GABA transaminase inhibitors have anticonvulsant activity.
- It forms receptor complexes with benzodiazepines but *not* with TCAs.
- Its action is enhanced/facilitated by benzodiazepine agonists, which reduce anxiety.
- Drugs causing a reduction in the action of GABA (benzodiazepine inverse agonists) increase anxiety.
- GABAergic neurones act in part as the **thalamic filter** that is hypoactive in schizophrenia.
- The actions of GABAergic neurones are:
  - decreased by dopamine
  - increased by glutamate.
- Vitamin B_6 deficiency can cause a lack of GABA and convulsions, as it is a co-factor for glutamic acid decarboxylase.

Gain, primary – Freedom from emotional discomfort brought about by *unconscious* defence mechanisms as a result of changes to the *internal* environment (ie it all goes on inside you own head and no-one else knows or is involved)
(eg reduced anxiety by *unconscious* denial of an exam).

Gain, secondary – Reduction in emotional discomfort brought about by the receiving of sympathetic attention of others, as a result of *unconscious* behaviours. It involves other people by definition (eg weak legs in conversion disorder leaving one bed-bound and therefore in the position of being waited on and cared for by others).

Galen – Proposed personality types, including:
Phlegmatic – apathetic.
Choleric – hot-tempered.

Ganser syndrome – A dissociative disorder with 4 central features:
- psychogenic physical symptoms (eg ataxia, limb flaccidity or rigidity, headache, backache, analgesia or anaesthesia) = somatic conversion symptoms
- (pseudo)hallucinations (usually visual and often elaborate)
- approximate answers
- clouding of consciousness – associated with perplexity.

Characteristic features include:
- disorientation
- inconsistent responses to questions, with some correct and some approximate answers
- amnesia for the duration of the illness.

It is a type of 'pseudod ementia'.

Gedankenlautwerden – Synchronous occurrence of thoughts and the same thought heard as an auditory hallucination.

Gegenhalten – *aka* opposition
A mild form of negativism.

Gender and development – Gender affects development:
- males compared with females are/have:
  - more aggressive
  - less verbal ability than females (in adolescence)
  - greater visuo-spatial ability
  - greater mathematical ability.

Gender identity – One's perception and self-awareness in relation to gender.
Is firmly established by 3–4 years old and is constant thereafter.

Gender role – The patterns of behaviour that a person adopts that identifies them as being male or female (eg clothes, social conventions).

Gender typing – The process by which individuals acquire a sense of gender and gender-related cultural traits appropriate to their cultural context. It starts with male and female infants being treated differently.

General paresis – Pathological features include:
- neuronal loss (especially frontoparietal)
- spirochaetes in brain (it is the only condition in which this happens)
- rod cells (iron-containing enlarged microglial cells)
- atrophied brain.

Generalised anxiety disorder – Differential diagnosis includes:
- thyrotoxicosis (all patients with suspected generalised anxiety disorder must be examined)
- neurasthenia
- alcohol dependence
- hypoglycaemia.

Is often associated with phobias.

Gerstmann's syndrome – Consists of:
- Acalculia.
- Agraphia (often as spelling errors).
- Finger agnosia.
- Right–left disorientation.

Cause:
- dominant parietal lobe lesions
- lesions of left angular gyrus.

Gestalt psychology Is based upon the idea that behaviour could not be studied by breaking it down into its constituent parts and analysing these (as behaviourism suggested). It has to be understood as a whole, by examining it in a broader context. It is holistic. Early work demonstrated this in the **phi phenomenon** (when two lights were lit sequentially and they appeared to be just one light that was moving).

The Gestalt movement did a lot of work on perceptual organisation.

Gestalt therapy – Was developed by Fritz Perls.
- Uses **dramatisation** instead of transference, to explore and express fuller awareness of the self in the **here and now**.
- Can be practised individually or in groups (ie is not dependent on groups).
- **Basic rules** include:
  - here and now
  - I and thou

- it language
- no gossiping
- dialogue
- making the rounds
- unfinished business
- exaggeration
- reversal.

Glomerular filtration rate (GFR) – Adult GFR is reached at 3–5 months of age.

Glossopharyngeal nerve – Innervates:
- the posterior one-third of the tongue
- the parotid gland.

Glutamate – Is an excitatory neurotransmitter.
- There are four types of glutamate receptor, including NMDA receptors.
- regulates GABAergic neurones.
- GABAergic neurones form part of the **thalamic filter**:
  - glutamate increases the activity of the thalamic filter
  - dopamine reduces its activity.

Goffman – Described the **betrayal funnel** (the patient's relatives act through the doctor to have the patient committed) and the **total institution**.

Goldstein – Concrete thinking.

Graphaesthesia – Ability to recognise letters or numbers traced onto one's palm or fingertip by sensation.

Grasping, forced – Is an involuntary phenomenon whereby the patient will not release something placed in their hand, forming part of frontal lobe dysfunction.

Grief – Those psychological and emotional processes, expressed internally and externally, that accompany bereavement.

Grief reaction, normal – A normal grief reaction may include:
- Stage 1
  - initial shock and disbelief, felt as 'numbness'.
- Stage 2
  - sadness
  - anger (which may be denied)
  - weeping

- poor sleep
- early morning waking
- loss of appetite
- motor restlessness
- poor concentration
- poor memory
- brief hallucinations
- social withdrawal
- sense of dejection
- weight loss
- loss of libido
- anhedonia
- loss of sense of purpose or meaning in life
- the experience that one is in the presence of the deceased
- identification phenomena – mannerisms and characteristics of the deceased may be taken on.
- Stage 3
  - symptoms resolve
  - social activity is resumed
  - memories of good times are retained.

Not usually seen are:
- suicidal thoughts
- retardation
- guilt about past actions.

Grief reaction, pathological – It's abnormal if:
- It's abnormally intense and meets the criteria for a depressive disorder.
  - suicidal thoughts are common.
- It lasts more than six months.
  - often stuck in first/second stages.
- It's delayed (ie first stage starts after two weeks).
  - this is related to pathological guilt
  - a risk factor for this is sudden/traumatic/unexpected death.
- It's inhibited or abnormal grief.
  - lacking some normal features (inhibited)
  - involves some (non-depressive) features that are unusual in degree or in nature (such as hostility, overactivity, extreme withdrawal)

Some social circumstances put people at risk of a pathological grief reaction:

- absent/unsupportive family
- immigrant (few religious/cultural supports)
- unemployment/unhappiness at work
- having dependent children
- low socioeconomic status.

Other risk factors for pathological grief reactions:
- sudden/unexpected death
- the survivor is coming to terms with another bereavement
- painful, horrifying or mismanaged death
- death of a parent (especially mother) leaving children aged 0–5 or 10–15 years.

Described by **Parkes** as three common patterns:
- **unexpected grief syndrome** – includes:
  - feelings of self-reproach
  - persistent sense of the presence of the dead person.
- **ambivalent grief syndrome** – includes:
  - prolonged/self-punitive grief.
- **chronic grief syndrome** – includes:
  - intense feelings of helplessness.

Lindemann described morbid grief reactions:
- delay of reaction
- distorted reactions:
  - overactivity without a sense of loss
  - the acquisition of symptoms belonging to the last illness of the deceased
  - a recognised medical disease
  - alterations in relationships
  - furious hostility against specific people
  - loss of affectivity
  - a lasting loss of patterns of social interaction
  - a colouring of activities that is detrimental to social and economic existence
  - agitated depression.

To describe depression also a grief reaction, the symptoms have to have been present for 2 months. The following factors also suggest depression superimposed on grief:
- guilt (about things other than one's actions at the time of death)
- thoughts of death (other than thinking that one would be better off dead or that one should have died with the deceased)
- morbid preoccupation with worthlessness

- marked psychomotor retardation
- prolonged and marked functional impairment
- hallucinatory experiences (other than thinking one can hear the voice of, or see the other person transiently).

Griesinger – Believed in *Einheitpsychose* (**unitary psychosis**), or one common disease underlying all psychoses
and
in **primary insanity** (*primare Verruckheit*) in the absence of mood disorder.

Group, large, setting –
- The emphasis is on sociocultural learning.
- There are only one or two leaders.
- Features similar to the unconscious are displayed (but this can be confronted with dialogue, for which there is much opportunity).

Groups – Compared with individuals:
- show less restraint
- are more likely to reach extreme conclusions.

Groupthink – Is the tendency of groups to reach decisions by putting aside differing opinions, due to the power of the leader of the group or lack of time.

Gyrus, angular – Is well connected to the:
- somatosensory
- visual $\Big\}$ association cortices
- auditory.

Lesions produce:
- inability to read
- inability to write.

Gyrus, inferior frontal – Is occupied by Broca's area (= motor speech area).

Gyrus, lingual – Bilateral lesions produce:
- achromatopsia.

Gyrus, post-central – Contains the primary somaesthetic area.

Gyrus, temporal, superior – Occupied by Wernicke's area.

Habituation – Getting used to something to make it less likely to provoke an undesirable response.

- Occurs in response to repeated presentation of a stimulus.
- In OCD, patients are told to think their obsessive thoughts or listen to a tape of obsessive thoughts spoken aloud as a means of reducing their subsequent carrying out of an associated obsessive ritual.
- Habituation training consists of **exposure** and **response prevention**.
- The habituation response is normal in phobic individuals.

Hall – Developed a theory of 4 zones of personal space.

Hallucinations – Are false sensory perceptions in the absence of a real external stimulus.
or
Are perceptions without an object (Esquirol).

They are:
- perceived as being located in objective space and as having the same realistic qualities as normal perceptions
- involuntary
- not amenable to argument by others
- not confined to the mentally ill, but usually represent an abnormal mental state.

Hallucinations suggestive of schizophrenia include:
- second- or third-person auditory hallucinations
- voices echoing the patient's thoughts (a first-rank symptom)
- poorly localised in space (or if well localised, there is no consistent lateralisation).

Correlate with increased electromyogram (EMG) activity in muscles associated with speech production in patients with schizophrenia and hallucinations. This supports the idea that hallucinations are associated with subvocalisation.

Include synaesthesiae – the perception of a stimulus from one modality in another.

Hallucinations, auditory – Can be:
- elementary
- second-person (usually organic or in schizophrenia)
- third-person (first-rank symptom)
- a running commentary (first-rank symptom)
- audible thoughts/thoughts repeated aloud/*echo de la pensée/gedankenlautwerden* (first-rank symptom).

Hallucinations, command – *aka* imperative hallucinations

Hallucinations, ecmnesic – Occur when the patient relives past experiences with great intensity.

Hallucinations, elementary – Are unstructured (eg simple noises).

Hallucinations, extracampine – Are located outside the limits of the sensory field (and so must be visual or auditory).
Are seen in schizophrenia, temporal lobe epilepsy or organic states.

Hallucinations, functional – Occur only with an unrelated external stimulus in the same modality.

Hallucinations, haptic – Are:
- tactile
- sensory
- superficial
- and usually have a delusional component.

Hallucinations, hypnagogic auditory – Are, very commonly, hearing one's name being spoken aloud.

Hallucinations, kinaesthetic – The feeling that the limbs are twisted – seen in schizophrenia.

Hallucinations, Lilliputian – Visual hallucinations of little animals or people.
- Occur in delirium tremens.
- Are sometimes described as pleasurable.

Hallucinations, olfactory – Are seen in depression (characteristically as a foul odour), schizophrenia (usually subordinate to hallucinations in other modalities), temporal lobe epilepsy (often as part of aura) and other organic states.

Hallucinations, reflex – Are said to occur when a stimulus in one sensory modality results in a hallucination in another. They occur with LSD or (rarely) in schizphrenia and are related to the normal phenomenon of synaesthesia.

For example, a patient may feel pain in a limb on (really) seeing a workman hammering.

Hallucinations, schizophrenic – Are typically:
- second- or third-person auditory
- poorly localised in space (or at least inconsistently lateralised)
- increased with reduced sensory input
- decreased by meaningful and interesting speech
- increased when the patient becomes drowsy
- heard by just over 50% of schizophrenic individuals at some stage.

Hallucinations, somatic – Are hallucinations of bodily sensation.

They can be:
- tactile/haptic = superficial
- visceral = deep.

Hallucinations, tactile – Occur in:
- cocaine psychosis
- delirium tremens.
  Do *not* occur in:
- temporal lobe epilepsy.

Hallucinations, visual – Characteristically occur in organic disorders.
- Include autoscopy.
- Include:
- positive scotomata
- fortification spectra
- after-image
- Lilliputian hallucinations.

Hallucinosis – Is the presence of hallucinations in clear consciousness.

Caused by:
- Psychoactive substances
  - show less restraint
  - amfetamines
  - alcohol
  - cocaine
  - hallucinogens (eg LSD) – these cause 'flashback' phenomena.

161

- Intracerebral pathology
  - neoplasia
  - head injury
  - migraine
  - infection (especially syphilis)
  - epilepsy (especially temporal lobe epilepsy).
- Endocrine disturbance
  - hypothyroidism (myxoedematous madness).
- Intoxication
  - amantadine
  - bromocriptine
  - ephedrine
  - L-dopa
  - lysuride.
- Sensory deprivation
  - deafness
  - blindness (Bonnet's syndrome)
  - torture.
- Other
  - Huntington's.

Hallucinosis, alcoholic –
- Characterised by auditory hallucinations.
- Usually voices uttering insults or threats.
- Occurs in clear consciousness.
- There is usually only one voice and the speaker is often identified.
- The patient is usually distressed by these experiences and appears anxious and restless.
- The problem responds poorly to neuroleptics, but remits spontaneously in the absence of alcohol.
- Increase with drowsiness and meaningful noise and are likely to be false perceptions of environmental noise.
- Usually manifests as simple words or second-person hallucinations.
- May occur while the patient is drinking.
- Does not include thought echo or running commentary.
- Is not a thought disorder.

Haloperidol – Was synthesised by Janssen.
- Is a butyrophenone and is therefore not sedating.

Harlow – Worked with infant chimpanzees and demonstrated the drive for attachment to objects. She showed that holding has primacy over feeding.

Worked with wire monkeys to overturn Bowlby's theory.
- Demonstrated that a fake monkey that was soft was preferred over a fake monkey that was made of wire, even if the wire monkey offered food.
- **Contact comfort** explained this.

Harm, deliberate self – Increases risk of suicide 100 times.

Head banging –
- Can occur at night time from 6 months of age.
- Usually vents frustration or aims to seek attention.
- Can be a sign of severe neglect.
- Is associated with the Lesch–Nyhan syndrome.
- Is associated with blindness.
- Is associated with mental retardation.

Head injury – Persisting cognitive impairment in head injury:
- correlates with duration of post-traumatic amnesia, coma and depth of coma (in severe closed head injury)
- typically occurs when there is post-traumatic amnesia of >24 hours in closed head injury
- is more likely with increasing age
- usually improves substantially during the first 6 months after injury
- is more likely after damage to the dominant hemisphere
- is in proportion to the amount of damage to the brain.

In (chronic) head injury due to boxing, there are several characteristic features:
- cerebral atrophy on CT antedates overt signs and is related to the number of bouts fought *rather* than number of knock-outs suffered
- cerebellar disorder
- pyramidal disorder
- extrapyramidal disorder.

There is no relationship with epilepsy, but schizophrenia-like psychoses are more common than expected and the trauma is believed to be a direct aetiological factor.

After head injury:
- the risk of suicide is 14%
- personality change can occur in the absence of brain damage and characteristically involves the following, which are common:
  - fluctuating depression
  - morbid anxiety

- obsessional traits
- persistent irritability
- the most common psychiatric disturbance is post-concussional syndrome
- amnesia recovers *gradually*
- injury at cortical sites distant to the impact occur as contrecoup injuries
- manic-depressive psychosis may result
- in recovery from *severe* closed head injury, > 5% of patients suffer from post-traumatic epilepsy
- following severe closed head injury, recovery can continue for three years
- after severe closed head injury, headaches are common
- after severe closed head injury, progressive dementia is a recognised sequel (eg boxers).

Hebephrenia – Described by Hecker in 1871.

Hecker – Described **hebephrenia** in 1871.

Heinroth – Described *verruckheit*.

Hemisomatognosia – *aka* hemisomatognosis
Is when the patient tends to neglect one side of the body, usually the left side, in threatened or actual left-sided hemiplegia.

Hemisomatognosis – *aka* hemidepersonalisation
The condition in which a patient feels that a limb which is actually present is missing.

Heroin – Use causes:
- miosis (= pupillary constriction)
- analgesia
- hypotension
- bradycardia
- respiratory depression.

Withdrawal causes:
- mydriasis (= pupillary dilation)
- sweating
- diarrhoea
- rhinorrhoea
- abdominal cramps
- yawning
- nausea

- vomiting
- lacrimation.

Sequelae are:
- endocarditis
- catastrophic reactions
- personality deterioration
- nephritic syndrome
- TB
- gangrene
- hepatitis
- thrombophlebitis
- HIV
- poisoning
- overdose
- emboli.

Herpes simplex encephalitis – Neuropathological changes include:
- perivascular inflammation with lymphocytes and histiocytes (seen in all encephalitides)
- main effects seen in cortex (especially frontotemporal)
- Cowdry type A inclusion bodies (seen in neurones, astrocytes and oligodendrocytes as large, eosinophilic intranuclear masses surrounded by a clear halo and displacing the nucleus to the periphery)
- medial temporal and orbital regions are affected
- typically symmetrical lesions.

5HIAA – 5-Hydroxy indole acetic acid(a 5HT metabolite).

Hippocampus – Lesions cause memory disturbance.

Histrionic personality disorder – Important features:
- Is a butyrophenone and is therefore not sedating.
- self-dramatisation
- craving for novelty and excitement
- self-centred approach to personal relationships
- suggestibility
- excessive concern with physical attraction.

Minor histrionic traits (conferring social advantages) are taken to extremes in this case. These people dramatise themselves as 'larger than life' characters and seem to 'play a part', incapable of being themselves. They are often unaware that other people can see through this. They search relentlessly for new experiences and have short-lived enthusiasms, are prone to boredom and crave novelty. They think only of themselves and appear vain, inconsiderate and demanding. 'Emotional blackmail', emotional scenes and apparent suicide attempts are common. They express emotions more than they feel them and forget them quickly, expecting other people to do the same. They maintain elaborate lies long after they have been revealed to be untrue. Sexual provocation is often combined with 'frigidity'.

HIV – Human immunodeficiency virus.

HLA – Human leukocyte antigen.

HMPAO – Hexamethylpropyleneamine oxime.

Hoch & Polatin – Pseudoneurotic schizophrenia.

Homeostasis – Was described by Canon.

Homosexuality – Is unique to humans as a predominant or exclusive mode of sexuality.

Arguments in favour of biological determinism:
- Endocrine
  - 21-hydroxylase deficiency:
    - in homozygous females causes congenital adrenal hypertrophy
    - in heterozygous females causes homosexuality
    - in males causes homosexuality.
  - luteinising hormone secretion:
    - in homosexual men causes positive oestrogen feedback (and therefore shows they have a female-differentiated brain)
    - there are similarly altered responses to ACTH stimulation in females.
- Neuroanatomical
  - interstitial nucleus of the anterior hypothalamus is more than twice the size in heterosexual men than in women or in homosexual men
  - the midsagittal anterior commissure is larger in homosexual men than in heterosexual men.
- Genetic
  - there is > 50% conformity between monozygous male twins for homosexuality
  - there are genetic markers.

Arguments against biological determinism:
- Endocrine

- • the results as above are arguably wrong.
- Neuroanatomical
  - • the above patients had AIDS and were therefore unrepresentative.
- Genetic
  - • the above results are preliminary, the group is very selected, the gene is hypothetical and the linkage has only been observed in one family.

Homosexuals do *not* identify exclusively with their same-sex parent.

Horney, Karen – Described psychosis as a serious consequence of neurotic development, leading to a repression of emotions and genuine thoughts.

5HT – 5-Hydroxytryptamine. *aka* serotinin

Humanism – *aka* **Phenomenological Approach**
Views humans as free and generous individuals with potential for growth and fulfilment. Arose in middle of the 20th century.

Some central concepts:
- The emphasis is on individual subject conscious experience (so it's phenomenological).
- Humans are unique and can choose their own destiny.
- The Scientific Method is inappropriate for the study of human behaviour.
- Psychology should aim to maximise potential for psychological growth.
- Let's be optimistic! Humans are all striving to reach their potential (to achieve self-actualisation).

Hunger – Is mediated by the lateral hypothalamus.

Huntington's chorea – Clinical features
- onset usually 35–45 years (onset is typically 25–60/'in the fourth to fifth decade' with the average in the mid–40s – ie in middle age)
- childhood onset in 10–20%
- insidious onset – fidgety movements in extremities and non-specific psychiatric symptoms
- neurology precedes psychiatric signs in just over 50% of cases.

movement disorder
- (starts distal)
- starts with clumsiness and facial twitching
- choreiform movements in the head, face and arms

167

- ill-sustained, jerky, voluntary and involuntary movements affect all muscles
- wide-based, lurching gait

psychiatric disturbance
- depression (early)
- prodromal personality changes then gross personality change
- antisocial behaviour
- substance misuse
- affective disorder
- schizophreniform disorder
- mild euphoria with outbursts of irritability and rage
- slowly progressive intellectual impairment – cognitive impairment occurs *late*, memory is relatively spared (subcortical dementia).

Pathology
- marked atrophy of striatum (head of caudate and putamen – part of lentiform nucleus)
- severe generalised neuronal loss causing cortical atrophy, especially of the frontal and parietal lobes and ventricular dilation
- atrophy of corpus callosum.

EEG
- flattened
- EEG shows complete loss of α rhythm (usually seen when relaxed with eyes closed) and flatter trace

Neurochemistry
- reduced GABA concentrations
- increased somatostatin concentrations
- unchanged dopamine concentrations.

Aetiology
- chromosome 4
- autosomal dominant gene with full penetrance
- occasional sporadic cases
- 20–40 CAG repeats are normal, more than about 45 is diagnostic
- age of onset is earlier if the father is the diseased parent.

Epidemiology
5/100, 000

Notes
Tetrabenazine helps reduce movement disorder.
Antidepressants, ECT and benzodiazepines may be useful initially.
Low-dose phenothiazines may control later behavioural problems.

12–20 years' life expectancy.

Early onset correlates with more rapid progression *and* unusual features (eg epilepsy and cerebellar ataxia), so if an exam question asks you if a specific (strange) symptom occurs in Huntington's disease in the young, the answer will probably be 'True'.

Differential diagnosis
- inherited cerebellar ataxia
- Creutzfeldt–Jakob disease
- Wilson's disease
- choreoacanthosis
- Parkinson's disease.

HVA – Homovanillic acid.

Hydrocephalus, communicating – Occurs when there is a communication between IV and the subarachnoid space
Causes increased pressure in the subarachnoid space and therefore increased pressure on lumbar puncture.

Hydrocephalus, normal pressure – *Characteristic* clinical features include:
- slowly progressive gait disorder (unsteadiness, impairment of balance, difficulty turning and initiating movements)
- urinary incontinence
- impairment of mental function (usually first and includes memory impairment)
- EEG is abnormal, with non-specific random θ (theta) or δ activity
- CT shows ventricular enlargement out of proportion to cortical atrophy, often with periventricular signal change.

Other features:
- abnormal posture is a feature (it's extrapyramidal)
- slowing of mental operations is a feature
- relative preservation of cortical associative functioning is a feature
- apathy, irritability
- affective disturbance is common, especially depression
- dysarthria.

Hyperactivity – Recognised treatments for hyperactivity in children include:
- imipramine
- clonidine
- dexamfetamine
- pemoline

- methylphenidate.

Hyperkinesis – Is seen in children and adolescents and includes:
- overactivity
- distractibility
- impulsivity
- excitability.

Hyperparathyroidism – Causes:
- depression (common)
- anergia (common)
- cognitive impairment.

Physical symptoms include:
- thirst
- polyuria
- fracture
- bony deformity
- renal colic
- muscle weakness
- diffuse headache
- anorexia
- nausea.

- The level of psychiatric disturbance is directly related to circulating concentrations of parathyroid hormones.
- Most patients present with physical symptoms.
- Skull X-ray occasionally shows calcification in the caudate nuclei and frontal lobes, but not nearly as often as in hypoparathyroidism, when large amounts of calcium are deposited.

Hyperprolactinaemia – Because dopamine reduces prolactin, antipsychotic drugs that reduce dopamine cause an increase in prolactin.

Clinical features:
- galactorrhoea
- gynaecomastia
- menstrual disturbances
- decreased sperm count
- reduced libido.

Hyperthyroidism –
- sleeping pulse more than 90 bpm
- sensitivity to heat

- preference for cold
- increased appetite and weight loss
- palpitations
- fine finger tremor
- mania.

Hypnagogic images – Hallucination-like images experienced while first falling asleep. They tend to occur when EEG patterns indicate Stage 1 sleep, but in the absence of the rapid eye movements (REM) typically seen during dreaming.

Hypnotism – A social interaction in which one participant responds to suggestions offered by another person for experiences involving alterations in perception, memory and voluntary action.

While in this altered state, the person is highly suggestible and the hypnotist can induce hallucinations.

Suggestions made during this state can be retained and acted on afterwards. For example, after the period of hypnosis, the subject may stand on a chair when the hypnotist taps the table, in response to a suggestion received during the period of hypnosis.

Hypnosis can overcome repression.

Estimation of time is well preserved in hypnotic states.

There are 2 theories of hypnosis:

- State theory – hypnosis is an altered state of consciousness, a dissociative state. There is a **hidden observer**, a part of the mind that is outside consciousness and not strongly influenced by hypnosis that monitors what is happening and can end the altered state if circumstances require it.
- Non-state theory – there is no distinct altered state of consciousness. The person is just being compliant and 'going along' with the hypnotist. The whole process can be explained in terms of motivation, imagination and compliance.

Hypochondriasis – Is a preoccupation with a fear of having a serious illness that is not based on real organic pathology but instead on an unrealistic interpretation of physical signs or sensations as being abnormal.

or

Increased subjective awareness resulting in a person taking excessive account of their symptoms.

May co-exist with a physical disorder.

Symptoms are left-sided in 75% of patients.

Hypochondriasis may be in the form of:

- primary/secondary delusions
- an over-valued idea
- obsessive/depressive ruminations
- an anxious preoccupation.

Mechanisms:
- misinterpretation of normal physiological sensation
- conversion of unwanted affect into physical symptoms
- mood disorder leading to changes in autonomic nervous system.

May be primary or secondary to:
- depression
- anxiety
- schizophrenia.

Risk factors:
- male gender
- Jewish religion
- low social class
- elderly
- medical student.

Hypoglycaemia – Can be a cause of episodic anxiety.
Can cause an acute or chronic organic reaction.

Hypomania – Features include:
- insomnia
- grandiose delusions
- unwise business investments
- increased libido
- euphoria
- infectious gaiety
- brief periods of depression
- anger
- irritability
- quick temper
- acute onset
- but *not* sustained affability.

Hypothalamus –
- Area of high 5HT concentration.
- Ventromedial nucleus = satiety centre.
- Lateral hypothalamus = hunger centre.
- Receives direct afferent fibres from the cerebral cortex.
- Controls hormone output from the pituitary gland by sending

major outputs there.
- Is part of the diencephalon.

Hypothesis, dopamine – Postulates excess mesolimbic-cortical dopamine activity as the cause of schizophrenia.

Hypothesis, frustration aggression – Was proposed by Dollard.
Proposes that aggression is always created by a frustrating situation, but that frustration does not always lead to aggression, with frustration being defined as anything interfering with the realisation of a goal.
It has been found that interference when one is close to one's goal is much more likely to result in aggression.
Regards aggression as an innate response.

Hypothyroidism – Associated psychiatric disorders include:
- organic psychosis:
  - most common
  - acute/subacute
- with:
  - delirium
  - florid delusions
  - florid hallucinations
  - confusion
  - impaired consciousness
  - dementia – insidious and progressive
  - depressive psychosis
  - schizophrenic psychosis.

Hysteria – Is much more common in developing countries, perhaps because a more somatic way of thinking about psychological distress predominates there.
Somatic expression correlates with low social class and low education.
The main defence mechanism is denial.

H

IBS – Irritable bowel syndrome.

ICD-10 – The International Statistical Classification of Diseases and Related Health Problems, 10th revision.
- was developed by the World Health Organisation (WHO)
- categorises neurasthenia under neurotic disorders (F48.0)
- schizoaffective disorder and post-schizophrenia depression are categorised under schizoaffective disorder, schizotypal and delusional disorders (F20–29)
- is *not* produced in a single and elaborate version
- the neurosis/psychosis division *isn't* adopted from ICD-9
- the chapter on mental disorder has 100 categories (not 50)
- does contain the terms neurotic and psychotic
- the classification is based on aetiology for some conditions:
  - delirium tremens and Korsakoff's syndrome
- but not for others:
  - Wilson's disease
  - Alzheimer's disease
  - Briquet's syndrome
- there were field trials, but these were not more extensive than ICD-9.

Idea, over-valued – Was described by Wernicke in 1900.
An isolated, preoccupying belief, neither delusional nor obsessional, which comes to dominate a person's life over many years and affect their actions. They are usually associated with very strong affect and carry a poor prognosis.
or
An unreasonable and sustained intense preoccupation maintained with less than delusional intensity (ie the patient can acknowledge that it may not be true), which is demonstrably false and not normally held by other members of the patient's subculture. There is a marked associated emotional investment.

or
Acceptable and understandable ideas that become dominant and are pursued beyond the limits of reasonableness.
- usually associated with abnormal personality
- includes:
  - morbid jealousy, dysmorphophobia, parasitophobia.

- different from delusions
- not obsessional
- not firmly held false beliefs.

Illusions – Are false perceptions (along with hallucinations and pseudohallucinations).
Are misperceptions of external stimuli. They are seen in normal people, delirium and depression.
May be secondary to delusions in psychosis (delusional illusions).

They include:
- mirage
- diplopia
- *jamais vu*
- *déjà vu*
- macropsia.

Completion illusion – unconscious filling in of gaps in a percept
Affect illusion – perception altered by mood state (eg scared person in dark room sees chair as intruder)
Pareidolic illusion – images are perceived from shapes and patterns.
- During inattention, completion and affect illusions can occur, but pareidolic illusions can increase in intensity during attention.
- They are seen in temporal lobe epilepsy.
- Are transformations of perception (Esquirol).
- Pareidolia is a false perception of a real external stimulus.
- Are not a feature of Capgras' syndrome.

Imagery – A fantasy, created voluntarily, not perceived as real and usually not acted upon.

Imaging, in-vivo receptor –
- PET is good, unlike MRI.
- Affinity of psychotropic drugs for receptors can be accurately calculated.

Imipramine – Was reported on by Kuhn.
Is a tertiary amine/TCA with noradrenaline and 5HT effects.

- can be used to treat hyperactivity in children
- has a quinidine-like action on ventricular ectopics
- has effects on 5HT reuptake.

Side-effects include:
- anticholinergic effects
- sedation
- seizures
- postural hypotension.

Imitation – Can be done by a newborn with respect to mouth movements.
From six months, social stimuli can be imitated.

Implosion – Putting a phobic patient in an imagined phobic situation. It's a type of flooding.

Impotence, secondary –
Can be caused by:
- TCAs
- antidepressants
- MAOIs
- typical antipsychotics (especially thioridazine)
- hypotensives
- diuretics
- ethanol
- cimetidine (but not ranitidine).

Imprinting – Is what happens (eg in geese) when the first moving object encountered after hatching is followed around. It is species specific and has not been described in humans.

Impulsive personality disorder – Involves:
- inadequate control of emotions
- sudden unrestrained outpourings of anger, with subsequent regret
- may involve violence
- no other difficulties in relationships (unlike dissocial personality disorder).

Regarded as subtype of emotionally labile personality disorder in ICD-10.

Impulsiveness – A central feature of antisocial personality disorder and borderline personality disorder.

Incongruous affect – Is seen more frequently in a schizophreniform psychosis than in an affective psychosis.

Inducers, hepatic enzyme – barbiturates
- phenytoin
- rifampicin.
- Decrease the concentrations of TCAs.

Infants –
- Can imitate adult facial expressions at 36 hours.
- Smile in response to their mother at 2 months (even if they're blind).

Infidelity –
- Men perceive sexual infidelity to be more of a betrayal than emotional infidelity and women see it the other way round.

Inhibition, reciprocal – Described by Joseph Wolpe in 1950. States that relaxation inhibits anxiety, so that they are mutually exclusive. It isn't true!
Is used to treat phobias – relaxation inhibits anticipatory anxiety. Patients identify increasingly anxiogenic stimuli (**anxiety hierarchy**), and **systematic desensitisation** couples exposure (imaginary or real) with relaxation to desensitise the patient. It's based on behaviour theory, which is associated with classical conditioning. What happens is that the CS is presented without the UCS and the CR fails to occur, leading to extinction.

Inhibitors, hepatic enzyme – phenothiazines
- butyrophenones
- MAOIs.

- Increase the concentrations of TCAs.

Instinct – Is inherited and unchangeable according to psychodynamic theory.

Intellect – Mental abilities, excluding feelings, emotions and perception.

Intelligence – The single generalised ability to adapt to the environment. Difficult to define in other terms and very political. Performance IQ declines with age; verbal IQ is relatively spared – this is the 'verbal-performance discrepancy'.

Cultural influences on IQ
- Cultures value and develop different abilities (accountants are slow but accurate).

- Tests measure assimilation of culture.

Effort depends on relationship between tester and subject.

Correlation coefficient for identical (monozygous) twins is 0.86, compared with 0.60 for non-identical (dizygous) twins.

Intelligence, heredity – Concordance for monozygous twins reared together is 0.85.
Concordance for monozygous twins reared apart is 0.70.

Intelligence tests – Raven's progressive matrices come in three versions – standard, coloured and advanced.

Interactionism – Represents the drawing together of other schools with regard to the understanding of the human condition. It aims to provide a complete account of human behaviour (in time). Included are biological, mechanical and social aspects of behaviour.

Interview, psychiatric typical –
As a first step, the interviewer should:
- ask the patient to give the history in his or her own words
- ask the patient about his or her main problem.

Intramuscular administration – Factors increasing absorption:
- lipid solubility
- low relative molecular mass
- increased muscle blood flow (eg exercise, emotion).

Disadvantages:
- pain
- not appropriate for self-administration
- collateral damage
- risk of sterile abscess formation (paraldehyde)
- reduced muscle blood flow reduces absorption
- tissue binding/precipitation reduces absorption (eg diazepam)
- unsuitable if patient taking anticoagulants
- increased CPK causes confusion with cardiac assays.

Intravenous administration –
Advantages:
- rapid action
- can titrate against response
- can give large volumes (albeit slowly)
- some drugs are for intravenous use only
- little first-pass metabolism.

Disadvantages:
- onset of adverse effects is also rapid
- dangerously high plasma concentrations possible
- you can't suck it back out if there's an adverse reaction
- sepsis
- thrombosis
- air embolism
- perivascular injection (necrosis)
- arterial injection
- no good for some drugs (ie insoluble formulations).

Invalidation – Describes denial of feelings of family members and is reported to be a risk factor for schizophrenia.

Inventory, Beck Depression – -Is *not* a diagnostic scale, but provides an indication of the depth of a depressive illness.

IQ – Intelligence quotient.

Ischaemia, vertebrobasilar – May cause drop attacks.

iv – Intravenous.

James–Lange theory (of emotion) – States that the experience of emotion is secondary to somatic responses (eg sweating, tachycardia, increased arousal) to the perception of emotionally important events. So if someone runs away from a mouse, it's because they find themselves tachycardic and sweating, not primarily because they want to get away from the mouse.

The theory states that we are able to differentiate the various emotions from one another because the physiological experiences caused by them are different. No other factors are needed, nor other cues involved.

Janet – First described the lowering of psychic energy as causing dissociation.

Janov, Arthur – Developed **Primal Therapy** (an emotional release therapy) and wrote *The Primal Scream*.

Janssen – Synthesised haloperidol.

Jealousy, morbid – *aka* Othello's syndrome is associated with:
- paranoia
- repressed homosexuality (it may be a projection of this)
- organic psychosis
- obsessional personality/neurosis
- hysteria
- feelings of inadequacy
- personality disorder
- schizophrenia
- manic-depressive psychosis
- Parkinson's disease
- cocainism
- dementia
- general paralysis of the insane
- cerebral tumour.

Johnston – Discovered ventricular enlargement in patients with chronic schizophrenia.

Jung, Carl Gustav – Concerned himself with the interpretation of unconscious material as represented in myths, dreams and culture.

His theory of the psyche has three levels:
- the **Conscious persona**
- the **Personal Unconscious**
- the **Collective Unconscious**.

He described **archetypes** as generalised symbols and images in the collective unconscious, inborn predispositions to perceive and act in a certain manner, including:
- **the Animus** – masculine prototype
- **the Anima** – feminine prototype
- **the Shadow** = unacknowledged and unacceptable (and therefore repressed) aspects of the self arising from animal instincts (either positive or negative, but some people say it's just disliked elements), related to the ego and the repressed opposite of the Persona
- **the Great Mother** – an all-nurturing caretaker
- **the Wise Old Man**
- **the Hero**
- **the Persona/Self**.

Coined the terms:
- **extroversion**
- **introversion**
- **individuation**

and was associated with the concepts:
- prominence of a general life force or libido (along with Freud), but believed this was the unitary force of every sort of psychic energy, rather than just sexually driven.
- **complexes** are related to archetypes – they are a mix of the Persona and archetypes that can dictate acts and feelings.

Differed from Freud, in that Jung believed

- in the **collective unconscious** (later called the **objective psyche**) that gives rise to consciousness, revealed in the myths and symbols of different cultures. There are **archetypes**, universal motifs seen in art, literature and religion around the world
- that the id was spiritual rather than sexual

- in personality types (extroverts – introverts)
- in **causality** as against Freudian psychic determinism:
  - causality explains things in terms of the past
  - teleology explains future potential
  - synchronicity explains things in terms of occurring at the boundary of the physical and psychical/mystical worlds.

Said there were four operations of the mind:

- Feeling – allowing feelings and judgements.
- Intuition – perception through unconscious processes.
- Sensation – allowing acquisition of factual data.
- Thinking – logic and reasoning.

J

Kahlbaum – Described catatonia in 1863.

Kane – Reported on clozapine.

Kasanin – Described schizoaffective psychosis.

Kaye – Described **scaffolding** and **framing**.

K_d – Inversely, measures affinity of an endogenous transmitter/drug for a receptor.

Kelly – Developed **fixed role theory**.

Klein, Melanie – Accepted orthodox Freudian theory, but claimed to have opened up unexplored regions in the pre-Oedipal stages. She traced the origins of the super-ego back to the first few months of life. She believed that the most important drives were aggressive ones and treated children as young as 2 years. She used the fantasy life of the child as expressed in play. The parents were not involved. Emphasised the defences of **splitting, introjection** and **projective identification**. She believed that the **paranoid-schizoid position** occupied the first six months and was characterised by anxiety about its own safety, which leads to the characteristic thoughts and behaviour of the stage and that 'the baby's notions of aggression are conditioned by the fact that it is at the oral stage of development'.

Analysed her own children and wrote them up as disguised clinical cases.
Her aim was to cure children of 'psychoses'.

She believed:
- Object relations were relevant in children.
- The **paranoid-schizoid position** – develops during the first six months and is characterised by isolation and persecutory fears, also aggression. It develops because the infant sees the world as **part objects** (the mother is split into good and bad objects, dependent

on whether she is satisfying the child's needs) and uses certain defence mechanisms:

- introjection (internalisation) – of good objects
- projective identification ▼ – of bad objects
- splitting ▼ – of bad objects – the breast is split into the **good breast** and a terrifying, frustrating bad object
- projection ▼
- omnipotence* ▼
- manic defence
- denial* ▼
- idealism*
- grandiosity ▼
  (* = main defences, ▼ = psychotic defences).
- Aggression was emphasised.
- The paranoid-schizoid position is seen in adults as aggression, terror of being hurt and a desire to retaliate.
- At 6 months comes the **depressive position** when the child moves on from part objects to perceive objects as whole (ie the mother) and realises that the world is not perfect. This is the prototype for working through adult losses. The depressive position is a normal feature and does *not* predispose to later depression.
- The depressive position may be held intermittently and transiently in adults.
- The oedipal situation is brought forward from age 4–5 years to the first year of life.
- The ego and a primitive super-ego exist during the first year of life.
- In stages of development:
  - oral frustration
  - oral envy (of parental oral sex and oral sadism, leading to an Oedipal impulse)
  - a longing for the oral incorporation of the father's penis and destruction of the mother's body
  - castration anxiety in boys and fear of destruction of the body in girls
  - primitive super-ego's emergence
  - introjection of pain-causing objects
  - development of a **cruel super-ego**
  - **ejection of the super-ego**.
- There are no anal, latency or pubertal stages.

Kleine-Levine syndrome –
- Hypothalamic disorder.
- Onset in second decade.
- More common in males.

Characteristic features include:
- periodic hypersomnolence (lasting several days) by day and night during an attack, with irritability and aggression if woken
- when awake, extreme hunger and hyperphagia
- hypersexuality
- attacks lasting from several days to several weeks
- average frequency is two attacks per year
- usually occurs in young men, with an onset in early adolescence
- occasional cases occur in women, in middle age
- the patient is normal between attacks
- visual and auditory hallucinations are present during attacks
- delusions.

Kline – Was one of the first to report on the use of MAOIs in depression.

Knight's move thinking – Is the transition from one topic to another with no logical relationship between the two.

Koro – *Common* culture-bound syndrome affecting men in South-West Asia, especially the Chinese.
It is characterised by:
- periods of acute anxiety with:
  - sweating
  - palpitations
  - pericardial discomfort
  - trembling
- belief that the penis will retract into the abdomen and cause imminent death
- this belief is *not* a delusion
- it occurs mainly at night
- it occurs in the context of sexual guilt
- the man may tie his penis up with string to prevent its retraction.

It may occur in epidemics

Korsakoff's syndrome – *aka* Korsakoff's psychosis
see Appendix 1.

Kraepelin – Proposed **dementia praecox, manic-depressive insanity/psychosis** and **Kraepelin's triad.**

K

Kretschmer, Ernest – Emphasised **morphological–physiological–psychological unity** of the individual, maintaining that an individual's temperamental reactions are reflections of their **body types**. His best known work is *Physique and Character*. His classes were:

- **pyknic** – relaxed/sociable
- **aesthetic** – solitary/self-conscious
- **athletic** – robust/outgoing.

Kuhn – Reported on imipramine.

Lability, emotional – Is seen in:
- delirium tremens
- BPAD
- 'hysterical personality'
- Alzheimer's disease
- pseudobulbar palsy
- postnatal blues
- puerperal psychosis
- Wernicke's encephalopathy
- bromism.

Laborit – Reported that chlorpromazine (synthesised by Charpentier) could induce artificial hibernation.

Lamotrigine – Has effects on voltage-sensitive sodium and calcium channels by inhibiting presynaptic release of glutamate and aspartate.

Langfeldt – Described **schizophreniform psychosis**.

Language – An organised system of sounds and words that permit the communication of information.
or
The sum of the skills required to communicate verbally.

Is strongly lateralised to the dominant hemisphere (99% in right-handers). In left-handers it can be bilateral (but the left hemisphere dominant in 60% of right-handers).

It consists of:
- phonology – words composed of phonemes
- syntax – sentences composed of words
- semantics – meaning of words.

Levels of language
- sentence units, including phrases

- words, prefixes and suffixes
- phonemes.

Assuming children are exposed to language, it is acquired in a predictable sequential manner according to the rate of individual developmental maturation (ie language development isn't affected by culture, geography, intelligence, cognition, training, etc).

Language, development of –
Within hours – distinguishing of mother's voice
0–3 months – random vocalisations – no meaning or structure
3–4 months – babbling
8 months – repetitive babbling
12 months – mama, dada and one other word
18 months – 20–50-word vocabulary with single word utterances = **holophasic speech**
2 years – 2–3-word sentences with basic grammar – **telegraphic utterances** (words and plurals, articles, prepositions left out) – **syntactic speech**
3 years – understanding of a 3-stage request.

Phases of language development
Phase 1
- Passive – child receives
  - 8–6 months
Phase 2
- Rapid vocabulary gain
  - 18 months – naming games, questions, under/over extension (eg 'bowow' = all animals)
Phase 3
- New kinds of words
  - relative values (eg under/over).

Influences on language development:
- Developmental maturation – determines extent of language development (factors such as cognitive ability, geographical location, culture and training are unimportant)
- Bilingual home – no problem
- Larger family size – slower speech development
- Pregnancy – intrauterine growth retardation and prolonged second stage of labour – slower language
- Gender – early language development is more common in girls
- Middle-class – faster
- Understimulation – slower

- Twins – slower speech development.
- Language development can only start properly after the concept of object permanence is achieved.

Language in relation to thought – There are four views:
- Language determines thought
  So people who speak different languages have fundamentally different views about the world. Examples given included the fact that Inuits (who have lots of words for snow) think about snow in a more complex way than non-Inuits, whereas Hopi Indians have the same word for insect, aeroplane and pilot – and can differentiate between them.
- Thought is internal speech (the behaviourist view)
  This idea is based upon the assumption that problem-solving involves use of an internal language, and the observation that, when people on their own are asked to perform difficult tasks, they often talk out loud to help themselves. However, it has been demonstrated that, even when someone is totally paralysed, they can still think, despite the fact that there is no capacity for subvocal speech.
- Thought determines language (by influencing linguistic development)
  Studied by Piaget, who found that children who understood the principle of conservation of volume (ie that a liquid stays the same volume whatever shape of vessel it's poured in to) understood 'more' 'as much as' and similar words and phrases much better than children who did not know the principle, even when these children were given specific linguistic training.
- Thought and language are not directly related, but both have effects on intellectual development
  Vygotsky said that, in infancy, thought must be independent of language as the infant trying to vocalise has no inner thought. By the age of 2 years, the child makes a connection between social speech and thought, and words act as symbols for thoughts. By the age of 7 years, language and thought separate again and language has 2 functions:
  - internal language as an aid to thought (egocentric speech) – sometimes expressed aloud
  - external language as a means of communicating thought to others.

L

Latah – Is a culture-bound condition seen in Malay women.
- onset is after a frightening experience
- there is an exaggerated response to minimal stimuli with an excessive startle reaction
- coprolalia
- echolalia
- echopraxia
- automatic obedience.

Lateral medullary syndrome – *aka* Wallenberg's syndrome
Characteristic features include:
- ipsilateral loss of pain and temperature sensation in the trigeminal distribution (due to involvement of the spinal trigeminal tract and its nucleus)
- contralateral loss of pain and temperature sensibility (because the lateral spinothalamic tract is interrupted in the spinal lemniscus)
- ipsilateral paralysis of muscles of the soft palate, pharynx and larynx s a result of destruction of the nucleus ambiguus.

LBD – Lewy body dementia; the same as DLB, dementia with Lewy bodies.

Leadership – There are several factors which will determine what sort of person will be a suitable leader:
- Personality – leaders are larger, healthier, more attractive (these are important), more intelligent (less so), more confident, talkative and feel more need for dominance.
- Situational – **task-oriented leadership** and **socioemotional leadership** demand different qualities.
- Behavioural (Lewin)
  - democratic leadership is best. It leads to greater productivity unless a highly original product is required
  - autocratic leadership is poor. Workers abandon the task in the leader's absence, but this style is good for situations of urgency
  - *laissez-faire* leadership is also poor, but can be suitable for creative, open-ended, person-oriented tasks.

Learned helplessness – Was described by Seligman.
Occurs when reward is no longer contingent on the desired behaviour.

Learning – Is a change in behaviour as a result of prior experience. It can occur in several ways:
- Associative learning.

- Classical conditioning.
- Operant conditioning.
- Cognitive learning.
- Observational learning.

Learning, avoidance – Occurs when two relationships have been learnt:
- What predicts an aversive event.
- How to get away from that aversive event.

Either of these two elements can be classical or operant.

Learning, cognitive – Occurs when current perceptions are interpreted in the context of previous information to solve unfamiliar problems.
It's more complex than associative learning.
Involves the formation of **cognitive maps**. These allow mental images to be formed that allow meaning and structure to be given to the internal and external environments.

Can occur in two ways:

- Insight learning – occurs 'out of the blue' when an understanding is reached of the relationships between different elements to a problem.
- Latent learning – cognitive learning takes place but is not manifest except in certain circumstances, such as when a basic drive needs satisfying.

Learning, insight – Characteristics include:
- suddenness
- transferability.

Learning, observational – *aka* vicarious learning
The optimal condition is when the individual sees that the observed behaviour is being reinforced.

Learning, state-dependent – Occurs when a memory was laid down (ie something was learnt) in a particular state (eg alcohol intoxication) and is later more easily retrieved in a similar state.

Learning theory – Is important in:
- phobias
  - classical conditioning – the fear object is present with a really fearful thing
  - operant conditioning – with reinforcement of the real fear.

- OCD
- fetishism.

Learning theory, observational – *aka* vicarious learning/modelling
Was described by Bandura.
The learning of behaviours occurring by observation without direct reinforcement.
Optimal conditions are:
- the individual sees the observed behaviour reinforced
- perceived similarity – the individual has to see that he/she can behave the same way as the perceived organism receiving reinforcement.

Learning theory, social – Explains how children learn new behaviour by imitating another person.
It highlights:
- Observational learning; works if the person observed:
  - is similar to the observer
  - exhibits power and control over a desirable commodity
  - is warm and nurturant.
- Necessary cognitive factors (on the part of the observer):
  - attending to important aspects of the behaviour and ignoring others
  - remembering critical features
  - accurate duplication of observed behaviour
  - motivation to duplicate the observed behaviour.
- Identification
  - Acting as others would act in the same position.

Leonhard – Distinguished schizophrenia from **cycloid psychoses**.
Described **cycloid psychoses**:
- anxiety-happiness
- confusion
- motility psychosis (either akinetic or hyperkinetic).

Lentiform/lenticular nucleus – Major part of basal ganglia, with caudate nucleus.

Lesch–Nyhan syndrome –
- X-linked recessive.
- Effects on purine metabolism due to enzyme defect causing excess production of uric acid.
- Children are normal at birth.
- Choreoathetoid movements, scissor position of legs,

self-mutilation.
- Prenatal diagnosis by amniotic fluid sampling.
- Postnatal diagnosis by enzyme estimation in hair roots.
- Death in second to third decade, from renal failure or infection.
- Hydroxytryptophan may reduce self-mutilation.
- Is associated with head banging.

Lethal catatonia – Is a differential for neuroleptic malignant syndrome. Features include:
- hyperthermia
- autonomic dysfunction
- extrapyramidal effects
- intense motor excitement
- violent destructive behaviour
- thought disorder
- auditory and visual hallucinations.

Lewy bodies – Seen in Parkinson's disease and Lewy body dementia.

LFT – Liver function test.

LH – Luteinising hormone.

Libido, loss of – Is often a symptom of depression.

Lidz – Described **marital schism** and **marital skew**.

Limbic system – Contains:
- grey matter
- part of the amygdaloid nucleus
- the limbic lobe (parahippocampal and cingulate gyri)
- hippocampal formation
- hypothalamus (especially mammillary bodies)
- anterior nucleus of the thalamus
- fibre bundles
- fornix
- mamillothalamic tract
- stria terminalis
- lots of 5HT.

Lithium –
- Use was first proposed by Lange in 1886.
- Was introduced by Cade in 1949.
- Is not a sedative, depressant or euphoriant.
- Has little effect on the EEG.
- Has similar efficacy to valproate when used in mania.

- Gives a better response in mania followed by depression than in depression followed by mania.

Acute toxicity reactions include:
- vomiting
- profuse diarrhoea
- *coarse* tremor
- ataxia
- coma
- convulsions
- arrhythmia
- dysarthria
- nystagmus
- renal impairment
- muscle weakness.

Treatment of toxicity can include:
- increase fluid intake
- give oral sodium chloride
- give iv mannitol
- if > 3 mmol/l, peritoneal dialysis or haemodialysis and forced alkaline diuresis.

Early side-effects include:
- mild polyuria (appears then disappears. In case of late polyuria, check the urea and electrolytes, it is usually reversible)
- nausea
- diarrhoea.

Late side-effects include:
- hypothyroidism (*not* hyperparathyroidism)
- benign and reversible T-wave depression
- nephrogenic diabetes insipidus (caused by increased vasopressin because of inhibition of vasopressin-sensitive adenylate cyclase) – presents as thirst and polyuria
- benign increase in polymorphonuclear leukocytes (reversible)
- weight gain
- oedema
- thirst.

Other effects:
- slight insulin-like action (ie hypoglycaemic)
- renal tubular damage (in therapeutic concentrations)
- memory disturbances (in therapeutic concentrations)

- choreoathetosis
- tardive dyskinesia
- nasal congestion
- *fine* tremor.

Should be avoided or carefully thought about in those with:
- Addison's disease (because of sodium imbalance)
- cardiac disease
- renal impairment
- myasthenia gravis
- pregnancy (not advised)
- surgery (discontinue 24–48 hours before operation).

Is highly water soluble and poorly lipid soluble, therefore it:
- does not bind to plasma proteins
- is cleared by the kidney, in contrast to **all other psychotropic drugs**
- is excreted in the urine (95%), with a half-life of 12–24 hours; excretion is biphasic: 33–66% over 6–12 hours and the remainder over 10–14 days
- passes the blood-brain barrier slowly
- is reabsorbed mainly by the *proximal* renal tubules
- is excreted in breast milk.

Concentrations can be increased by:
- some NSAIDs (eg indomethacin, phenylbutazone) – increase resorption at proximal convoluted tubule
- loop diuretics
- thiazides
- phenytoin.

Concentrations are decreased by:
- theophylline.

Use in pregnancy:
- increased risk of Ebstein anomaly (= tricuspid effects) in 1st trimester
- subtherapeutic concentrations may be caused by increased volume of distribution
- glomerular filtration rate is increased during pregnancy, therefore toxic concentrations can be seen in the puerperium.

Lobe, frontal – Prefrontal cortex:
- problem solving
- perceptual judgement

- memory
- programming and planning sequences of behaviour
- verbal regulation
- level of response emission
- adaptability of response pattern
- tertiary motor control.

Frontal eye fields:
- voluntary eye movements.

Motor and premotor cortex:
- contain primary and secondary motor areas respectively
- primary and secondary motor control
- design fluency.

Broca's area (motor association area):
- expressive speech.

Orbital cortex:
- personality
- social behaviour.

see Appendix 4.

Lobe, occipital – *see* Appendix 4.

Lobe, parietal – *see* Appendix 4.

Lesions cause:
- Gerstman's syndrome
- finger agnosia
- left–right disorientation
- a homonymous hemianopia.

Lobe, parietal, non-dominant – Functions include:
- drawing together of elemental visual percepts into complete percepts (ie seeing objects as a whole) – but there is no attribution of meaning.

Lesions here cause:
- apperceptive agnosia
- sensory inattention
- anosognosia
- constructional apraxia (lesion in posterior area of lobe)
- homonymous hemianopia
- topographical agnosia
- visuo-spatial problems.

Lobe, parieto-occipital – Functions include:
- attribution of meaning in visual perception, meaning being supplied by the dominant parietal lobe.

Bilateral lesions cause:
- associative agnosia
- apperceptive agnosia.

Lobe, temporal –
- Lesions cause memory loss.
- Bilateral lesions can cause Kluver–Bucy syndrome.

Lobe, temporal, non-dominant –
- Lesions cause:
  - inability to learn new roads
  - diminution of musical appreciative ability
  - difficulty in reproducing visual designs from memory.

Lobe, temporo-occipital, dominant – Stores visual verbal short-term memory.

Locus caeruleus – Group of neurones in reticular formation involved in regulation of circadian rhythm.
- activity is decreased just before sleep
- activity is decreased just before waking,

so it seems that they have a central role in arousal, rather than in sleep regulation.
- Neurones stop firing during REM sleep.
- Contains noradrenergic cell bodies.

Logoclonia – Repetition of the last syllable of every word.
Occurs in Parkinson's disease and catatonic schizophrenia.

Logorrhoea – *aka* volubility
Fluent rambling speech with many words.
or
Voluble pressure of speech
- a feature of mania.

Loosening of associations – *aka* formal thought disorder
Was described by Bleuler.
May be considered to be a schizophrenic language disorder.

Includes:
- knight's move thinking
- word salad/schizophasia (described by Bleuler)/speech confusion

- derailment
- drivelling
- fusion
- condensation
- flight of ideas
- perseveration
- transitory thinking
- 'woolly thinking'.
- Occurs most often in schizophrenia.
- Evidence for formal thought disorder includes:
- loosening of personal constructs (as measured with the repertory grid).

Lorazepam – Has a shorter half-life than diazepam.

Lorenz, Konrad – Was an ethologist.
Wrote about imprinting in *King Solomon's Ring*.

LSD – Lysergic acid diethylamide.
Is a 5HT antagonist.
- causes visual hallucinations
- can cause a schizophreniform psychosis.

Magnification – Inflation of the magnitude of the individual's problems.

Main, Tom – First used the term **Therapeutic Community** in 1946.

Malignant hyperpyrexia – Is a differential diagnosis of neuroleptic malignant syndrome (NMS). It is an inherited muscle disorder in which administration of a general anaesthetic leads to:
- widespread rhabdomyolysis (less than in NMS)
- hyperpyrexia (less than in NMS)
- muscle contraction
- delirium
- tachycardia
- increased creatine kinase.

Mamillary bodies – Lesions cause memory loss.

Mania – The following have been described in mania:
- stupor (rare)
- (Kurt) Schneiderian first-rank symptoms (in 10–20%)
- delusions of persecution
- delusions of grandiosity
- delusions of reference
- formal thought disorder (ie flight of ideas)
- loosenings of association as seen in mania include punning, rhyming, clang associations
- transient depression
- passivity phenomena
- thought broadcasting
- expansiveness
- somatic passivity
- physical overactivity
- a 'made' affect
- infectious humour

- real suicidal risk
- anger
- hallucinations.

Mania, primary – Family history of affective disorder is present in >85% of cases.

Mania, secondary – Causes of (secondary) mania:
- steroids
- L-dopa
- bromide
- influenza
- pyrexia
- amfetamines
- amantadine.

- There is typically a negative premorbid history.
- It has been described postoperatively.
- The average age of onset is later than in primary mania.
- Has been described as secondary to steroids.

Mania vs schizophrenia – Symptoms more suggestive of:
Mania
Normal syntactic structure
Pressure of speech
Clanging
Distractible speech
Circumstantiality

Schizophrenia
Poverty
- of speech
- of content of speech

Tangentiality (does not discriminate between the two)

MAO – Monoamine oxide.

MAOI – Monoamine oxide inhibitor.

Maprotiline – Is a tetracyclic antidepressant.
Is cautioned in epilepsy.

Mannerisms – Are repeated involuntary movements that appear to be goal-directed.

Marital schism – Described by Lidz.

Describes hostility/conflict between the parents resulting in difficulties in allegiance for the child.

Marital skew – Described by Lidz.
Occurs when an individual has a dominating mother and a passive father.

Maslow's hierarchy of needs – Maslow described 2 kinds of motivation:

- **deficiency motivation** – corrects deficiency (eg hunger/thirst) – satisfied first
- **growth motivation** – satisfaction of (higher) needs (eg to be loved) – come second.

The hierarchy stratifies needs, with basic needs being satisfied before **meta-needs**:

- Self-actualisation needs ⎫
- Aesthetic needs   ⎬ Meta-needs
- Cognitive needs   ⎭
- Esteem needs   ⎫
- Love and belonging needs ⎪
- Security needs   ⎬ Basic needs
- Physiological needs.   ⎭

- Everyone is capable of self-actualisation, but few achieve it.
- High-level needs create later evolutionary developments.
- Self-actualisation is linked to life experience rather than the biological character of need.

Self-actualising people have some characteristics:
- detachment
- resistance to enculturation
- democratic philosophy.

Maslow was an idiographic person.

Maternity Blues – Seen in 50–70% of recently delivered women.
More common in primiparous women.
Occurs after home or hospital births, with about the same incidence.
Do not correlate with obstetric complications.
Typically reaches its peak on the 3rd or 4th day postpartum (but weeping and depression may persist for several weeks).

Maturation – Orderly changes in behaviour resulting from biological development, the timing and form of which are relatively independent of external experience.

Maturational tasks – Are influenced by biological growth, the drive for independence and other people's general expectations.

Mayer-Gross – Described **oneirophrenia**.

McClelland – **Need for achievement** (nAch).

Measurement, principles of –
- Decide what you are measuring.
- Define it.
- Set a scale with two ends and a middle.
- Find some way of measuring it, including:
  - standardised administration
  - standardised scoring
  - collection of normalised data
- Evaluate the quality.

Sources of error:
- Response set (ie the tendency always to agree *or disagree* with the questions asked).
- Bias towards the centre (ie the tendency to avoid extreme responses).
- Extreme responding (ie the opposite).
- Social desirability (ie the giving of responses that the individual believes the tester will find desirable).
- Defensiveness (ie the individual avoids giving self-related information).
- Halo effect (ie the tendency to see a person as consistent – in an interview the observer may allow their expectation to distort their judgement).
- Hawthorne effect – the presence of the interviewer alters the situation.

MCV – Mean corpuscular volume.

Media – Especially TV, influences aggression:
- there is a relationship between boys' exposure to TV violence and aggressive behaviour
- the ways in which filmed violence may increase aggressive behaviour are:
  - teaching aggressive styles of conduct
  - increasing arousal
  - desensitisation to violence

- reducing restraint
- distorting views about conflict resolution.

Medial medullary syndrome – Features include:
- contralateral hemiparesis.

Median eminence – Is located on the floor of the 3rd ventricle (III) and is lined with tanycytes.

Meditation – The focussing of consciousness on a stimulus (external, internal) to exclude external stimuli and exert control over one's state of mind.
Physiological changes can take place.

Medulla – Contains the:
- nucleus ambiguus
- inferior olivary nucleus.

Medulla oblongata – Contains:
- nucleus of the hypoglossal nerve (XII)
- nucleus ambiguus
- origin of the cranial root of the accessory nerve (XI)
- dorsal motor nucleus of the vagal nerve (X)
- lateral, medial and inferior subnuclei of the vestibular nerve (VIII).

Melatonin – From the pineal gland.
- Acts at the raphe nuclei to increase serotonin production.

Memory – Memory is the storage of an internal representation of knowledge.

It occurs as a result of 3 related processes:
- Encoding/registration/reception – the transformation of stimuli into a form that memory can accept.
  - Problems can occur due to:
    - inability to understand perceptions (acute confusion)
    - anterograde amnesia after head injury
    - palimpsest.
- Storage – ability to store new material.
  - Problems can occur due to:
    - retrograde amnesia after head injury
    - temporal lobectomy.
- Retrieval – capacity to return stored material from memory.
  - Problems can occur due to:
    - Korsakov syndrome
    - anxiety

M

- dissociative fugue.

Long-term potentiation involves NMDA receptors and is important in memory formation.
Recognition isn't important in memory formation.

Storage is the retention of coded information.

It is made up of:
- sensory memory
- short-term (primary/working) memory
- long term (secondary) memory.

Primary/short-term memory (STM) and secondary/long-term memory (LTM) are described by the **multi-store model** (*aka***dual memory theory**).

Accessibility is not the same as availability. Information can be available (ie stored) but not immediately accessible (ie temporarily forgotten).

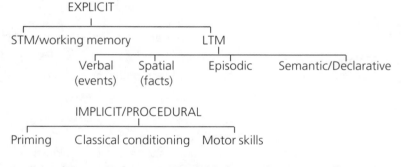

Explicit = facts and information available for recall. Requires effort and can be reported verbally.

Procedural = capacity to perform a task, not available for conscious thought (eg riding a bike).

Priming = capacity to profit from prior exposure to cues (eg partially completed words) in an executive task.

Classical conditioning – *see* Conditioning, classical.

Motor skills – associated with basal ganglia.

Anterograde = Acquiring new information.
Retrograde = Recalling what was previously learnt.

Memory retrieval

Is the recovering of information from memory when needed. It is error prone and can be influenced by emotion in several ways:

- Emotionally charged memories are more easily recalled (they are rehearsed more often when remembered and subsequently remembered more).
- Negative emotions and anxiety hinder retrieval.
- **State-dependent learning** refers to the fact that things are more likely to be remembered if an attempt is made to remember them in the same context as that in which they were first encountered.
- Repression of emotionally charged information hinders retrieval.

Forgetting

- This is usually retrieval rather than storage failure, explaining why hypnosis can aid remembering and 'tip of the tongue' feelings.
- Interference theory – **retroactive interference** is when you learn something and later learn something similar but different – this can cause you to forget the first thing you learnt.
- **Proactive interference** – occurs when something previously learnt causes you difficulty in learning something new and similar.
- Distortions of memory tend towards the familiar and towards social norms.

Memory loss is caused by lesions of the:

- temporal lobe
- uncus
- amygdala
- mammillary bodies.

Memory, declarative – Concerns knowledge of facts.

Memory, delusional – A type of delusional perception when a true memory is remembered accurately and invested with delusional significance.
or
The 'remembering' of something that never happened to one and is entirely delusional.

Memory, dissociative – Loss of memory of a traumatic nature not attributable to organic mental disorder, intoxication or ordinary forgetfulness.

Memory, episodic – Concerns knowledge of autobiographical events.

Memory, explicit – Requires the medial temporal lobes to be intact.

M

Memory, echoic – Exists in the auditory association cortex.

Memory, iconic – Exists in the visual association cortex.

Memory, long-term – *aka* secondary
- More or less permanent.
- Does not have to pass through short-term memory first.
- (Almost) unlimited capacity for storage, if not for retrieval.
- There are different types:
  - **semantic** – verbal information is stored as meanings rather than a list of specific words. Less personal and deals with organised knowledge of the world (eg vocabulary, facts, etc). It is not time specific and is usually acquired in early life.
  - **episodic** – long-term memory for events, specific and personally experienced.
- More effort required for input and retrieval relative to short-term memory.
- Forgetting is usually retrieval failure (ie 'tip of the tongue' experience).
- Schizophrenia and depression have effects.
- Anatomy:
  - episodic = limbic
  - semantic = temporal neocortex.

Memory, 'photographic' – *aka* eidetic imagery
5% of children possess this and can retain a detailed visual image for 30 s.
It is *common* among children.
Is *not* a hallucination or an illusion.
May be perceived in relation to a real object.
Is voluntary.

Memory, sensory – *aka* sensory buffer store/sensory storage
Modality specific – stored *within the receiving sensory system* and not centrally.
- additional sensory information entering the same sensory system disrupts the storage
- visual sensory memory lasts 0.5 s (= iconic memory)
- rapid decline in quality/quantity of information stored
- large capacity and accurate
- auditory sensory memory = echoic store
- touch sensory memory = haptic store
- both iconic and echoic stores store information based purely on its physical characteristics, and no processing occurs.

Memory, short-term – *aka* working memory/buffer memory
- Can store 7 (±2) chunks of information (eg letters), but if these are 'chunked' into words, then each word can be stored in a slot. Number of chunks is restricted, but not their contents.
- Made up of aspects of sensory information that receive active attention. Encoding is mostly acoustic (phonological loop – in dominant parietal lobe – auditory association cortex), as visually encoded information (visuo-spatial sketch/scratch pad – in visual association cortex) fades rapidly.
- Lasts 20 s unless rehearsed.
- Displacement principle/interference hypothesis – new information results in loss of old information and forgetting is item dependent.
- Primacy effect – chance of recalling information is higher if it was one of the first pieces of information.
- Recency effect/decay hypothesis by time – more likely to be recalled if encountered recently, as high trace strength and forgetting are time dependent.
- Serial position effect – items in the middle are most easily lost.
- Verbal is in left hemisphere.
- Visual is in right hemisphere.
- Retrieval is effortless and error-free.

Memory disturbance – Episodic
- amnestic syndrome (eg Korsakoff's psychosis)
- psychogenic amnesia
- transient global amnesia.

Semantic
- herpes simplex virus (HSV)
- major head injury
- vascular
- Pick's disease
- early Alzheimer's disease.

Mesolimbic–mesocortical pathway – Blockade of dopamine receptors here causes akathisia and therapeutic effects of antipsychotics.
Mediates the reward effects of stimulants.

Metabolism – *aka* biotransformation
- Occurs in the:
  - liver
  - kidney
  - adrenal cortex

M

- gastrointestinal tract
- lung
- placenta
- skin
- lymphocytes.
- Hepatic phase I metabolism
  - Changes the molecular structure by *non-synthetic* reactions:
    - oxidation (by microsomal mixed function oxidases, eg cytochrome p450 isoenzymes)
    - hydrolysis
    - reduction.

- Hepatic phase II metabolism
  - Is a *synthetic* reaction that *conjugates* a drug or drug metabolite with an endogenous polar molecule/group to make a *water soluble* conjugate
  - Endogenous groups are:
    - glucuronic acid
    - sulphate
    - acetate
    - glutathione
    - glycine
    - glutamine.

- If the resultant molecular mass is < 300 it is excreted by the kidney, otherwise in the bile.

Metabolism, first pass – *aka* first pass metabolism/presystemic elimination
The metabolism undergone by an orally absorbed drug during its passage from the hepatic portal system through the liver before entering the systemic circulation.
- Inter-individual variation.
- Reduced by:
  - Hepatic disease
  - Food
  - Drugs that increase hepatic blood flow.

Methadone – At 80–120 mg, overdose gives peak plasma concentrations of 440–1600 ng/ml.

Metonym – The substitution of the name of an attribute or adjunct for that of the thing meant (eg 'crown' for king, 'the turf' for horse-racing).

or

The use of ordinary words in unusual ways.

- A schizophrenic thought disorder.

Meynert – Concerned himself with neuroanatomy and behaviour.

Meynert's nucleus – Contains cholinergic cell bodies.

MHA – Mental Health Act.

Mianserin –
- Recognised side-effect is arthritis.
- Has no cardiotoxic effects and is safe in overdose.
- Is a tetracyclic antidepressant.
- Stimulates α_1-adrenoceptors on 5HT cell bodies.
- Is an α_2-adrenoceptor antagonist when acting on 5HT nerve terminals.
- Antagonises 5HT2 and 5HT3 receptors.

Micropsia – Objects are seen smaller or farther away than is actually the case.

Midbrain – Includes:
- Corpora quadrigemina (ie superior and inferior colliculi, on dorsal surface of midbrain).
- Oculomotor nuclear complex (near superior colliculus).
- Red nucleus (prominent motor component of the tegmentum).

Midbrain raphe nuclei – Contain serotonergic cell bodies.

Milestones of social development –
Social smiling
- 4–6 weeks – voluntary in response to attention
Specific facial recognition
- 2–3 months
Stranger anxiety
- *aka* wariness, open distress, 8-month anxiety
- 8 months – when faced with strange adult
- Separation anxiety
- 8 months – when separated from an attachment figure
- Proceeds from 'protest stage' of distress and anger to 'despair stage' of depression and dejection to 'detachment stage' of becoming responsive again = **acute separation reaction, syndrome of distress**.
Social attachment
- A bond of affection directed by a child towards a specific individual

Mutual reciprocity
- (described by Schaffer) the patterns of interaction between an infant and a caregiver.

Minimisation – Underestimation of the individual's performance, achievement or ability.

Minnesota Multiphasic Personality Inventory – Is a standardised self-report personality inventory with 550 statements as True/False/can't say.
It has:
- 10 clinical scales
- 3 validity scales.

Miosis – Pupillary constriction.

Mirtazepine – Reduces REM sleep.
Is a presynaptic α_2 antagonist.

Misidentification, delusional – Frequently has an organic cause (especially dementia).

Mitchell, Juliet – Wrote *Psychoanalysis & Feminism*.

Mitgehen – Is moving a limb in response to slight pressure despite being told to resist the pressure.
Is an exaggerated form of *mitmachen*.
A feature of catatonic schizophrenia.

Model, Internal Working – A complex mental understanding of a child's relationship between its care givers and itself. There are affective and cognitive components. They are largely unconscious and stable but may change after experience, self-reflection or psychotherapy.

Modelling – Involves a phobic person watching someone coping well and not showing anxiety in a phobic situation.

Monoamine oxidase (MAO) – Comes in two forms: MAO-A and MAO-B:
- MAO-A
  - Has 5-HT and noradrenaline as preferred substrates, then tyramine.
  - Is found in gastrointestinal mucosa.
  - Is what reversible inhibitor of monoamine oxidases (RIMAs) act on.

212

- MAO-B
  - Has dopamine as its preferred substrate – present in the gastrointestinal tract wall and liver.
  - Is found in platelets.
  - Causes problems when inactivated by MAOIs.

Monoamine oxidase inhibitors (MAOI) –
- Were developed after the use of iproniazid (an MAOI) in TB was noted to improve mood.
- Kline was one of the first to report on beneficial effects in depression.
- Were introduced in 1958.
- Are the treatment of choice for atypical depression.

Include:
- Hydrazine compounds:
  - phenelzine
  - isocarboxazid
- Non-hydrazine compounds:
  - tranylcypromine – also acts like an amfetamine to stimulate.

(Moclobemide is a selective MAO-A inhibitor (in fact it's a RIMA).)

M

Increase brain concentrations of:
- 5HT
- noradrenaline
- dopamine.

Recognised side-effects include:

- dangerous food reactions/cheese reaction (see below)
- REM suppression (therefore used in narcolepsy)
- peripheral neuropathy
- hypotension
- hypertension
- antimuscarinic effects:
  - central:
    - convulsions
    - pyrexia
  - peripheral:
    - dry mouth
    - blurred vision
    - urinary retention
    - constipation
    - nasal congestion

- hepatotoxicity
- appetite stimulation
- weight gain
- dependency (with tranylcypromine)
- drowsiness.

The following should be avoided while taking MAOIs:

- TCAs – there have been deaths
- opioid analgesics (can cause hyper- or hypotension) – including codeine
- ethanol
- insulin
- disulfiram (can cause CNS excitation and hypertension)
- ephedrine (a sympathomimetic with effects potentiated by MAOIs, leading to hypertensive crisis)
- tyramine – ie:
  - all cheese except cream and cottage
  - yeast extracts (eg Marmite, Bovril)
  - meat extracts
  - beer (especially Guinness)
  - wine (especially Chianti, fortified wines)
  - non-fresh fish (eg pickled/smoked herring)
  - snails
  - non-fresh meat/poultry (eg pheasant, venison)
  - offal
  - avocado
  - banana skins
  - beef/chicken liver
  - 'going off' food
  - broad bean pods
  - fermented sausage (eg pepperoni, salami)
  - large quantities of coffee
  - citrus fruits
  - chocolate and cream
  - caviar.

The **cheese reaction** is caused by the fact that inhibited MAO cannot break down tyramine from the diet. This therefore acts as a powerful hypertensive agent and can cause subarachnoid haemorrhage.

Contraindications:
- hepatic failure.

Monoamines –
Include:
- dopamine
- noradrenaline
- 5HT/serotonin
- tyramine
  - histamine.

Monomania – Is a pathological obsession with a single object.

Mood – Is a prolonged and prevailing state.

Moody, Dr Raymond – Coined the term **near-death experience**.

Moral development – Theories of moral development include:
- Piaget's cognitive developmental view
  - There are stages of moral thought through which children pass sequentially:
    - < 7 years – egocentric and solitary play.
    - Sharing and rules for games only appear after 7–8 years.
    - Rules provided by adults are 'sacred'.
    - 11–12 years – rules are mutually agreed and clearly understood.
  - **immanent justice** – 6-year-olds (but not 11-year-olds) believe that doing wrong invariably leads to punishment.
- Kohlberg's stage theory
  - He presented moral dilemmas to a variety of people.
  - The results suggested six developmental stages of moral judgement categorised into three levels:
    - Pre-moral/pre-conventional morality – < 7 years.
      Stage 1 – **Punishment/obedience orientation** – actions judged solely by their consequences, also egocentric.
      Stage 2 – **Reward orientation** – 'right' = good for child.
    - Conventional morality – 7–13 years.
      Stage 3 – **Good boy orientation** – motivated by anxiety about disapproval of others – ie wants to 'be good' – intentions judged now rather than just outcome.
      Stage 4 – **Authority orientation** – laws/social rules upheld due to fear of authority and guilt about not doing one's duty.
    - Post-conventional morality – may never be reached as requires Piaget's formal operational stage to have been reached.
      Stage 5 – **Social contract/legalistic orientation** – actions guided by principles generally felt to be good for public

M

welfare – these are upheld for respect of peers and self-respect.

Stage 6 – **Ethical principle orientation** – actions are guided by one's own principles (eg dignity, equality and justice) – so avoiding self-condemnation.

- Social perspective taking and Piaget's formal operational stage are both necessary for higher levels of reasoning.
- Criticisms of Piaget and Kohlberg:
  - Piaget disregards social factors.
  - Training can alter the individual's moral judgements.
  - Immanent justice *increases* with age in some cultures.
  - They overgeneralise.

- Psychoanalytic theories
- Freud (1914) – ego-ideal/super-ego is the result of repressed hostility towards a frustrating parent.
- Parental rules and prohibitors are therefore internalised.
- Self-punishing guilt is felt when the child transgresses.

Factors affecting moral development:

- Socialisation – girls are better than boys.
- Intelligence correlates with altruism.
- Self-esteem correlates with helpfulness and resistance to temptation (in boys).
- Social class – middle-class children aren't as immediate as working class children.
- Poor children are more generous than those from wealthy families.

Morals – Areas of thought and conduct in which issues of right and wrong are concerned, including:
- Conformity to social standards of behaviour.
- Personal principles.
- Emotions specific to right and wrong – (especially guilt and shame).
- Pro-social attitudes (eg helpfulness, generosity and altruism).
- Conscience, internalised mental structures responsible for moral beliefs and behaviour.

Morel – Described *demence precoce*.

Moreno – Developed **Psychodrama**.

Morpheme – Sound as a subunit of a word, changing the meaning of it (eg the 's' at the end of 'cups').

Motivation – Motivations are causes; they energise, explain, direct and sustain behaviour. They can be about survival, competence or socialising.
- Needs are measurable physiological concepts.
- Drives are psychological and more hypothetical.

There are several theories of motivation:

Extrinsic theories
Deal with external factors such as food and drink.
They are based on **Canon's drive reduction theory** and state that the motivation for behaviour is the reduction of the level of arousal associated with a *basic drive* (eg hunger/thirst), to maintain homeostasis.

There are:
- *primary biological drives* (activated by homeostatic imbalance mediated by brain receptors – hunger/thirst centre has a lateral hypothalamic location; satiety centre is located in the ventromedial nucleus of the hypothalamus)
- *secondary drives* (eg anxiety), which result from generalisation and conditioning.

Intrinsic theories
- Suggest that activities have their own intrinsic rewards and deal with behaviour such as:
  - play
  - sexual behaviour
  - curiosity
  - gambling
  - addiction
  - risk-taking.

- **Optimal arousal** – people manage their arousal level to achieve maximum performance. Moderate arousal is best, with over- or under-arousal being counterproductive ('boring' or 'stressing'), as in the Yerkes-Dodson curve.
- **Cognitive dissonance** – described by Festinger. Discomfort results when two or more cognitions are held that are inconsistent with one another. Motivation is felt to achieve cognitive consistency by changing the weaker of the inconsistent cognitions.
- **Attitude-discrepant behaviour** – is when attitude and behaviour are inconsistent. Attitude changes to cause cognitive consistency.
- **Need for achievement (nAch)** – McClelland proposed this to

M

explain why people are motivated by pleasure to achieve mastery. It is linked to early deprivation.

Mowrer described secondary drives. Hull's theory was that of primary drives being activated by brain receptors tied up in homeostasis.

Motor neurone disease – Recognised features include:
- dysarthria
- dysphagia (*not* dysphasia)
- muscle wasting
- fasciculation
- difficulty of micturition (but *not* incontinence)
- exaggerated tendon reflexes
- muscle atrophy.

Mourning – Culture-bound social and cognitive processes through which we must pass to resolve grief and return to normal functioning.

Movements, abnormal involuntary – Occur in:
- tardive dyskinesia
- Parkinson's disease.

Movements, abnormal voluntary – Occur in:
- echopraxia
- chronic schizophrenia.

MRI – Magnetic resonance imaging.

MRI, functional –
When using the water proton signal, MRI is sensitive enough to detect changes in cerebral blood flow related to neuronal activation.
- Has demonstrated diffuse reduction in grey matter in people with schizophrenia.

Munchausen's syndrome –
- Was first used by Asher in 1951 to describe those patients who present dramatically to hospitals with histories typical of acute organic emergencies.
- Is named after an 18th century German cavalry officer.
- Is more common in men.
- Has a poor prognosis.
- May present with psychiatric symptoms.
- There is no established treatment – it's difficult to treat.
- Is classified under factitious disorder in DSM-IV and under *personality disorder* in ICD-10.
- Does not correlate strongly with opiate addiction.

- Is often associated with alcohol dependence.
- Personal history is important in aetiology.
- Confronting the patient is recommended.
- Discourage self-discharge to encourage appropriate follow-up.

Murray – Described **neurodevelopmental schizophrenia**.

Mutism – Complete loss of speech in a conscious patient.
Wide range of causes, including:
- Organic disorders, drugs, catatonic schizophrenia, depression, personality disorder.

Mydriasis – Pupillary dilation.

Myelinosis, central pontine –
- Is a rare cause of psychosis.
- Seen rarely in alcoholism, usually after over-rapid correction of hyponatraemia.
- There is massive progressive demyelination of the basal pons.
- Clinical features include:
  - confusion
  - cranial nerve palsies (especially IV, V and VI – gaze palsies and bulbar signs)
  - pyramidal signs in limbs
  - cerebellar signs
  - vasomotor disturbances
- 75% of those affected are dead within one month.

Myxoedema – Can cause an acute or chronic organic reaction.

M

Narcissism – Occurs when the person's libido is invested in the ego. Freud thought this would account for schizophrenia.

Narcissistic personality disorder – (A DSM-IV term). Features include:
- grandiose sense of self-importance
- preoccupation with fantasies of unlimited success, power and intellectual brilliance
- craving of attention from others, with little return of feeling
- exploitation of others, with unreturned favours.

There is a large overlap with histrionic personality disorder, but also with dissocial and borderline personality disorder.

Narcolepsy – Is characterised by:
- episodes of uncontrollable sleep
- one or more of:
  - cataplexy (loss of muscle tone)
  - sleep paralysis (transient with spontaneous recovery)
  - hypnagogic hallucinations
- nocturnal sleep is disrupted
- early REM sleep (ie decreased REM latency)
- REM sleep in the daytime
- normal routine EEG
- 1/3 have a positive family history
- occasionally autosomal dominant (with HLA-DR2, chromosome 6)
- the sleep during the sleep attacks is refreshing.

Treatment:
- amfetamines
- modafinil
- methylphenidate.

NART – National Adult Reading Test.

Near-death experience – A normal experience in rarely encountered situations, especially when dying or when one nearly dies, often encompassing depersonalisation, increased alertness and various descriptions of 'mystic consciousness', including out-of-body experience with autoscopy and passage of consciousness into a foreign region or transcendental experience. Term coined by Dr Raymond Moody in 1970s.

- associated with the name Moody
- seen in life-threatening experiences
- are features of altered state of consciousness
- are not a basis for reincarnation
- do not occur in death.

Neck stiffness – Suggestive of:

- subarachnoid haemorrhage
- meningitis.

Need for achievement – *aka* nAch

Was described by McClelland.

Nefazodone – Is an SSRI and blocks serotonin receptors (specifically 5HT2A receptors).

It does *not* cause priapism, because it has a low affinity for peripheral α_1-adrenergic receptors.

Negativism – A motiveless resistance to commands and to attempts to be moved.

or

Accentuated opposition to movements.

- It is a more marked form of *gegenhalten*
- Seen in:
  - catatonia
  - dementia
  - severe mental handicap.

neo-Freudians – Included:

- Fromm
- Horney
- Sullivan
- Erikson.

Neologisms – Is a new word constructed by the patient.

or

Existing words used in novel ways.

A type of loosening of association characteristic of schizophrenia but also seen in:

- Wernicke's aphasia
- Gilles de la Tourette syndrome
- mania.

Neurasthenia – Core symptoms are:
- excessive fatigue
- lethargy.

but anxiety and depression also occur.
- Is categorised under neurotic disorders (F48.0) in ICD-10.

Neurites – Are projections from perikaryons (ie neurone cell bodies) and include axons and dendrites.

Neuritis, retrobulbar – *aka* optic neuritis
Inflammation, degeneration or demyelination of an optic nerve caused by a wide variety of diseases.
Causes visual loss.

Neuroleptic malignant syndrome – Clinical features of NMS include:
- motor
  - muscle rigidity in throat and chest
  - akinesia
- mental
  - (akinetic) mutism
  - stupor
  - fluctuating level of consciousness
- autonomic
  - tachycardia
  - labile blood pressure
  - pallor
  - urinary incontinence
  - pyrexia
  - sweating
- *not*
  - cholestatic jaundice.

Investigations reveal:
- increased CPK
- increased WBC – neutrophilia
- abnormal LFTs
- electrolyte changes:
  - reduced calcium
  - reduced magnesium
  - reduced phosphate

N

- It is a rare idiosyncratic reaction to any antipsychotic with onset at 2–28 days.
- There are no CSF changes.
- MRI is normal.

Differential diagnosis includes:
- lethal catatonia
- tetanus
- malignant hyperpyrexia
- encephalitis
- hallucinogen ingestion
- delirium tremens.

Neurolinguistic programming – Is primarily conducted via hypnosis.

Neurone – At rest there are:
- high potassium
- low sodium
- low chloride
- the opposites of these outside the cell
- the inside is strongly negative.

Neurones, lower motor –
- Compose the anterior grey column of the spinal cord.
- Innervate the muscles of the hand.
- Are selectively destroyed by polio.

Neuropeptides – Are neurotransmitters made of small proteins or peptides.
They include (among others):
- corticotrophin releasing hormone (CRH)
- cholecystokinin (CCK)
- endogenous opioids.

Neurosis, compensation – aka accident neurosis
Psychologically determined physical/mental symptoms occurring in the context of unsettled claims for compensation.
- There's no resolution of symptoms on settlement.
- Features include:
  - frontal headaches
  - fainting
- Not seen:
  - severe insomnia
  - seeking compensation after minor injury.

Neurotensin – Found in CNS and gut. As a neurotransmitter, it:

- reduces body temperature
- reduces food intake
- reduces locomotor activity.

Nicotine –
- Increases prolactin and growth hormone at higher doses only.

Night terror – Is the phenomenon of sitting up apparently terrified while in Stage 3–4 of sleep. There may be screaming, and confusion is usual. There is tachycardia and tachypnoea.
There is no dream recall and normal sleep follows after a few minutes. They may be familial, are uncommon and usually end in childhood. Treatment includes regular bedtime routine and improved sleep hygiene. Benzodiazepines and imipramine can help.
δ waves are seen on EEG.
Occurs during first third of the night.
It is genetically related to sleep-walking.

Nightmare – An awakening from REM sleep to full consciousness with detailed dream recall accompanied by strong subjective feeling of unpleasantness and fear.
- Precipitating factors include:
  - frightening experiences during the day
  - anxiety
  - PTSD
  - pyrexia
  - psychotropic drugs
  - alcohol withdrawal.

Nigrostriatal area – Contains dopaminergic neurones; when blocked by antipsychotic drugs, causes EPSEs.
The nigrostriatal tract connects the substantia nigra in the midbrain with the striatum in the basal ganglia.

NMDA – N-methyl-D-aspartate.

NMDA receptors –
- Are a type of glutamate receptor.
- They are involved in memory formation.
- When blocked (by phencyclidine), schizophrenia-like effects are seen.
- Are excitatory and involved in the **thalamic filter**.
- Are anxiogenic and convulsant when agonised
- Glycine (which is inhibitory) increases calcium flux at NMDA receptors.

225

Non-compliance

Sources of non-compliance include:
* early recovery
* fear of addiction
* failure to warn and explain about side-effects
* long intervals between consultations.

NMS – Neuroleptic malignant syndrome.

Noradrenaline – Is produced:
   tyrosine
   ↓ (trosine hydroxylase)
   DOPA
   ↓ (DOPA decarboxylase)
   dopamine
   ↓ (dopamine-β-hydroxylase)
   noradrenaline

Is degraded:
   noradrenaline
   ↓ (COMT/MAO)
   vanilylmandelic acid
   (VMA; or others – it's complicated!)

Inactivation is by presynaptic reuptake.

Normal experiences – Normal experiences include:
* *Jamais vu*
* Derealisation
* *Déjà vu*

Normative social influence – Refers to situations in which the individual publicly conforms to the consensual opinion and behaviour of the group but has a different view in his or her own mind. Social pressure forces compliance to avoid social rejection.

Nortriptyline – Has effects on noradrenaline pathways.

NSAID – Non-steroidal anti-inflammatory drug.

Nucleus accumbens – Dopamine activity here has a major role in pleasurable and reinforcing effects of cocaine, amfetamine, phencyclidine, nicotine and ethanol.

Nucleus basalis (of Meynert) – Contains cholinergic cell bodies.

Obedience – Studied by Millgram. He found that most people would obey an experimenter's orders to deliver increasingly powerful electric shocks.

Factors increasing obedience:
- The presence of the person demanding obedience.
- The belief that prior arrangement was binding.
- Increasing distance from the 'victim'.

Obesity – Obese people think they're thinner than they really are.

Object, transitional – Described by Winnicott.
An object, neither oneself nor another person, that is selected by an infant at 4–18 months for self-soothing and anxiety reduction.
- Helps with separation-individuation.

Object constancy – *aka* perceptual constancy
Is the tendency to perceive objects as unchanged under different conditions.

Is the principle by which we recognise the inherent nature of objects we perceive and the fact that, although they can be perceived differently according to our physical relationship to them, there are inherent aspects to them which remain the same.

Incorporates:
- Shape constancy
  - The realisation that an object is the same shape although it appears to be a different shape when viewed from different angles.
    (If ambiguous can result in illusions.)
- Size constancy
  - Objects look smaller the further away they are, but we know how big a cup is whether it's pressed against our forehead or is on the other side of the room.

- Familiarity with the object and other cues are used to assist this process (eg comparing it with another object at a similar distance, the size of which is known).
- Brightness/colour constancies
  - However an object is illuminated, it will appear the same colour/brightness (grass appears green, even if someone shines a red light on it).
- Location constancy
  - When we move our heads, we know that things around us are staying still, rather than moving. Stratton wore inverting lenses and grew accustomed to them.

Object relations – Theorists suggested that the primary motivational drive in humans is to seek relationships with others.

Theorists included:
- Fairbairn
- Guntrip
- Winnicott
- Balint
- Weston – believed personality disorder arose from his 'level 3'.

The ego is at the centre of object relations.

Obsessional doubts – Repeated themes expressing uncertainty about previous actions, eg whether they turned off an electrical appliance that might now cause a fire.
Whatever the nature of he doubt, the person realises that they have in fact done whatever it was they doubt having done.

Obsessional impulses – Repeated urges to carry out actions, usually aggressive, dangerous or socially embarrassing in nature, eg to pick up a knife and stab someone or shout obscenities in church.

Obsessional phobia – An unsatisfactory term
It describes obsessional symptoms associated with avoidance as well as anxiety. For example, obsessional impulses to stab someone with a knife might lead to avoidance (= obsessional phobia) of knives.

Obsessional ruminations – Repeated worrying themes, more complex than obsessional thoughts (eg about the end of the world).
- are usually associated with rituals
- are characteristically distressing
- are a normal experience.

Obsessional slowness – Usually the result of compulsive rituals or repeated doubts, but it can occur without them as primary obsessional slowness.

Obsessional thoughts – Repeated and intrusive words or phrases that are usually upsetting to the patient (eg repeated obscenities or blasphemous phrases coming into the awareness of a religious person).

- they are rarely pleasurable
- they occur in healthy people
- they are *not* usually acted on.

Obsessions – Recurrent persistent thoughts, impulses or images that enter the mind despite the person's efforts to exclude them. There is a sense of a struggle, when the patient resists the obsession that enters the awareness anyway. Obsessions are recognised as coming from the person's own mind. They are often realised to be untrue or senseless (as distinct from delusions). They are usually about unpleasant or distressing things and often lead to compulsions. Over time, the resistance diminishes.

There are several forms:
- thoughts
- ruminations
- doubts
- impulses
- obsessional phobias.

There are six categories of themes of obsessions:

- Dirt and contamination – associated with idea of harming others by spreading disease.
- Aggression – assaulting someone/shouting in public.
- Orderliness – about arrangement of objects or approach to work.
- Illness – usually fearful, eg dread of cancer or STD (*aka* illness phobia – although it's not a phobia!).
- Sex – concerning practices the patient would find shameful.
- Religion – doubts about fundamental beliefs or about whether sins have been adequately confessed (= scruples).

They are closely related to compulsions.
They are ego alien.
They are best treated by exposure and response prevention when occurring with rituals. The rituals do *not* respond well to behaviour therapy.
Obsessional thoughts alone are best treated by medication and

229

usually respond best to SSRIs.

The rituals reduce anxiety.

The characteristic defence mechanism is reaction formation.

Occur in:
- early dementia
- encephalitis lethargica
- anorexia nervosa
- post-encephalitic parkinsonism
- head injury.

Obsessive-compulsive disorder (OCD) – Characteristic features include:
- anxiety
- depression (30%)
- depersonalisation

Obsessional thoughts in OCD are:
- usually unpleasant and often abhorrent
- resisted (a required symptom)
- intrusive
- either primary or secondary to external events
- recognised as patient's own thoughts
- take the form of:
  - words
  - rhymes
  - phrases.

- Occurs more often than expected in families of OCD patients.
- Overall, it has equal sex incidence, but this is not true of some subtypes.
- Mean age of onset is 20 years, earlier in males.
- Onset over the age of 35 years is very rare.
- Often has a fluctuating course.
- Best treatment is exposure to environmental cues, together with response prevention.
- Correlates with above average social class and intelligence.

Ego defence mechanisms include:
- magic doing and undoing
- reaction formation
- isolation.

Drugs used include:
- SSRIs

- clomipramine.

- 80% of patients ritualise.
- 50–60% have motor compulsions.
- Anti-depressants may be of use.
- The compulsions often relieve anxiety.
- Obsessional thoughts may *not* be enjoyable to the patient.
- Anxiety *increases* if thoughts are resisted.
- Is associated with anankastic personality disorder in 15–30% of cases.
- The family are often involved in the rituals, by way of providing reassurance.

Obsessive-compulsive personality disorder – Is the DSM-IV version of anankastic personality disorder.

Obsessive traits – *aka* anankastic traits
Include:
- dependability
- punctuality
- precision →preoccupation with detail
- setting of high standards → bigotry
- adherence to social rules
- determination/persistence → obstinacy
- constant mood → humourlessness.

- may be associated with significant family distress
- may be advantageous
- may pre-date a depressive illness
- are associated with OCD.

OCD – Obsessive-compulsive disorder.

Oculomotor nerve (III) –
- Supplies all extraocular muscles except superior oblique and lateral rectus.
- Also supplies:
  - levator palpebrae superioris
  - sphincter pupillae
  - Mueller's muscle (sympathetic – lifts eyelid)
  - ciliary muscles.
- Complete lesion causes:
  - ptosis (due to effects on levator palpebrae superioris)
  - external strabismus
  - diplopia

- pupillary dilation (due to effects on sphincter pupillae)
- failure of accommodation (due to effects on the ciliary muscle).

Oedipal phase – One of Freud's phases. It corresponds with Erikson's third stage (initiative vs guilt).

Offending – Peak ages in the UK:
- Girls = 14 years.
- Boys = 17–18 years.
- Half of all indictable crimes committed by those under 21 years.
- By age 30 years, 30% of UK males have been convicted of an indictable offence.
- Conviction: male : female ratio is 5 : 1.

Omission – Described by Carl Schneider.
Missing out large parts of a thought.

Oneiroid state – Is a dream-like state in which the patient remains awake.
Is associated with tactile hallucinations.

Oneirophrenia – Described by Mayer-Gross.

Opisthotonos – The position of the body in which the head, neck and spine are arched backwards. It is assumed involuntarily by patients with tetanus and strychnine poisoning.

Oral administration – Mechanisms of absorption:
- passive diffusion
- pore filtration
- active transport.

Factors influencing absorption:

- gastric emptying
- gastric pH
- intestinal motility
- presence/absence of food (food and antimuscarinics delay gastric emptying)
- intestinal microflora
- area of absorption
- blood flow.

- Small intestinal absorption is most common.

Organic reaction, acute – Features suggestive of an acute organic reaction include:

- fluctuation in consciousness with nocturnal worsening
- prominent illusions and visual hallucinations
- pyrexia
- neck stiffness (suggestive of subarachnoid haemorrhage or meningitis)
- rich intrusive fantasies
- ability to establish emotional rapport
- emotional response (commonly fear, tension, perplexity and agitation)
- disorientation.

Organic reaction, chronic – Suggestive features include:
- poverty of thought.

Orientation – The awareness of one's setting in time, place and person.

Orientation, double – Refers to a schizophrenic's behaviour contradicting his beliefs.

Overeating – Is seen in:
- anorexia nervosa (50% binge)
- bulimia nervosa
- depression
- Kluver-Bucy syndrome
- Kleine-Levine syndrome.

Overgeneralisation – Drawing a general conclusion on the basis of a single incident.

Pain –
- Psychogenic pain can be differentiated from physical pain because:
  - it *increases* in severity with time
  - it does not have a precise anatomical location.

Pairing – Is guided by certain principles:
- Homogamous mate selection – from within the same socioeconomic, religious and cultural group.
- Reinforcement theory – people are attracted to those who reinforce the attraction with rewards. This is a reciprocal process.
- Social exchange theory – relationships with a minimum cost : benefit ratio are preferred.
- Equity theory – the cost:benefit ratio is usually perceived to be equal.
- Matching hypothesis – although everyone would like to pair with the most attractive person, they choose one as ugly as they are so that their partner doesn't subsequently run off with someone more attractive. There is also less chance of rejection in this case.
- Men prefer attractive partners, women prefer ambitious, industrious and therefore potential high earners.
- In Africa/Asia – chastity, home-keeping potential and desire to have children are paramount.
- Western countries – love, character, emotional maturity are important. Chastity is unimportant.

Palimpsest – *aka* alcoholic blackouts
Is an early feature of alcohol dependence.

Palilalia – A perseverative error of speech that entails reiterations of single words, usually with increasing frequency.
A feature of catatonic schizophrenia.

Palsy, III – 'Down and out'.
- Loss of direct and consensual reflexes in the affected eye (efferent problem).
- Accommodation in the affected eye.
- Dilation of the pupil in the affected eye due to parasympathetic interruption.
- Unopposed action of the dilator pupillae muscle (this has sympathetic innervation).
- Marked ptosis due to levator palpebrae paralysis.
- Lateral strabismus due to unopposed action of the lateral rectus muscle

Palsy, Bell's
- facial paralysis
- ptosis
- drooling
- hyperacusis.

Palsy, bulbar – Lower motor neurone weakness of IX–XII.
- features:
  - reduced palatal sensation/movement
  - choking
  - weak sternomastoid and trapezius
  - weak, wasted and fasciculating tongue – points to the affected side.

Palsy, pseudobulbar – Bilateral supranuclear (= upper motor neurone) lesions of lower cranial nerves.
- causes:
  - tongue and pharyngeal weakness
- features:
  - stiff, slow, spastic tongue (which is not wasted)
  - dysarthria (as gravelly voice)
  - exaggerated jaw jerk
  - emotional lability
  - facial fasciculation
- aetiology:
  - motor neurone disease
  - multiple sclerosis
  - cerebrovascular disease.

Panic disorder – Characteristic features include:
- depersonalisation
- feelings of choking

- trembling or shaking
- dizziness
- fear of losing control.

Papilloedema – Causes include:
- central retinal vein thrombosis
- cavernous sinus thrombosis
- hypercapnia.

Paralysis, general of the insane –
- Rare.
- Develops 5–25 years after initial *Treponema pallidum* (ie syphilis) infection.
- Clinical features:
  - insidious onset
  - depression
  - slowly progressive memory and intellectual impairment (simple dementia is the most common presentation)
  - frontal lobes are involved, causing characteristic personality change (differential diagnosis is hypomania):
  - disinhibition
  - uncontrolled excitement
  - overactivity
  - grandiose delusions (in 10%)
  - dysarthria
  - tremor of lips/tongue
  - Argyll Robertson pupil (in 50%)
  - increasing leg weakness leading to spastic paralysis.
- CSF Wasserman reaction is *always* positive initially, then it's negative.
- CSF also shows:
  - lymphocytosis
  - increased protein
  - increased globulin.
- Neuropathology
  - marked cerebral atrophy – due to neuronal loss
  - meningeal thickening – due to astrocyte proliferation
  - iron pigment in the microglia and the perivascular space is pathognomonic
  - spirochaetes are seen in the cortex in 50%.
- Management
  - high-dose penicillin under steroid cover to prevent Jarisch–Herxheimer reaction

- can lead to some improvement.
- Neurological signs are inconspicuous in early cases.
- FTA test and TPHA are positive.

Paramnesia – A distorted recall leading to falsification of memory. Including:
- **Confabulation** – a completely false memory is added to fill a gap
  - memory falsifications in clear consciousness in amnesia due to organic disorders
  - typically seen *early* in Korsakov syndrome
  - subjects give elaborate details of events that did not occur
  - there is marked suggestibility.
- *Déjà vu* – a feeling of familiarity with events not previously experienced – normal experience, also associated with anxiety and temporal lobe epilepsy.
- *Déjà entendu* – false feeling of auditory recognition.
- *Déjà pensé* – the feeling that one has had a thought before, when really one hasn't.
- *Jamais vu* – loss of feeling of familiarity when stored material is returned to consciousness (usually due to organic disorder, eg Korsakov syndrome).
- **Retrospective falsification** – false details are added to an otherwise true memory
  - also seen in affective disorder, when selective forgetting and paramnesia occur, consistent with current mood state
  - pseudologica fantastica – fluent untruthful statements – associated with hysterical behaviour.

Paranoia – Means self-referent.
- Includes persecutory, grandiose or other ideas referent to the self.
- Describes only the content of an idea or belief, not the form (eg delusion, over-valued idea, etc).
- Projection is the characteristic defence mechanism.

Paranoid personality disorder – Features include:
- suspiciousness
- sensitivity
- mistrust
- argumentativeness
- stubbornness
- self-importance
- jealousy
- combative and tenacious sense of personal rights.

- *Weak* familial association with schizophrenia.
- Does involve persecutory overvalued ideas.
- Doesn't involve persecutory delusions, but can be mistaken for these.
- Patients are reluctant to become close to others.

Unlike minor obsessional and histrionic traits, paranoid traits can never add desirability to a personality. A person with paranoid personality disorder, when severely humiliated, may develop 'sensitive ideas of reference'.

- The main defence mechanism used is projection.

Paraphrenia – Described by Kraeplin.
A psychotic condition characterised by relatively late first onset, chronic delusions and hallucinations, the preseveration of volition and lack of personality deterioration.

Paraphrenia, late – Described by Roth.
A condition with first onset after 60 years, well-organised delusions with or without hallucinations and a well-preserved personality and affective response.

Risk factors:
- Female sex (it's possible that oestrogens protect and that this protection is lost after the menopause; there is also a relative excess of dopamine D2 receptors in females).
- Conductive hearing loss in early life causes social deafness (ie deafness impeding social interaction).
- Paranoid personality disorder.
- Schizoid personality disorder.

There are more women affected than men.
Patients are more likely to be unmarried and are known to have lower fecundity.

Features:
- thought disorder and catatonia are almost never seen
- delusions are *always* seen
- hallucinations are usually seen
- 50% have at least one first-rank symptom
- negative symptoms are mild.

Not seen:
- thought disorder
- catatonia

- inappropriate affect.

Aetiology
- Genetic – increased risk of schizophrenia in first-degree relatives.
- Personality – paranoid personality disorder predisposes.
- Sensory impairment – duration and extent of hearing loss correlate with paraphrenia.
- Brain disease – larger ventricles and cognitive impairment are more common in late paraphrenics.

Parapraxes – *aka* slips of the tongue, Freudian slips
eg 'Let us say a prayer for our Queer Dean'.
An outward sign of the conflict between id and ego.

Parasomnias – Include nightmares, night terror and somnambulism.

Parasympathetic nervous system – Has a secretomotor function.
Controls:
- gut motility
- micturition
- peristalsis
- salivary secretion.

Pareidolia – Is the occurrence of vivid imagery without effort while looking at a poorly structured background.

- It may occur against one's will
- Attention may increase it.

Parenteral administration – Is *not* by the gastrointestinal tract.
It includes:
- intramuscular
- intravenous
- subcutaneous
- inhalational administration
- topical administration.

Parenting – Is influenced by:
- The parent's cultural beliefs about parenting (including their own early experiences).
- Parental genetic factors influencing parenting.
- Child's genetic factors influencing the parents with regard to parenting.

It is *not* influenced by:
- Sex hormones.

Parenting, abusive – Is a strong predictor of later psychopathology.

Parietal lobe – *see* Appendix 4.

Parkinsonism, drug-related – Antimuscarinics may be used to treat it:
- procyclidine
- benzhexol
- benztropine
- orphenadrine
- biperiden
- methixene.

Treatment of drug-related parkinsonism with anticholinergics leads to subjective, but not objective, improvement.

Paroxetine – Side-effects include:
- dry mouth
- sedation
- headache
- nausea
- vomiting.

  Decreases the efficacy of codeine.

Parsimony – Excessive care in spending money.

Parson – Developed theories about the sick role.

Partnerships – Were examined by Winch, who said that a dominant partner paired with a submissive partner produces a good relationship. There is no good evidence for this.

Passive aggressive personality disorder – A DSM-IV term.
This describes a person who passively resists demands placed on them by:
- procrastination
- dawdling
- stubbornness
- deliberate inefficiency
- pretended forgetfulness
- unreasonable criticism of people in authority.

Passivity phenomena – The delusional belief that an external agency is controlling aspects of the self that are normally under one's own control.
Includes:
- Disorders of thought possession:

- Thought insertion ⎫
- Thought withdrawal ⎪
- Thought broadcasting ⎪
- Made feelings ⎬ First-rank symptoms
- Made impulses ⎪
- Made actions ⎪
- Somatic passivity. ⎭
- They occur in schizophrenia and manic-depressive psychosis.
  - They do *not* include thought echo.
  - They are *not* recognised in obsessional neurosis.

Peer relationships –

Piaget – cognitive-based theory, underestimated social aspects.
Hays – best friends are organised by elders.
Hartrup – friendships are very important to later social adjustment.

2 months
- Look at peer.

6 months
- Smile and vocalise in response to peer.

7–12 months
- Co-ordinate behaviour.

9 months
- More interested in peer than in mother.
- Imitation of peer's gesture/laughter.

Preschool children
- Adults select and influence friends.
- Offer support if peer distressed.
- More likely to interact with others if encouraged by mother.

Primary school
- More selective about friends, with more complex friendships and more joint interests.
- Greater familiarity and closer friendships.
- They like talking.
- Groups still imposed (classrooms, etc).

Secondary school
- Increasing influence of peers.
- Peer groups – social structure and hierarchy.
- Conflict in relationships – emotional lability.
- Reasoned argument used more in peer groups than in families.

Anna Freud described sibling and peer attachments.

Percept, sensory – Caused by a real stimulus, perceived as real and acted upon.

Perception – Is the means by which the brain makes representations of the external environment.
It is an active process involving the awareness and interpretation of sensations received through sensory organs.
It is an active process in which there is search for meaning.

There are 3 stages:
- Awareness of stimulus (ie a sound or image).
- Awareness of configuration (ie the sensory percept).
- Awareness of entity.

Perception, delusional – *aka* apophanous perception
Described by Jaspers *or* Kurt Schneider.
Is a disturbance of thought, when some abnormal significance, usually with self-reference, is attached to a genuine perception without any justification.

- The object is perceived normally and then invested with delusional significance.
- Is not readily understood, not being related to a particular emotional state.

According to Schneider, delusional perception:
- is often preceded by a delusional atmosphere
- is made up of 2 stages (perception then attachment (investing) of delusional significance)
- may occur as a delusional memory – when a delusional meaning is attached to a true memory (this is really delusional retrospective falsification and delusional memory is really the describing of delusional experience as memory)
- is always a 'schizophrenic symptom', but is seen in:
  - epileptic twilight states
  - toxic psychoses
  - morbid cerebral changes.
- Is a first-rank symptom.
- Is a type of primary delusion.

Perception, depth – Is the process by which a 3-dimensional image is formed by integration of two 2-dimensional images. A variety of cues are used:
- convergence
- relative size

P

- relative brightness
- motion parallax
- object interposition
- linear perspective.

Perception, false – Includes illusions, eidetic images, hallucinations and pseudohallucinations.

Perception, visual – Takes place at different levels in different locations:
- Occipital lobes
  - shape
  - colour
  - spatial orientation
- Non-dominant parietal lobe
  - complete percepts (without meaning)
- Parieto-occipital areas
  - meaning ascribed to object.

Perception, visual, development of –
Birth
- discrimination of brightness
- eye tracking
- preference for complex visual stimuli (eg human faces)
- pupillary reflex
- focus fixed at 20 cm
- optokinetic reflex (ability to follow a moving scene as evident by optokinetic nystagmus – this is the smooth, slow following of a moving scene (eg a tree passed in a car), followed by a rapid movement in a new direction.

2 months
- depth perception (as seen in visual cliff experiments)
- accommodation begins
- (but also reported as developing at 3–6 months – anyway, a child can't crawl until they're 7 months old, so it doesn't matter).

4 months
- colour vision.

6 months
- 6 : 6 acuity (develops between 6 and 12 months)
- adult-like accommodation.

Innate abilities include:
- visual scanning
- visual tracking

- visual fixating
- figure–ground discrimination.

Learnt abilities include:
- size/shape constancy
- depth perception
- shape discrimination.

Perceptual organisation – Gestalt psychology describes a number of perceptual phenomena:
- *Prägnanz* – the whole of perception is greater than the sum of the parts, as the brain brings all the parts together to perceive them in the most meaningful way.
- **Law of simplicity** = Occam's razor applied to perception.
- **Law of closure** = partial outlines are perceived as whole.
- **Law of continuity** = interrupted objects are perceived as continuous.
- **Law of similarity** = like items are grouped together.
- **Law of proximity** = adjacent items are grouped together.
- **Figure–ground differentiation** = patterns are perceived as figures differentiated from their background with contours and boundaries, and so as simulating objects (can apply to auditory stimuli, eg hearing a specific conversation over background noise).

Perceptual organisation (especially depth perception and perceptual constancy) is altered in schizophrenia, depersonalisation, derealisation, temporal lobe epilepsy and delirium.

Perls, Fritz – Described **Gestalt therapy**, which is influenced by
- Gestalt psychology
- psychodrama
- existentialism
- psychoanalysis.

Perplexity – Is more likely to be seen in schizophrenia than in affective psychosis.

Perseveration – The persistent and inappropriate repetition of the same thoughts.
or
The persistence of cued speech/behaviour beyond its relevance.

- Occurs most commonly in dementia.
- Is a function of clouding of consciousness.
- It is *pathognomonic* of organic psychiatric disorder.

245

Includes:
- palilalia
- logoclonia.

Person perception – The way in which an individual regards another. There are 3 aspects:
- Selection (eg focusing on an aspect of their appearance or behaviour).
- Organisation (ie trying to integrate impressions of the person into a coherent whole).
- Inference (ie attributing characteristics to them for which there is no direct/immediate evidence).

Personalisation – Relating external events to oneself in an unwarranted way.

Personality – The sum of enduring qualities of an individual that are shown in his ways of behaving in a wide variety of circumstances. In clinical practice, it is best judged on clinical interview (with the patient and with informants (especially by talking about the patient's state *before* he became ill) rather than with psychological tests of personality. These are not useful when used on a mentally ill person and often do not measure traits that are important in clinical practice.

'Relatively stable internal factors which make one person's behaviour consistent from one time to another and different from the behaviour other people would manifest in comparable situations' (Child).

Personality change – There are three causes:
- Injury or organic disease of the brain.
- Severe mental disorder, especially schizophrenia.
- Exceptionally severe stressful experiences (eg being a hostage or undergoing torture).

Personality disorders – Deeply ingrained maladaptive patterns of behaviour recognisable by the time of adolescence or earlier and continuing through most of adult life, although often becoming less obvious in middle or old age. The personality is abnormal either in the balance of its components, their quality and expression, or in its total aspect. Because of this, the patient suffers or others have to suffer and there is an adverse effect on the individual or on society.

Distinct from mental disorders in that, when a person has always behaved abnormally, they are said to have a personality disorder. If they have previously behaved normally and then start behaving abnormally, they are said to have a mental disorder.

Because normality is broader and less precise than the specific pathological processes that cause abnormality, specific examples may defy categorisation.

DSM-IV has 'clusters' of personality disorders:
Cluster A (MAD):
- paranoid
- schizoid
- schizotypal

Cluster B (BAD):
- antisocial (= dissocial in ICD-10)
- borderline
- histrionic
- narcissistic

Cluster C (SAD):
- avoidant (= anxious in ICD-10)
- dependent
- obsessive-compulsive (= anankastic in ICD-10)

Persecutory ideation in personality disorder can be explained by Freud's projection.

Personality theory, idiographic – These theories are person-centred. Emphasises differences between people. Allport is the main man, with Rogers, George Kelly and Freud. They all built their theories of personality on case studies, rather than from general observations. They lack scientific rigour.

Allport's trait approach
Not purely idiographic as he recognised some common traits.
- Personality traits – cardinal, central and secondary dispositions.
- Whole person – very important to Allport – scales are meaningless.
- Personality assessment – is done by studying the person, for example by reading all their letters over a period of time, not by a questionnaire.
- People say he's just a biographer and that there is no such thing as a unique human because humans all have a lot in common.

P

Carl Rogers' self theory
He *wasn't* a psychoanalyst.
The individual's view of himself (the **perceived self**) is the most important thing. It is compared with the **ideal self**. If there is a great difference (ie **incongruence**) between the two, then problems arise with neuroticism.
Everyone has an **actualising tendency** which drives us to grow, develop, mature and realise our full capacities as humans within our **phenomenal field**. There are different levels to this, as seen in Maslow's hierarchy of needs.
Positive regard is also seen as important – if it is unconditional from others, we will hold ourselves in unconditional positive regard and this is optimal. Usually positive regard is conditional. We then try to live our own lives in accordance with others' principles and attach **conditions of worth** to ourselves. If we fail to meet these, we suffer the psychological consequences.

The Q sort technique:
- Was used to assess changes in a client's perception of self.
- The person sorts many cards with statements about himself into *up to* 9 piles (some items use less than 9), from 'agree strongly' to 'disagree strongly' , with most near the middle.
- They are then re-sorted by the person to provide a profile of the ideal self.
- The two sets of results are then correlated to give the degree of **incongruence**.
- Is a personality rating.
- Explicitly compares traits *within* an individual.
- Allows personal disposition and individuality to be identified.
- Reliability can be assessed by using two Q sorts.

- Concerns are:
  - people aren't often fully aware of the truth about themselves.
  - that they may be guided by the expectations of the investigator.
  - there is little evidence for Rogers' techniques and his ideas are poorly defined.

George Kelly's personal construct theory
He *wasn't* a psychoanalyst.
Kelly believed that people put forward hypotheses and theories about their world in an attempt to understand it. These are tested and help each person to develop their own rules of behaviour and their own personal view of the world. The person's particular hypotheses are

their **personal constructs**. To investigate someone's personality, you have to gain access to their personal constructs and this is done through the use of a **repertory grid**.

Repertory grids are a systematised way to explore the way people think about aspects of their lives. If one was drawn up to see how a person viewed significant others in his life, the names of these people would be listed as columns in the grid. The person would be asked to consider these people (the **elements**) in groups of three, and say what made one of the three different from the others. He might say that, while two were understanding, the third was unsympathetic. The first row (**construct**) would be labelled understanding-unsympathetic. The procedure is repeated many times to reveal how someone viewed the world.

- Sees man as a scientist.
- Is based on constructive alternativism.
- Stipulates the use of personal constructs to predict the future.

Problems with personal construct theory:
- it fails to account for the effects of strong emotions on someone's constructs
- it can only be used to investigate conscious traits
- it is self-validating in that, so long as Kelly's methods are used, it is impossible to find evidence to dispute it.

Personality theory, nomothetic – Emphasises similarities between people. Assumes that the same traits or dimensions of personality apply to everyone, differing only quantitatively. There are laws of behaviour that can be applied to anyone.
Associated with Cattell and Eysenck.

Trait approaches/multi-trait approaches – nomothetic theories.

Cattell and Eysenck are trait theorists. The aim is to identify the range of traits which are central to the personality and devise tests of these traits. People share the same central personality and differ only in their expression of various traits.

Orthogonal Factor analysis is used by Eysenck; **oblique factor analysis** is used by Cattell.

Eysenck's theory
Using **orthogonal factor analysis** (ie second-order factor analysis to identify a small number of powerful independent factors) on battle-shocked soldiers, he described personality on 2 dimensions:

P

- Extraversion–introversion (E scale).
  - Extroverts – sociable risk-takers, impulsive and unreliable.
  - Introverts – serious and reserved, solitary, orderly, restrained, pessimistic.
- Neuroticism–stability (N scale).
  - Neurotics – touchy, irritable and anxious, headaches and sleeping difficulties.
  - Stables – calm, even-tempered and controlled.
- (Psychoticism (P scale) was added later as another dimension – solitary, cold and hostile; is not evenly distributed throughout the population, with criminals and schizophrenics having a lot of it.)

There is a continuum between the extremes in both cases.

There is a **hierarchy** linking specific responses to situations (at the bottom) to habitual responses (next up) to traits (near the top) and types (at the top) – *BUT* these types *aren't* categories but quantitative variations (ie it's hierarchical, not categorical).

Eysenck proposed a biological theory to justify his ideas. Extroverts have less active ascending reticular activating systems (ARASs) and therefore need to seek excitement to achieve an optimum level of arousal. Their cortices are also at a lower level of arousal. The level of E therefore depends on the nature of the ARAS. N is explained by the autonomic nervous system, in that neurotic individuals respond more to stimulation.

Cattell's theory
There are 20 different traits. He collected 18, 000 words used to describe personality and used **oblique factor analysis** (ie first-order factor analysis to identify a large number of non-independent factors that correlate with one another) to reduce these to 15 **primary traits**/first order factors (L data). Questionnaires based on these traits were used to develop the theory and these confirmed 12 of the primary traits and added another 4. The findings at this level were called Q data. Some situational tests on people revealed a third set of criteria, T data, which do not seem to correlate well with L and Q data.

So Eysenck looks at things on three scales (**N, E, P**) and Cattell looks at things in 16–23 areas. A compromise between the two (by Costa & McCrea) shows that there are **five universal factors** that are most important in personality:
- extroversion
- agreeableness

- conscientiousness
- emotional stability
- culture.

State approaches (considered here as 'type' approaches)
The classification of a person into one or another groups. There is no quantitative element to it. Started with Hippocrates's fluids. Sheldon suggested a classification based on body type (endomorphic = fat *bon viveur*; ectomorphic = thin intellectual; mesomorphic = muscular leader). Jung suggested introverts and extroverts. Kretschmer suggested pyknic, aesthetic and athletic, which is too simplistic.

Personality, type A – (Friedman & Rosenman)
Describes behaviour patterns displayed by patients with coronary vascular disease. Relative risk of coronary vascular disease is 2.5 in men. Behaviours include being/doing things:
- appearing 'driven'
- ambitious
- competitive – even in leisure pursuits
- alert
- impatient
- aggressive
- talking quickly
- frequent gestures
- highly aroused
- deadline urgency.

There are two types of behaviour pattern:
- achievement strivings
- impatience irritability.

Personality, type B – May be as ambitious, but don't appear 'driven'. Job ambitions don't dominate their entire lives.
More time for family and friends and less competitive leisure pursuits.

PET – Positron emission tomography.

Phaeochromocytoma – Can cause episodic anxiety.

Pharmacokinetics –
Zero order
- Rate of decay limited by enzyme systems.
- Rate of decay remains constant.
- Elimination half-life varies according to how much drug there is.
- Drugs include:

P

251

- phenytoin
- ethanol.

1st order:
- Simple exponential decay, rate proportional to the amount in the body.
- Rate proportional to the concentration of the drug.

2nd order:
- Bi-exponential; implies a multicompartmental model.

- Steady state is achieved within 4–5 half-lives.
- Dosage interval should be dependent on half-life after steady state has been achieved.

Phenelzine – Is an MAOI
Causes:
- swelling of ankles
- peripheral neuropathy (and therefore paraesthesia)
- hypomania
- *not*:
  - hypocalcaemia
  - purpura.

Phenomenology – The study of psychic events and psychological feelings as phenomena without exploring the underlying causes.

Phenytoin – Side-effects include:
- Dose related side-effects:
  - sedation
  - ataxia
  - dysarthria.
- Chronic use causes:
  - folate deficient (ie macrocytic) anaemia
  - osteomalacia
  - cerebellar atrophy
  - gingival hyperplasia
  - hypertrichosis.

Phobia – A persistent irrational fear or anxiety, object or situation leading to avoidance. The fear is out of proportion to the real danger and cannot be reasoned away.
There is anticipatory anxiety.
- The defence mechanism is different than that seen in conversion disorder.
- The defence mechanism is similar to agoraphobia and social

phobia.
- Repression is the main defence mechanism.
- Oedipal conflict plays a part.

Aetiological factors include:
- preparedness
- avoidance learning
- repression
- stimulus generalisation
- incubation.

- CBT can help in 90% of cases.
- They're most common in women in their 20s.
- The anxiety or focus often generalises.
- Frequently associated with generalised anxiety disorder.
- Associated with childhood fears and enuresis.
- The habituation response is normal in simple phobias.
- Phobic symptoms are seen in 5–25% of the population.

Phobia of excretion – A special type of social phobia.

Phobia of vomiting – A special type of social phobia.

Phonation – Is more common in frontal lobe seizures than in temporal lobe seizures.

Phoneme – Unit of sound.

Phonology – Is the study of the basic sound units of speech (= phonemes).
These are produced in the left superior temporal lobe.

Phosphene – Flash of light seen on direct stimulation of the visual cortex.

Physostigmine –
- Is an anticholinesterase.

Piaget – Developed a stage theory of cognitive development.
- Involved **schemata** – a means of organising one's experience that makes the world more simple, predictable and knowable. They change as we do, by:
  - **Assimilation**
  - **Accommodation**
  - **Equilibration** – when pre-existing schemata are inappropriate to deal with new situations, the child is in disequilibrium and has to restore the balance by changing one or more existing

schemata (ie **accommodate** new experience).

- When something outside an existing schema is encountered, a shift of equilibrium results. The **disequilibrium** prompts **accommodation** and the development of new schemata, which are incorporated by **assimilation** to regain equilibrium.

Piaget's stages:

Sensorimotor period – 0–2 years

- **Circular reactions** – voluntary repeated motor activities (eg shaking a toy) – from 2 months.
- **Primary circular reactions** – 2–5 months – purposeless.
- **Secondary circular reactions** – 5–9 months – purposeful/experimental.
- **Tertiary circular reactions** – 12–18 months – original behaviour patterns and purposeful quest for new experiences.
- **Concept of the permanent object** – ie the child becomes aware that a hidden object still exists at 12–18 months and will look for it, whereas at 4–8 months it will think it has ceased to exist.
- Problems – at 4–8 months, the child doesn't comprehend 'in' or 'behind' and at this age can already cry to get attention from the mother he cannot see.

Preoperational stage – 2–7 years

- Learns to use language and represent objects with **images and words**.
- **Egocentricity** – believes own view of world is only one.
- Thinking characterised by:
  - **Realism** – belief in dreams, imaginary situations.
  - **Animism** – attributes consciousness to toys, etc.
  - **Artificialism** – natural events believed caused by people.
  - **Authoritarian morality** – teleological, based on outcome not intention, and negative events seen as punishments.
  - **Creationism** – teleological – eg moon exists to provide light at night.
  - **Finalism** – all things have a purpose.
  - **Fails on conservation tasks** – believes liquid's volume changes when in different sized/shaped glasses due to **precausal reasoning** – beliefs based more on internal schemes than observation.
- Problems – failure on conservation task may be due to inability to understand question – when asked non-verbally, they do better. They may also be forgetful.

Concrete operations period – 7–12 years
- Thinking characterised by:
  - **Logical thought.**
  - **Concept of conservation.**
- **Understands relational terms/logic of class hierarchy** (this is the ability to compare a superclass with a subclass).
- **Less egocentric.**
- **Abstract thinking.**
- A mental structure – an **operation** – is developed which comprises **compensation, reversibility** and **identity.** It is the **ability to conserve,** but can only be performed in the presence of actual objects:
  - Number/liquid quantity at 6–7 years.
  - Substance/quantity and length at 7–8 years.
  - Weight at 8–10 years.
  - Volume 11–12 years.
- Operations are acquired by **decalages,** which are slips in levels of performance which can be horizontal (conservation) or vertical (causing inconsistencies between different abilities or operations).
- **Transitivity tasks** – eg If John is taller than Susan and Susan is taller than Charlie, is John or Charlie taller? – can only be solved with real objects.

Formal operational stage – > 12 years
- **Abstract thinking.**
- **Logical propositions, hypothetical reasoning,** hypothetical problems, future and ideological problems – the ability to discuss things never encountered.
- Only ever achieved by 1/3 average adolescents and adults.

Criticisms of Piaget's theory
- More than one stage can exist in an individual.
- There are formal aspects in preoperational children.
- Pure motor abnormalities occur in the sensorimotor stage, but affected children may be intellectually normal.
- All work was done on 'average' children.

Piblokto – Is a culture-bound dissociative state seen in Inuit women.
- occurrence associated with food shortage
- associated with symptoms of depression
- clothing is torn off and the patient screams and runs about wildly, often jumping into water
- life is endangered by hypothermia

- suicidal/homicidal behaviour may also be seen.

Pica – Up to 50% of those affected have a first-degree relative with pica. There is an association of the following in relatives:
- obesity
- alcoholism
- drug addiction,

and the sufferers of the above often have a childhood history of pica in this case.

May present with problems of iron, zinc or other deficiency, lead poisoning or gastrointestinal problems (diarrhoea, constipation, obstruction or parasitosis).

It has no effects on the desire for food.

Pick's disease – Characteristic features include:
- early personality deterioration
- early incontinence
- normal EEG
- transcortical motor aphasia is seen
- occasional apraxia and agnosia (but these are more common in Alzheimer's disease).

- Is more common in women than in men.

Pathology
- Macro
  - selective asymmetrical frontotemporal atrophy with cerebellar sparing
  - knife-blade gyri
  - ventricular enlargement
  - atrophy of basal ganglia and thalamus.
- Micro
  - Pick's bodies
  - neuronal loss ⎫ seen in ⎧ cerebral cortex
  - reactive astrocytosis ⎭ ⎨ basal ganglia
  ⎩ locus caeruleus
  substantia nigra
  - balloon cells
  - loss of myelin in white matter of affected lobes
  - Pick bodies (affected neurones lose Nissl substance, swell and develop irregular argentophilic inclusions, which are the Pick bodies).

Characteristic neuropathological features include:
- Generalised cortical atrophy, especially frontotemporal with

cerebellar sparing.
- Balloon cells.
- Atrophy of basal ganglia and thalamus.
- Loss of myelin in white matter of affected lobes.
- Pick bodies (affected neurones lose Nissl substance, swell and develop irregular argentophilic inclusions, which are the Pick bodies).

Pick's bodies consist of:
- straight neurofilaments
- paired helical filaments
- endoplasmic reticulum.

Apraxia and agnosia are seen but are more common in SDAT.
It's a *common* cause of pre-senile dementia.

Pineal gland –
- Situated at the top of the brainstem.
- Receives afferents from retina conveying light/dark information.
- Secretes melatonin in response to fading light.

Placebo –
- The effect is strongest with very small or very large tablets.
- For the purposes of exams, everything responds to placebo treatment.

Placebo, active – Contain substances that induce side-effects similar to those of the experimental drug.
They are rarely used.

Plaques, senile –
- are extracellular
- are seen in:
  - Alzheimer's disease
  - normal ageing.

Play – Is difficult to define, but has several characteristics:
- It is enjoyable and associated with positive affect.
- It is done for its own sake and contains its own goals.
- It is spontaneous, voluntary and controlled by oneself.
- It requires active involvement.
- It is different from 'real life'.

Seems not to be crucial to development, as children play little in some cultures. The enjoyment that results from it may be important in contributing to psychological well-being.

Play behaviour – Was described by **Patten**:

Unoccupied behaviour – Not playing but may pay brief attention to activities around.

Solitary play – Plays alone, more or less oblivious.

Onlooking behaviour – Watches others, doesn't join in, but may speak.

Parallel play – Plays with others, little organisation, no joint goal.

Co-operative play – Plays as part of group, roles/tasks shared out, sense of exclusivity about group.

Pons – Structure lying between the medulla and the midbrain that is about 2.5 cm in length. It contains the:
- spinal trigeminal tract and nucleus
- pontine trigeminal nucleus
- trigeminal motor nucleus
- trapezoid body
- superior olivary nucleus.

Contains the nuclei of the:
- abducens nerve (VI)
- facial motor nucleus nerve (VII).

Porphyria, acute intermittent – Features include:
- autosomal dominant inheritance (but incomplete penetrance)
- precipitation by of acute episodes by:
  - carbamazepine
  - acute infection
  - anaesthesia
  - barbiturates
  - amitriptyline
  - phenytoin
  - nitrazepam
  - steroids
  - oral contraceptive pill
  - oestrogens
  - tetracyclines
  - sulphonamides
  - methyldopa
- 20% of patients have epileptic seizures
- psychiatric symptoms may resemble schizophrenia.

Differential diagnosis:
- acute organic reaction

- functional psychosis.

Porropsia – The perception/belief that objects are retreating from oneself but retaining their size.

Positive scotomata – Are a form of hallucination. They consist of simple percepts that obliterate part of the visual field (eg flashes and stars after a blow on the head).

Possession state –
- Belief one is possessed.
- Most often occurs in trance/altered state of consciousness.
- Usually dissociative.
- Distinction of normal from pathological:
  - unwanted
  - distressing
  - prolonged beyond immediate triggering event.

Posterior column damage – Causes ipsilateral loss of:
- vibration sense
- proprioception
- tactile discrimination/discriminative touch, below the level of injury.

- Also reported to cause 'loss of sensation of body image'.

Postnatal blues – A brief psychological disturbance characterised by:
- tearfulness
- emotional lability
- confusion.

It occurs in 50% of women, peaking at 3–5 days postpartum.
It is associated with:
- history of premenstrual tension (PMT)
- calcium deficiency
- monoamines, tryptophan, platelet α_2-adrenoceptors
- progesterone withdrawal post-delivery
- poor social adjustment
- poor marital relationship
- neuroticism
- fear of labour
- anxious/depressed mood during pregnancy.

Postnatal depression – Characteristically:
- occurs in 10–15% of women
- occurs within 6 weeks *or* 3 months of birth.

P

There is a correlation with:
- young age
- poor marital relationships
- absent social support
- past psychiatric history.

There is no correlation with:
- assisted delivery
- age
- social class
- parity
- biology (ie it's a relatively pure psychological condition).

Post-schizophrenic depression – Prominent depressive symptoms are present for at least 2 weeks while some symptoms of schizophrenia (either positive or negative) remain. Depressive symptoms must be distinguished from the effects of antipsychotic drug treatment or the impaired volition and flattened affect occurring in a schizophrenic disorder.

Post-traumatic stress disorder (PTSD) – Prolonged and abnormal response to exceptionally intense stressful circumstances such as a natural disaster or a sexual or other physical assault.

Intense, prolonged and delayed reaction to intensely stressful event. Features include:
- hyperarousal
- re-experiencing images of the stressful event ('flashbacks')
- avoidance of reminders.

The original concept of PTSD was of a reaction to such an extreme stressor that anyone would be affected. Epidemiological studies have shown that not everyone exposed develops PTSD, therefore personal predisposition is felt to play a part. Physical injury is believed to increase the risk of developing PTSD.
Concept originated in the USA post-Vietnam, and meant soldiers could receive medical and social help without being labelled/diagnosed with another psychiatric disorder.

Clinical picture
hyperarousal (but *not* autonomic signs of severe anxiety – that's an acute stress reaction)
- persistent anxiety
- irritability
- insomnia

- poor concentration.

intrusions
- difficulty in recalling stressful events at will
- intense intrusive imagery (flashbacks)
- recurring distressing dreams
- plus depression.

avoidance
- avoid reminders of the event
- detachment from others
- emotional blunting.
- numbness
- unresponsiveness to surroundings
- diminished interest in activities
- plus guilt in survivors, eg of a disaster.

other
- anhedonia.

There may also be maladaptive coping responses – eg excess alcohol consumption, drugs, deliberate self-harm, persistent aggressive behaviour or suicide.

After traumatic events, survivors often reconsider their beliefs about the meaning and purpose of life.

Dissociation and depersonalisation are felt to be important.

Symptoms may begin very soon after the event or after an interval of days, occasionally months; very rarely more than 6 months.

If the patient experiences a second stressful event, then the symptoms may return even if the second event was less severe. Most cases resolve in 3 months, but some persist for years.

PTSD can be diagnosed in people who have history of mental disorder before the stressor (unlike acute stress disorder).

Combat-related guilt increases risk of suicide.

Other responses to stressful events may be seen, such as:
- depression
- somatisation disorder
- alcohol and drug abuse.

Epidemiology
1–2.6% prevalence and lifetime prevalence.
Rates are higher in groups with exposure to greater stress, being common immediately after the stress and then declining: eg 3.6% population prevalence after a volcanic eruption.

Present in 30% of firefighters.
Present in 45% of battered women.

After a road traffic accident, generalised and phobic anxiety disorders are more common than PTSD.
90% of Vietnam veterans had PTSD and 43% had at least one other diagnosis, most commonly atypical depression, alcohol dependence, anxiety disorder, substance abuse and somatisation disorder.
• is *not* common after childbirth.

Aetiology
The stressor – could be anything.
Intensity of involvement in incident seems unimportant.

Personality vulnerability
Genetic factors
Susceptibility found to be 30% genetic in twin studies.

Other predisposing factors
Temperament – especially neuroticism.
Young or very old age increases risk.
History of psychiatric disorder increases risk.
Child and adolescent environment felt not to contribute to susceptibility.

Neurophysiological factors
Animal experiments in which animal exposed to severe aversive stimuli – seem to trigger flashbacks by smell and sounds (as in humans).
Therefore classical conditioning may be involved (subcortical).
Animals subjected to uncontrollable stress show increased noradrenaline turnover in limbic and cortical areas and increased dopamine release in nucleus accumbens and frontal cortex.
No evidence that these changes cause symptoms of PTSD.

In patients with PTSD, the main findings are hyperarousal and increased noradrenaline activity.
Contradictory evidence of abnormalities of hypothalamic–pituitary–adrenal axis in these patients.

Psychological explanation
Psychodynamic theory – role of previous experience determines individual response to stressful events.
Cognitive theory – normal processing of emotionally charged information is overwhelmed to the point that intrusive memories

persist; high arousal leads to increased liability to interpret ambiguous information as threatening. This theory has not been critically tested.

Treatment

Immediate

Encourage to recall the event, express emotions; benzodiazepine as required to reduce anxiety; hypnotic at night-time in the short term for sleep. Work through the event as many times as is needed before the symptoms begin to subside. No evidence for counselling, although widely used.

Later treatment

Counselling

Once PTSD is established, treatment is difficult.

Give emotional support, encourage recall, facilitate working through associated emotions. Deal with feelings of guilt the patient may have *re* survival, grief, perceived shortcomings, and with existential concerns *re* the meaning and purpose of life and death.

Behavioural techniques

Desensitise to the intrusive memories, by encouraging recall while relaxing/flooding.

Psychodynamic psychotherapy

Helps patients to work through the events, also to understand how the initial event has increased their vulnerability to recent stressors.

Drug treatment

Anxiolytics – avoid for established PTSD as they may lead to dependence.

MAOIs – have been recommended for PTSD, but evidence is contradictory.

TCAs – have only small effect, even in big doses.

Fluoxetine – one trial showed it to be effective; more work needed.

Poverty of content of speech – Occurs most often in schizophrenia.

Poverty of speech – Is a restricted amount of speech, which may be monosyllabic.

Occurs most often in schizophrenia.

Praecox feeling – Refers to empathic rapport with the patient.

Refers to a subjective sense by the clinician that the patient is odd.

Preconscious – *aka* subconscious

Is part of the unconscious and involves cortical activity. It has several

roles, eg:
- To carry out conscious but well-rehearsed tasks semi-autonomously (eg driving along a well-known road in a familiar car).
- To act as a buffer for consciousness (eg only one interpretation of a stimulus can be held in consciousness, but the preconscious holds the others, so that they can be made conscious quickly).
- To carry out background processing of tasks (eg when you think about a problem, fail solve it but find that the answer 'pops back' into consciousness some time later).

Pregnancy – Protects against psychiatric illness and suicide.

Prejudice – Making assumptions about a person's characteristics on the basis of the identification of a salient characteristic and behaving in accordance with these assumptions.
or
Prejudgement of others that is not amenable to discussion and is resistant to change.
or
An attitude towards a person or group of people, a negative emotional response and consequent intolerant, unfair and unfavourable attitude towards them.
or
A preconceived set of beliefs held about others who are pre-judged on this basis. It is usually used in a negative sense.

Prejudice can be the result of inadequacy, with an attempt to increase self-esteem by denigrating another. It can be displaced frustration or an attempt to gain acceptance, affiliation, security or superiority.

To eliminate prejudice from oneself, conscious control must be exerted to limit the negative response. Encounter between the two groups is not enough. They must work towards a common superordinate goal and therefore encounter non-competitive contact on equal terms.

Physical separation increases hostility.

Runciman's relative deprivational theory is associated with believing that the group to which you belong is being treated unfairly compared with other groups.

Conditions needed to reduce prejudice:
- cooperative effort

- potential for personal acquaintance
- equal status
- exposure to non-stereotypic individuals
- non-competitive contact.

Pressure of speech – An increase in both the amount and rate of speech, which can be difficult to understand.

Primal Therapy – A type of emotional release therapy pioneered by Arthur Janov.

Primitive idealisation – In psychoanalytic theory, a defence mechanism in which an object about which one is ambivalent is split into two conceptual representations, one wholly bad and one completely, ideally good.
Is one of the characteristics of borderline syndrome.

Problem-solving strategies – These are applied to complete tasks. There are several elements:
- Understanding the problem.
  - Coherence – the plan has to fit properly together and be followable.
  - Correspondence – the plan as understood internally has to be the same as the plan that will be acted on externally (ie we have to know how to carry out the internal plan).
  - Relationship to background knowledge – the plan has to be in keeping with background knowledge and be understandable in the light of it.
- Representing the problem – by the use of:
  - Symbols – (eg $= + - < >$, etc).
  - Lists – good if there are only so many solutions, as you can list them all and see which works.
  - Matrices.
  - Hierarchical trees.
  - Graphs.
  - Visual representation.
- Using a strategy to solve the problem.
  - Random search.
  - Heuristic strategies = trial and error made more efficient because of previous experience.
  - Algorithms – use of a specific set of attempts to solve the problem, which must be carried out in a certain order.

Processing, information – The way in which external signals arriving at

the sense organs are converted into meaningful perceptual experiences.
Can be:

- Data driven – starts when data arrive and includes template matching (a form of pattern recognition and classification) when the perception is matched with an internal template.
- Conceptually driven – when data are incomplete a concept is formed of what *might* be present and confirmatory evidence is sought, biasing the result and potentially leading to a misperception.

Prolactin – Release is inhibited by dopamine released from the hypothalamic-hypophyseal pathway.

Prolixity – Flight of ideas/pressure of speech.

Prosody – Is concerned with intonation, cadence and emotional expression through tone of voice. It is frontal in origin and frontal lesions can cause aprosody.

Prosopagnosia – Is defective recognition of faces, associated with bilateral lesions of the ventromedial occipitotemporal regions.
In advanced Alzheimer's disease, the patient may fail to recognise their own mirrored reflection. This is 'the mirror sign'.

Proteins, G- –
- Have 7 transmembrane-spanning sites.

Protein, G-, -coupled receptors –
- Are distinct from the effector proteins.
- Have extracellular recognition sites for ligands.
- Link cell surface receptors to a variety of enzymes and ion channels.
- Can increase in number after blocking.

Prototype – A cluster of schemata relating to an individual person or a group of individuals, enabling the identification of a person belonging to a particular group (eg a 'yuppie').

Proxemics – Relates to 'personal space'.

Pseudodementia – Is an imprecise, potentially confusing word with a range of meanings.
Most often, it refers to apparent (but not real) dementia, often in depressed people.
- Anxiety.

- Includes the Ganser syndrome.
- Is different from dissociative pseudodementia.
- Has onset with depressive features.
- Normal EEG.
- No focal neurology.
- Associated with past or family history of manic-depressive psychosis.
- Has a relatively acute onset.

Pseudohallucination – Was described by Kandinsky.
Pseudohallucination (like pseudodementia) is an imprecise and poorly defined word with several meanings that is best avoided. It is preferable simply to describe the psychopathology.

Either means
located in inner, subjective space
or
are figurative 'as if' experiences located in external space.
- Are not created voluntarily.
- Are not subject to conscious manipulation.
- Are not pathognomonic of any illness and were first described by Kandinsky in 1885, but later discussed by Jaspers.
- Are a type of mental image.
- *Don't* occur in dreams.

Includes:
- **Eidetic imagery** – a vivid and detailed reproduction of a previous perception.
- **Pareidolia** – the occurrence of vivid imagery without effort while looking at a poorly structured background. It can occur against one's will.

Pseudohallucinations are a feature of:
- bereavement
- the Ganser syndrome.

Pseudomutuality – A disorder of communication within a family in which a superficial pretence of closeness and reciprocal understanding belies a lack of real feeling.
Alleged but not proved to be a risk factor for schizophrenia.
Is a method by which a family system maintains equilibrium.

Pseudoseizures – *aka* psychogenic/hysterical seizures
Characteristic features include:
- maintenance of consciousness

- normal EEG.

The following are more common in schizophrenics than in epileptics:
- Family psychiatric history of psychiatric disorder.
- Past history of attempted suicide.
- Current affective disorder.
- Sexual maladjustment.

Psychoanalysis – Suggests that active forces within individuals (conscious or unconscious) are the determinants of behaviour.

Fosters:
- regression
- transference of feeling towards the analyst
- recollection of forgotten memories.

Psychoanalytic approach, the – Developed from Freud's theories and relies heavily on the influence of the unconscious mind. There was a rejection of the strict, objective reproducible scientific method.

Principles:
- The unconscious mind and its repressed/forgotten memories are hugely important.
- The preconscious is also present, and represents memories to which we have access.
- There are instinctual drives such as the libido that drive behaviour.
- the **id** (wild primitive biological drives), ego (represents id in a socially acceptable way) and **super-ego** (conscience) are present.
- Experience in early childhood is critically important.
- Personality development proceeds through several stages, as the libido is attached to different parts of the body. Problems in a given stage result in fixation at that stage and characteristics of that stage are retained during later years, causing problems.

Psychoanalytic technique, basic model of –
- The patient is encouraged to talk as freely as possible.
- The major therapeutic interventions of the analyst are:
  - interpretations
  - confrontations
  - clarifications.
- The patient experiences transference.
- The working relationship is the **therapeutic alliance** or the **working alliance**.
- Resistance is typically experienced by the patient.

Psychodrama – Was developed by Moreno.

Psychology, self
- External relationships maintain:
  - self-esteem
  - self-cohesion.
- There's mirror- and idealising-transference.
- *Is* of use to narcissists.
- Is different to object relations theory.

Psychometrics – Clinical uses:
- to save time in assessment
- to confirm clinical hypotheses
- provides objective assessment (use of standardised tests puts one's own clinical experience in context)
- aids clinician in unfamiliar area
- sets up dialogue with patient.

Psychopathology – Systematic study of abnormal experience, cognition and behaviour.
Descriptive vs dynamic/analytic psychopathology.

Descriptive psychopathology categorises abnormal experiences based on patient's subjective description (based on conscious experience) or on observed behaviour and is based on the *form* of the experience.

Dynamic/analytic psychopathology emphasises the unconscious processes that may influence conscious experience. The relationship between the patient and the therapist is most important and the emphasis is on the *content* of the experience rather than the form.

Psychoses, cycloid – Distinguished from schizophrenia by Leonhard. He said they were non-affective psychoses and had a good outcome.

Psychosis – Has been said to have several characteristics:
- a gross disorder of basic drives
- impaired insight
- personality distortion
- impaired reality testing.

Psychosis, acute organic – Features suggestive of this rather than schizophrenia include:
- misidentification of people (because organic psychotics have impaired consciousness, thinking, concentration, attention and distorted visual perception)

269

- visual hallucinations
- absence of delusions.

Psychosis, manic-depressive – Described by Kraepelin.

Psychosis, monosymptomatic hypochondriacal – Is characterised by any of:
- Delusion of halitosis.
- Delusions of the dysmorphic type.
- Delusions of infestation.

Psychosis, puerperal – Distinctive symptoms are:
- abrupt onset (first 2 weeks)
- marked perplexity
- rapid fluctuations in mental state (hourly)
- marked restlessness, fear and insomnia
- rapid development of delusions, hallucinations and disturbed behaviour.

Risk factors are:
- caesarean
- higher social class
- older age at birth of first child
- primiparity.

- 80% are affective psychoses.
- Occurs in 0.2% of mothers (recurrence is much higher).
- Can last longer than eight months if untreated.

Psychosis, schizophreniform – Was described by Langfeldt.
Can occur in:
- myxoedema
- encephalitis lethargica/von Economo's encephalitis/sleeping sickness
- Wilson's disease.

Psychotherapy, brief dynamic – (Malan & Horowitz)
- Focuses on the conflict.
- Is good for circumscribed neurotic problems.
- The main indication is difficulties in personal relationships.

Psychotherapy, clientcentred – Provides an enabling relationship to allow the individual to realise his/her capacity for growth and self-realisation.
- Main activities include:
  - reflecting what the client says

- paraphrasing the words
- Is non-directive.
- Is associated with Carl Rogers.
- Effective therapists have three characteristics:
  - **accurate empathy**
  - **non-possessive warmth**
  - **genuineness**.

Psychotherapy, exploratory – Includes:
- unburdening of problems
- ventilation of feelings
- discussion of current problems
- confrontation of defences
- regression
- support within the working alliance.

Psychotherapy, insight-oriented – Prerequisites include:
- verbal fluency
- a degree of introspectiveness
- adequate ego strength
- average intelligence (*not* above average intelligence).

Psychotherapy, psychoanalytic –
- the therapist remains neutral
- transference phenomena are explored
- talking in an unstructured way/free association
- **working through** (which is an elaboration of insights into various areas of the patient's functioning)

Psychotherapy, supportive – Includes:
- unburdening of problems
- ventilation of feelings
- discussion of current problems
- support for and reinforcement of defences
- support within the working alliance.

PTSD – Post-traumatic stress disorder.

Puerperal psychosis – Risk factors include:
- family history of mental illness
- primiparity
- past history of major psychiatric illness
- unmarried mothers.

80% of cases are affective, but there are also schizophrenic and

organic causes. Onset is acute and usually in the first 2 weeks postpartum. Compared with manic psychoses, puerperal psychoses show more:
- delusions
- hallucinations
- disorientation
- agitation
- emotional lability.

Puncture, lumbar – Increased pressure may be secondary to:
- hypertensive encephalopathy
- cortical vein thrombosis
- communicating hydrocephalus
- subarachnoid haemorrhage.

Punning – A type of loosening of association seen in mania.

Purkinje cells –
- Have high GABA concentrations.
- Degenerate in Marie's hereditary cerebellar ataxia.
- Send efferents to the lateral vestibular nuclei.

Quotient, Intelligence – Among people with IQ < 50, males are more common than females at all ages.

Rabbit syndrome – A late-onset movement disorder that can be confused with tardive dyskinesia. It involves rapid, fine, rhythmic movements of the mouth that resemble the chewing movements of rabbits. Unlike tardive dyskinesia it improves with anticholinergics.

Rape – Psychiatric consequences can involve:
- Anxiety disorder.
- Depressive disorder.
- Psychosexual dysfunction (two-thirds of rape victims reported less sexual activity; 40% gave up intercourse or had no orgasm for six months).
- PTSD – most common (in 97% of victims mmediately and 47% at three months). No correlation with level of violence or nature of sexual act(s) experienced. 'Treatment' involves:
  - prolonged exposure by reliving the events in imagination.
  - overcoming feelings of vulnerability and self-blame.

Raphe nuclei – Are midbrain structures containing serotonergic cell bodies.
These are associated with non-REM sleep in the monoaminergic theory of sleep.

RDC – Research Diagnostic Criteria.

Q
R

Reaction, adverse drug – There are four types:
- Intolerance
  - consistent with the known pharmacological actions of the drug
  - may be dose-related.
- Idiosyncratic reactions
  - not characteristic or predictable
  - relate to patient's characteristics, which are unusual.
- Allergic reactions
  - drug interacts with a protein to form an antigen
  - this causes sensitisation and an immune response
  - suggested by:
    - delayed onset
    - onset after repeated exposure
    - no dose related effect (a very small dose can cause it)
    - hypersensitivity unrelated to the usual effects of the drug
  - types:
    - I – anaphylaxis
    - II, III, IV can present as haematological:
      - haemolytic anaemia
      - agranulocytosis
      - thrombocytopenia
  - II and III can present with hepatic damage
  - IV can present as skin rashes or generalised SLE-like disease.
- Drug interactions
  - pharmacokinetic
  - mixing causing precipitation or inactivation
  - chelation
  - changes in gastrointestinal motility
  - drug displacement from binding sites
  - enzyme induction/inhibition
  - renal tubular transport competition
  - changes in urinary pH changing drug excretion
  - pharmacodynamic
  - inhibited uptake
  - inhibited transport
  - interaction at receptors
  - synergism
  - changes in fluid and electrolyte balance.

Reaction, catastrophic – Sudden emotional reaction to frustration. Characteristic of dementia.

Reaction, sensitivity – Includes:

- agranulocytosis
- leukopenia
- leukocytosis
- haemolytic anaemia.

Reaction formation – A defence mechanism acting when an unacceptable impulse is mastered by an exaggeration of the opposing tendency (eg solicitude as a reaction formation to cruelty).

Reasoning, deductive – The process by which new facts are discovered, based solely on known facts rather than on new experiences.

Reasoning, dichotomous – *aka* all-or-nothing reasoning
Displayed by anorexics who think that if they put on *any* weight they'll put on an excessive amount of weight.

Reasoning, inductive – The process by which new facts are discovered/assumptions made about the world based on experience of it. For example, if someone with a large bunch of keys is seen trying them in a locked door, inductive reasoning leads us to believe that they are trying to unlock the door.

Reciprocal inhibition – States that anxiety and relaxation are mutually exclusive. Relaxation techniques are practised and performed in an anxiogenic situation so that the person cannot become anxious.

Recognition – Is the sense of familiarity occurring when one recalls previously memorised material in response to a cue.

Rectal administration –
Advantages:
- no swallow necessary
- bypasses gastric factors
- good for gastric irritants
- reduced first-pass metabolism
- no co-operation needed
- can be used during seizures.

Disadvantages:
- patients aren't keen
- faecal load affects absorption
- local inflammation occurs with frequent use.

Referencing, criterion – A measurement according to an agreed standard. If there is a pre-set pass mark, then the exam is criterion referenced.

Referencing, norm – A measurement according to the average mark. If it is predetermined that 50% of people will pass, then the exam is norm referenced.

Reflex, pupillary light – Involves:
- optic nerve
- Edinger–Westphal nucleus
- oculomotor nuclei.

- It isn't cortical.

Regulation, up/down – Relates to changes in the rate of synthesis of a neurone's neurotransmitter receptors. If rate of synthesis is increased, it's upregulation, and *vice versa*.

Reich, Wilhelm – Developed the idea of **muscular armour/character armour** (repetitive unconscious behaviours that protect against both internal and external dangers to the individual) and **organ energy accumulator**, which has developed into bioenergetics.
- One of the original followers of Freud.

Reinforcement theory – Reciprocal reinforcement of attractions occurs with rewards in both directions and *vice versa* (ie punishment diminishes the probability of interpersonal attraction).

REM – Rapid eye movement.

Reserpine – Is an alkaloid that depletes stores of:
- noradrenaline
- dopamine
- 5-HT
- histamine.

Resistance – Is everything done or said by the patient that stops them gaining access to their unconscious.
In psychoanalytic theory:
- Is a clinical concept (*not* psychological).
- Can provide information on the patient's mental functioning (emphasised by Anna Freud – it reflects the type of conflict and defences used).
- May arise because of the threat resulting from the psychoanalytic procedure.
- May be an obstacle to treatment.
- Includes absenteeism.

Resonance – The movement of protons to a higher energy level in response to a radio-frequency impulse.

Response, galvanic skin –
- Anxiety is only one component of this measure of arousal.
- Increased in chronic schizophrenia.
- Is unreliable as a lie-detector test.
- Is not a sensitive measure of anxiety.

Response, orienting – Occurs in phasic alertness and involves:
- decrease in heart rate
- decreased ventilatory rate
- desynchronised EEG.

Retardation, mental – In ICD-10:
- IQ 50–69 = mild mental retardation
- IQ 35–49 = moderate mental retardation
- IQ 20–34 = severe mental retardation
- IQ <20 = profound mental retardation.

Reticular formation – A key arousal control centre. Inhibited by serotonin.

Rigidity, clasp-knife – Is a pyramidal (ie upper motor neurone) feature.

RIMA – Reversible inhibitor of monoamine oxidase.

Risk, cardiovascular – Is increased in employed vs unemployed women.
Is proportional to the number of children in employed women, but inversely proportional to the number of children in unemployed women.

Risperidone –
- Blocks:
  - D2 receptors
  - 5HT2 receptors.
- The serotonergic effects probably limit EPSEs.
- Is metabolised by cytochrome p450 2D6 to an active metabolite.

Rogers, Carl – Developed **client-centred therapy** and the **Encounter movement**.
- Was *not* a psychoanalyst.

Effective Rogerian therapists have three characteristics:
- accurate empathy

- non-possessive warmth
- genuineness.

Room, Ames – Used in experiments to demonstrate that size constancy can be broken down.

Rotter, Julian – Developed a social learning theory that emphasised the role of cognitive factors and also mentioned the **locus of control**, which describes whether people believe internal or external factors control their lives (**internals** and **externals**).

SANS – Scale for the Assessment of Negative Symptoms.

Satiety – Ventromedial hypothalamic nucleus.

Scaffolding – *aka* framing
Described by Kaye.
Is the process by which the infant learns its appropriate skills of social interaction from its parents and other adults.

Good parents provide the framework in a variety of ways:

- Nurturing for physical and emotional needs.
- Protection.
- Helping.
- Feedback on behaviour.
- Modelling.
- Encouraging discourse.
- Acting as a memory.

Scale, Depressive Signs – Is good for depression in dementia as it's behavioural.

Scale, Hamilton Rating for Depression – Is a diagnostic observer-rated scale for depression.
Contains somatic items, so may therefore be less good for old-age patients.

Scale, Montgomery–Asberg – Is a diagnostic observer-rated scale for depression.
Does not contain somatic items and is therefore better in old age.
Is not reliable in dementia.

Scale, Wakefield – Is a self-rated scale.

Scale, Zung Depression – Is a self-rated scale.

Scales, ratio measurement – Measure things that can be compared

with one another by ratios (eg degrees Kelvin but not degrees Celsius, or height). You can say that someone is twice as tall or heavy, but not that they're twice as hot (in Celsius, at least).
Have some characteristic properties:
- categories are mutually exclusive
- categories are logically ordered
- there is an equal distance between adjacent categories
- there is a true zero point.

Scaling – The conversion of raw data into types of scores more readily understood (eg ranks, centiles, standard scores).

Scan, CT – Useful indications include:
- suspicion of cerebral tumour
- suspicion of subdural haematoma
- focal neurology
- normal pressure hydrocephalus
- cerebral oedema.

Schaffer – Described mutual reciprocity.

Schema – A cognitive plan of a person/situation/thing that helps in reacting appropriately to it, built on the basis of previous experience of it. It includes the characteristics of the thing and the relationships between these.

Common examples are:
- Person schemata – characteristics of people.
- Role schemata – define characteristics of people in certain jobs (eg teachers, policemen, astronauts, etc).
- Scripts – schemata relating to events, eg going out for dinner (wait for table, be seated, order wine before food, eat, ask for the bill, etc).

In the absence of an appropriate schema, situations more easily lead to confusion and disorientation.
Schemata allow us to infer and therefore form complete ideas about situations much more quickly than we would otherwise manage.

Schism – Described by Bleuler.
Fragmentation of mental functioning.

Schizoaffective disorder – A disorder in which there are:
- definite schizophrenic
- definite affective symptoms
  which are

- equally prominent
- present simultaneously *or* within a few days of each other.

First-degree relatives have a higher incidence of both schizophrenia and mood disorders. The outcome of schizoaffective disorder is better than that for schizophrenia, especially if manic symptoms are prominent.
Beware confusion due to post-schizophrenic depression.
Patients recovering from recurrent manic-type schizoaffective disorder rarely develop a defect state.

Schizoaffective psychosis – Described by Kasanin.

Schizoid personality disorder – A person with this disorder is:
- introspective
- prone to engage in autistic fantasy rather than take action
- emotionally cold
- self-sufficient
- emotionally detached
- aloof
- humourless
- apparently incapable of expressing affection or tenderness
- unlikely to make intimate friendships or to marry – they withdraw from close relationships
- unlikely to concern themself with other people's opinions
- eccentric.

There is no aetiological relationship between this and schizophrenia. Excessive social anxiety is seen, *not* in schizoid personality disorder, but in *schizotypal* personality disorder.

Schizophasia – *aka* word salad
Described by Bleuler.
Was originally used by Bleuler to describe a form of schizophrenia in which disorder of speech was the main feature.
Now it means 'word salad'.

Schizophrenia – Described by Bleuler in 1911.
Positive symptoms include:
- Delusions (including delusional perception).
- Hallucinations.
- Incongruity of affect.

Negative symptoms include (and can be assessed by the Scale for the Assessment of Negative Symptoms – SANS):

S

- flat/blunted affect
- poverty of speech
- avolition
- anhedonia
- apathy
- abulia
- derailment
- age disorientation
- indifference to the environment.

Neither positive nor negative (ie orthogonal) symptoms include:
- Thought disorder.

Type I schizophrenia (**Crow**)
Predominantly positive symptoms of acute onset with a good response to treatment. Normal ventricles, normal cognition and good prognosis. There is a positive family psychiatric history.

Acute schizophrenia – Features include:
- delusional perception
- incongruity of affect.

Chronic (defect state) schizophrenia
Important features include:
- Formal thought disorder (and cognitive impairment/slowing and behavioural slowing)
- Depression
- Emotional blunting
- Reduced drive
- Social withdrawal
- Recurrent psychotic episodes.

Other features include:
- formal thought disorder
- behavioural slowing.

Movement disorder in schizophrenia includes
- stereotypy
- mannerism
- ambitendence
- *mitgehen*
- automatic obedience
- waxy flexibility
- *Schnauzkrampf*
- negativism

- perseveration
- echopraxia
- choreiform movements.

Bleuler's view of schizophrenia
- Fundamental symptoms:
  - As: Associative disturbance.
          Affective changes.
          Ambivalence (existence of 2 opposing drives).
          Autism.
- Bleuler's accessory symptoms
  (mechanisms patients may develop to cope with fundamental symptoms):
  - Hallucinations
  - Delusions
  - Catatonia/Abnormal behaviour.
- Non-schizophrenic symptoms
  - Emotional disturbances not uniquely associated with schizophrenia.
    - Anxiety
    - Tension
    - Agitation
    - Guilt
    - Depression
    - Disorientation
    - Somatisation.

- Loosening of associations seen in schizophrenia include neologisms, word salad and paraphrasias, *not* punning, metonyms or parapraxes.

(Kurt) Schneider's first-rank symptoms are:
- auditory hallucinations
- repeating thoughts aloud
- in the third person
- running commentary
- (all) delusions of passivity
- thought insertion/withdrawal/broadcasting
- made feelings/impulses/actions
- somatic passivity
- delusional perception.

They all result from the loss of ego boundaries.
They are highly suggestive of schizophrenia, but not pathognomonic.

They *don't* include formal thought disorder or incongruity of affect.
- Lead to high reliability in the diagnosis of schizophrenia.
- Give a narrow definition of schizophrenia.

Second-rank symptoms:
- perplexity
- emotional blunting
- other hallucinations
- other delusions.

Neurological abnormalities
- cerebral atrophy
- abnormalities in proprioception
  - astereognosis
  - graphaesthesia
  - difficulties with balance
  - proprioception
- medial temporal lobe structural changes
- smooth pursuit eye movements are abnormal in a proportion of patients
- abnormal event-related evoked potentials
- soft signs in up to 60%, with no specific abnormalities.

Neurochemical abnormalities
Those that have been suggested include:
- Lack of:
  - glutamate
  - aspartate
- Excess of:
  - serotonin/5HT
  - dopamine
  - dimethyltryptamine.

Good prognostic indicators
- no previous psychiatric history
- being married
- prominent affective symptoms
- older age of onset
- acute onset
- short duration of episode
- normal neuropsychological profile
- female gender
- normal premorbid personality
- living in a developing country

- high socioeconomic status
- predominantly positive symptoms
- good compliance
- good response to treatment
- female gender (unless treated with clozapine)
- clear precipitating factor(s)
- presence of affective symptoms
- positive family psychiatric history of affective symptoms
- fewer relapses are experienced by those living in hostels compared with those living with their families.

Epidemiology
- Incidence is fairly stable across a wide range of cultures, climates and ethnic groups, if narrow criteria (eg (Kurt) Schneider's) are used, but if wider criteria are used, incidence varies significantly.
  - equal sex incidence
  - it is associated with winter/early spring births, especially in those without a family psychiatric history
  - there is a negative association with rheumatoid arthritis
  - incidence is higher in the unmarried
  - average ages of onset: 28 years in men, 32 years in women
  - incidence is 15–20/100, 000 per year
  - lifetime risk is 1%
  - age of onset is 15–45 years
  - patients are more often single and have low fertility.

Cultural variations in presentation
- Catatonic schizophrenia is vanishingly rare in the West, but seen in 10% of developing countries.
- Hebephrenic schizophrenia – 4% in developed countries; 13% in underdeveloped.
- Acute schizophrenia is more common in developing countries.

Notes
- The course is more favourable in less developed countries (perhaps because families are more tolerant there and levels of expressed emotion decrease).
- There is an increase in life events in the 3 weeks before first episodes and relapses.
- An understimulating hospital environment is associated with the clinical poverty syndrome.
- An overstimulating environment is associated with relapse.
- Maintenance neuroleptic drugs reduce the effects of both life

events and high expressed emotion in precipitating relapses.
- There is an association between expressed emotion in a relative and arousal in the patient.
- Almost half the homeless have schizophrenia.
- Memory defects involve mainly semantic memory.
- Schizophrenia is associated with:
  - TB
  - rheumatoid arthritis (negatively)
  - suicide
  - obstetric complications at birth
  - substance misuse.

Diagnostic criteria
- Feighner/St Louis.
- DSM-IV – restrictive, continuously unwell for at least six months, therefore defining patients with poor prognosis.
- CATEGO – computer program, (Kurt) Schneiderian approach; takes no account of duration/affective symptoms and therefore doesn't predict outcome well.
- (Kurt) Schneider's symptoms – give consistent inter-rater performance, but don't predict outcome.
- RDC – 2-week duration of symptoms with presence of thought disorder and specific types of hallucinations and delusions.

50% of schizophrenics have abnormal attention span.

Liddle's syndromes (a **dimensional** approach):
- Lack of:
  - glutamate
- Psychomotor poverty syndrome:
  - poverty of speech
  - flatness of affect
  - decreased spontaneous movement.
- Disorganisation syndrome:
  - disorders of the form of thought
  - inappropriate affect
  - poverty of content of speech
  - incoherent speech.
- Reality distortion syndrome:
  - delusions
  - hallucinations.
- These correlate with patterns of perfusion on PET scanning.

Schizophrenia, aetiology of – Genetics – 70% of heritability is genetic.

- Family studies

Relationship (to index case)	Lifetime risk (%)
Parent	6
Sibling	10
Sibling (parent also has it)	17
Child	13
Child (when *both* parents have it)	46
Grandchild	4
Uncle, aunt, niece, nephew	3

- Twin studies
  - Concordance: monozygous = 45%, dizygous = 10%.
  - Phenotypically normal monozygous co-twins' children have the same risk as those of the phenotypically abnormal co-twins' children, so they have the gene(s) but don't express them.
- Adoption studies
  - Children of schizophrenic mothers adopted soon after birth by normal families have the same risk of developing schizophrenia as if they had stayed put.
- Possible modes of inheritance:
  - Single major locus – none discovered, only very few at most.
  - Polygenic – there is a threshold for schizophrenia.
  - Multifactorial – heterogeneous mix of genetic and environmental subtypes, with the range stretching from wholly genetic to wholly environmental.
- Linkage studies
  - A man was identified who had physical abnormalities *and* schizophrenia, both shared with a maternal uncle.
  - Chromosome 5 had a translocation – was this the locus?
  - Subsequent investigation of schizophrenic families in England and Iceland revealed a link with chromosome 5, but this has not been reproduced and the method was questionable.
- Difficulties:
  - Schizophrenia is probably heterogeneous.
  - Linkage studies are a good technique for simple Mendelian inheritance patterns (which schizophrenia hasn't got).

Prenatal factors
- Excess of late winter/early spring births – prenatal infection (eg influenza) is known to increase risk.
- Minor physical abnormalities are more common in schizophrenics:

S

- Low-set ears.
- Eyes wide apart (hypertelorism).
- single transverse palmar crease < br > (2nd trimester origin).
- Finger/palm/sole prints (ie dermatoglyphs) are significantly more abnormal in schizophrenics (even in abnormal monozygous twins compared with the normal twin).
- That prenatal infection plays a part is suggested by:
  - 2nd trimester fetuses caught in a flu epidemic are more likely to get schizophrenia later.
  - Late-winter birth babies are more likely to have had exposure to 2nd trimester infections.
  - Eearlier onset in males may be due to their greater susceptibility to neurodevelopmental problems.
  - Suggestions that less male schizophrenia is genetically determined (concordance rates are lower in males).
- Obstetric difficulties increase your risk of schizophrenia, especially if you have no family psychiatric history.

Personality
- Schizotypal personality disorder is related to schizophrenia and may be a milder phenotype.

Social factors
- There are significantly more life events in the three weeks before relapse, or first episode.
- High expressed emotion is significantly more common in families who have a member with schizophrenia (Vaughn & Leff) – with over-involvement and critical comments.
- Second-generation West Indians have a greater risk.

Groups with high rates of schizophrenia:
- southern Irish
- north-west Croatians
- Roman Catholic Canadians.

Group with low rates:
- Hutterites.

Neurotransmitters
Dopamine
- The mesolimbic-mesocortical system is in the ventral tegmental area.
- The mesolimbic system projects to the limbic system.
- Mesocortical system projects to the:

- Cingulate cortex
- Entorhinal cortex
- Medial prefrontal cortex

(Mesolimbic and mesocortical mediate reward effects of stimulants).

Dopamine hypothesis – central dopamine hyperactivity in the mesolimbic-mesocortical system causes schizophrenia.
- Evidence includes:
    - All effective antipsychotics occupy D2 receptors (70–80% of striatal D2 occupancy at therapeutic doses).
    - Amphetamine is a dopamine agonist and can cause something like acute schizophrenia.
    - Dopamine agonists exacerbate psychosis.
    - There are two isomers of flupenthixol and only the one with dopamine antagonist action works.
    - There are more D2 receptors in basal ganglia and limbic regions of the brains of schizophrenics than in normal people (at postmortem) and there are two to three times more D2 receptors in drug-na(239)ve schizophrenics than in normal people (measured by PET).
    - Dopamine agonists cause something like psychosis in animals, reversed by antagonists.

- Evidence countering the hypothesis includes:
    - Concentration of the dopamine metabolite HVA is no greater in the CSF of schizophrenics than in the CSF of anyone else.
    - D2 blockade is acute, whereas the therapeutic effects are chronic.
    - 15–30% of schizophrenics don't respond to dopamine antagonists.
    - Antipsychotic drugs have a better effect on positive than on negative symptoms.
    - Clozapine blocks D2 receptors weakly, but is an effective antipsychotic.
    - Some studies haven't confirmed Wong's finding of high D2 receptors in the striatum of living schizophrenic individuals.

- Rationalisation of the above:
    - Schizophrenia is heterogeneous and more complex than suggested above.
    - There may be reduced dopamine in prefrontal cortex and compensatory overactivity in the subcortical/limbic areas.
    - There are problems with methodology in every study.

- During treatment with haloperidol, the ratio of HVA (a dopamine metabolite) to 5HT and noradrenaline metabolites increased significantly and the ratio correlated with symptom reduction. This suggests that interactions between these neurotransmitters are involved in psychosis.

5HT
- May be associated with schizophrenia because LSD (acting at 5HT receptors) is hallucinogenic.
- Risperidone is a potent 5HT2 receptor antagonist (also blocks D2 receptors).

Glutamate
- Stimulates NMDA receptors.
- Phencyclidine blocks NMDA receptors.
- Postulated to be lacking/underactive in schizophrenia.
- Is excitatory.

Aspartate
- Postulated to be lacking/underactive in schizophrenia.
- Is excitatory.

Structural cerebral abnormalities
- Suggest a neurodevelopmental rather than degenerative process.
- Non-progressive ventricular enlargement (small differences overlapping with normal and more marked in males – not caused by treatment, present from the start) and cortical sulcal enlargement.
- Thickening or thinning of the corpus callosum.
- Limbic structural abnormalities.
- Suggest early acquired hypoplasia.
- Suggest change in normal pattern of programmed cell death resulting in defective migration of neurones.
- Diffuse reduction in cortical grey matter seen with MRI.
- Other structural changes seen:
  - reduced frontal lobes (whole or part)
  - reduced temporal lobe (especially dominant)
  - reduced hippocampus/amygdala (especially dominant)
  - reduced parahippocampal gyrus
  - reduced globus pallidus.
- changes *NOT* seen:
  - small caudate
  - small putamen
  - small nucleus accumbens.

- Ventricular enlargement correlates with:
  - early age of onset
  - poor prognosis
  - poor cognitive performance
  - male gender.
- **Murray** suggests that prenatal neural dysplasia causes:
  - premorbid cognitive defects
  - abnormal personality
  - negative symptoms
  - abnormal CT scans,
  - then maturational changes occur and make things worse so that delusions and hallucinations occur.

Neuropathology
- Postmortem studies suggest that schizophrenics have:
  - lower brain weight
  - reduced brain length
  - reduced size of parahippocampal gyrus.
- Histological studies suggest:
  - abnormal pyramid cells in hippocampus
  - reduced total hippocampal cells
  - reduced size of hippocampal cells
  - reduced total entorhinal cortical cells
  - disturbed cytoarchitecture in entorhinal cortex.

Functional abnormalities
- Hypofrontality:
  - associated with presence of negative symptoms and autism
  - reduced increase in cerebral blood flow during Wisconsin Card Sorting Test (impaired performance noted).

Schizophrenia, catatonic – Features:
- Predominantly motor abnormalities.

Schizophrenia, hebephrenic – Features:
- Thought disorder.
- Prominent disturbance of affect.

Schizophrenia, International Pilot Study of –
Conducted by the WHO in 1973.
Found 1-year incidence to be 0.7–1.4/10, 000 aged 15–54 years in *all* countries.
Diagnosed twice as often in USA and USSR as those in 7 other countries (including UK).

This led to the realisation of the need for **operational definitions**.

Schizophrenia, paranoid – Features:
- Delusions and hallucinations with relatively well-preserved personality.

Schizophrenia, residual – Features:
- apathy
- emotional blunting
- the eccentricity of a defect state.

Schizophrenia, simple – Characteristically:
- lacks positive psychotic symptoms
- there is a gradual deterioration with increasing eccentricity
- has insidious onset
- leads to social isolation.

Schizophrenia spectrum disorders – Include:
- schizophrenia
- schizotypal personality disorder
- schizoid personality disorder
- schizoaffective disorder
- schizophreniform disorder
- paranoid personality disorder
  - may also include:
    - delusional disorder
    - brief reactive psychosis
    - psychogenic psychosis.

Schizotypal personality disorder – A person with this disorder shows:
- social anxiety
- inability to make close friendships
- eccentric behaviour
- oddities of speech (eg vague and excessively abstract speech)
- inappropriate affect
- suspiciousness
- ideas of reference (*NOT* delusions)
- other ideas (eg telepathy/clairvoyance) that are odd for his culture
- unusual perceptual experiences (eg sensing the dead when not bereaved).

This is the type of personality disorder most closely linked to schizophrenia.

Schneider, Carl – Described:
- substitution
- derailment
- drivelling
- fusion
- omission.

- As a prominent Nazi, was 'Professor of Racial Hygiene' at Heidelberg University.

Schneider, Kurt – Described first- and second-rank symptoms of schizophrenia.

Schneiderian first-rank symptoms – (Kurt) Schneiderian first-rank symptoms are:
- auditory hallucinations
- repeating thoughts aloud
- in the third person
- running commentary
- delusions of passivity
- thought insertion/withdrawal/broadcasting
- made feelings/impulses/actions
- somatic passivity
- delusional perception.

- They all result from the loss of ego boundaries.
- They are highly suggestive of schizophrenia but not pathognomonic.
- Occur in 10–20% of manic patients.

Sclerosis, multiple –
- Often presents with transient ocular symptoms (diplopia, optic neuritis).
- Usually progresses over 20–30 years.
- Can produce *any* upper motor neurone sign, including spastic paraplegia.
- Is the most common demyelinating disease.
- Causes increase of CSF (but not plasma) gamma globulin (eg IgG) and can therefore cause oligoclonal bands in the CSF, but not in the plasma.

Scruples – Type of obsessive doubt about whether sins have been adequately confessed.

SDAT – Senile dementia of Alzheimer's type; the same as Alzheimer's disease.

Seasonal affective disorder – Characteristic features include:
- hypersomnia
- increased appetite with carbohydrate craving
- weight gain
- fatigue
- main occurrence in women between 20 and 40 years.
    - There is usually complete summer remission.
    - Light is given at 2500 lux in morning and late evenin
    - Bright lights are not as good as summer light.
    - Bright lights reduce total sleep time and increase δ-wave sleep.
    - Response is extremely rapid with a 50% reduction in symptoms in 4 days.
    - Relapse is also rapid – continue the treatment.
    - There is a bipolar form, with summer hypomania or mania.
    - There is also a subsyndromal form, with winter vegetative symptoms, but falling short of diagnosis of major depression.
    - Rosenthal's original **criterion of seasonality** was that major depression should be present in at least two consecutive previous years during autumn or winter and remit in the following spring or summer.

Security, in relation to relationships – Secure people approach relationships with confidence and freely enjoy them. They have wide-ranging skills and are confident, flexible, versatile and adaptive. They have good self-esteem.
Insecure people are uncertain of their ability to make or keep relationships. They are cautious, restricted, rigid and have fewer skills, avoid some areas and people and seek reassurance.

Sedative – Drug acting as anxiolytic and hypnotic, with muscle relaxant and anticonvulsant properties. Examples include benzodiazepines, zopiclone, zolpidem, etc. but *not* buspirone.

Withdrawal/abstinence produces:

Psychological problems:
- insomnia
- nightmares
- dysphoria
- restlessness
- agitation

- impaired memory
- impaired concentration.

Physiological problems:
- profuse sweating
- lethargy
- shakiness.

Seizure, petit mal –
- A dissociative state is *not* seen.
- Ethosuximide and sodium valproate are the treatments of choice.
- Triphasic waves are seen.

Selective abstraction – Focusing on a detail and ignoring more important features of the situation.

Selective serotonin reuptake inhibitors – *aka* SSRIs
Were introduced in the 1980s.

Self-concept – A set of attitudes one holds about oneself, not necessarily corresponding with reality (Rogers).
or
Is one's own idea of who and what one really is, based on what other people's impressions, comments and reactions to us are.
In children it is very physically oriented, but in adults is very much defined in terms of role.

Self-esteem – The aspect of the self concerned with how we value ourselves. From the age of 8 years, children can discriminate between several aspects of this and attach different levels of importance to them:
- scholastic competence
- athletic competence
- social acceptance
- physical appearance
- behavioural conduct.

Their general level of self-esteem relates to a person's perceived competence *in areas important to them.* So if someone believes they're hopeless at football but doesn't think that football skills are important, then they'll still have good self-esteem. Physical attractiveness is generally important to most children.

Self-image – A set of beliefs held about oneself, based on achievements and social interactions, which influences personal meaning and behaviour.

Self-perception theory – One applies the same practice of observation and inference about attitudes to oneself as one does to others. For example, if you see someone jogging regularly and hear that they go to the gym every day, you might infer that they like to keep fit. If you yourself go jogging and attend the gym every day, then you might infer that you yourself like to keep fit.
You define your self-image as a result of inferences based on observed behaviour.

Semantics – Relates to the meanings of individual words. It is regulated by poorly localised areas in the left temporal lobe.

Sensitisation – The process by which repeated administration of the same amount of a drug leads to a greater response

Sensory inattention – Is caused by parietal lobe lesions.

Serotonin – *aka* 5-hydroxytryptamine (5HT)
Is an **inhibitory** neurotransmitter acting particularly on the reticular formation.
Produced at the raphe nuclei in response to melatonin produced by the pineal gland:

tryptophan
↓
5-hydroxytryptophan
↓
serotonin (5HT)

Degraded:

serotonin (5HT)
↓ (MAO-A)
5-HIAA

- Found mostly in the gastrointestinal system and platelets (only 5% is in the brain).
- Highest brain concentrations are in the hypothalamus and limbic systems.
- Is associated with the raphe nuclei.
- Concentration is increased by MAOIs.
- Is produced from tryptophan.
- Is metabolised to 5HIAA.
- Has effects on:
  - appetite
  - sleep

- sexual behaviour
- (ie vegetative functions).
- Reuptake is blocked potently by:
  - secondary amines (not so much tertiary amines)
  - clomipramine (selective)
  - fluoxetine.

Serotonin syndrome – *aka* 5HT syndrome
Features:
- hyperpyrexia
- rigidity
- myoclonus
- coma
- death.

Set, perceptual – Is the motivational state of mind in which certain aspects of stimuli are perceived according to expectation.
- is a function of signal detection theory
- is determined by:
- expectation
- past experience
- cultural factors
- motivation
- emotion.

Sexual development – Determinants of gender:
Chromosomes.
Testis-determining factor is the *SRY* gene on the Y-chromosome.
Over-ripe ovum at fertilisation has fewer primordial germ cells, so females will be somewhat masculinised.
Endocrine – excess masculine/feminine hormone (eg in congenital adrenal hyperplasia (CAH), enzyme deficiency) or insensitivity to the hormone (eg androgen insensitivity syndrome) may cause genotype/phenotype differences.

Puberty – a series of physical and physiological changes that convert a child into an adult capable of reproduction.
- Physical changes
  - growth spurt
  - change in body proportion
  - development of sexual organs
  - development of secondary sexual characteristics
  - (Tanner developed standard for recording physical changes).
- In girls – 95% between 9 and 13 years; 80% = breasts, 20% =

pubic hair. Menarche = 13.5 years.
- In boys – 95% between 9.5 and 13.5 years = testicular/scrotal enlargement, then penis and pubic hair. Ejaculation at 13 years.

Physiological changes
Adrenarche (suprarenal androgen release) is at 6–8 years old.

Sexual drive – Is the desire to achieve sexual pleasure through genital stimulation. It exists from birth to 7–8 years and resurfaces in adolescence.

Sexual dysfunction – (Masters & Johnson)
- They described a 2-week residential treatment programme with two therapists per couple.
- Treatments were:
  - graded stimulation for impotence
  - super stimulation for ejaculatory failure
  - graded stimulation for vaginismus
  - the squeeze and the stop–start techniques for premature ejaculation.

Sexual response, phases of – (Masters & Johnson)
- 4 phases:
  - excitement
  - plateau
  - orgasm
  - resolution.

Shadowing experiment, the – You will hear more of something unfamiliar played into one ear if something familiar is played into the other ear, than if something unfamiliar is played into the other ear. The fact that one ear hears something familiar means that you have more processing capacity left over to hear what is being played into the other ear.

Shaping – Reinforcement of behaviours that are successively closer to desired behaviour, to reinforce desired behaviour. Used in patients with learning difficulty who have undesirable behaviour. Basically, the goal-posts are moved so that more and more desirable behaviour has to occur to obtain the same positive reinforcement.

Sheldon – Suggested endomorphic, ectomorphic and mesomorphic body types as indicating relaxed/sociable, self-conscious/solitary and robust/outgoing respectively.

Shock, spinal – Follows sudden complete section of the spinal cord.

- All spinal reflexes are reduced and return in the following order:
  - stretch
  - flexor
  - postural
  - stepping
- Resting membrane potential of motor neurones is increased by 2–6 mV.

'Shocks' – People demonstrate less arousal and distress when awaiting predictable than unpredictable 'shocks'.

Siblings – Were investigated by Dunn.
- Sibling relationships centre on love and envy.
- Children younger than 2 years can learn to placate, please, tease and comfort a younger sibling.
- Sibling de-identification is the idea that siblings will try to be as different as possible from each other.
- Are not as important as adults in social development for children.

Sick role – Theories were developed by Parson.
He said that the illness needed to be legitimised by someone in order for the individual to be exempted from normal social role responsibilities.
Is prominent in children.

Sign, Lhermitte's – A sensation like an electric shock radiating down the trunk and limbs on neck flexion.
- indicates a cervical cord lesion
- often associated with an acute exacerbation of multiple sclerosis.

Signal detection theory – States that perception is not solely dependent on stimulus intensity, but is also a function of biological factors such as:
- motivation
- previous experiences
- expectations.

These factors are the defining elements of the perceptual set.

Simon, Herbert – Was awarded a Nobel prize for work on psychology based on computer experiments.

Simple phobias – Are more common in women (lifetime prevalence = 4–5% in men and 9–26% in women).
They are usually a continuation of a childhood phobia, but may arise in adulthood after a stressful event.

They are best treated by exposure techniques (*not* relaxation training). They do *not* lead to depersonalisation and are not related to mitral valve prolapse.

Simultanagnosia – Is the inability to recognise the overall meaning of a picture despite being able to understand individual details.

SLE – Systemic lupus erythematosus.

Sleep – Is an altered state of consciousness. It is *not* a state of unconsciousness.
- There are sleep cycles – 90 min each.
- All 'deep sleep' (ie stages 3–4) is done in first 3.5 hours.
- Later cycles only get to stages 1 and 2.

Stages 1–4 are non-REM.
- Reduced neuronal activity.

Stage 0
- Quiet wakefulness with shut eyes.
- Alpha activity on EEG.

Stage 1
- Falling asleep.
- Irregular EEG.
- Low amplitude, slow waves at 2–7 Hz (theta).
- Slowed heart.
- Slowed breathing.
- Easily woken.

Stage 2
- Light sleep.
- Higher amplitude at 2–7 Hz.
- Sleep spindles/spindle patterns at 13–15 Hz lasting 20 seconds.
- K-complexes – sudden brief but dramatic deviations in the EEG, which often relate to auditory stimuli.
- Easily woken.

Stage 3
- Difficult to rouse.
- Slow heart and breathing, low blood pressure.
- Long, slow δ waves.

Stage 4
- Very difficult to rouse.
- Low blood pressure and pulse, slow breathing.

- Largely long, slow, rhythmic δ waves (by definition, $> 50\%$ δ waves).

Stages 3–4 are slow-wave sleep.
REM sleep
- When dreams occur.
- Inhibition of brainstem motor neurones by locus caeruleus paralyses us during REM sleep.
- Increased sympathetic activity – pulse, blood pressure, ventilatory rate, cerebral blood flow increase.
- Occasional myoclonic jerks, but generally minimal muscle tone.
- Erection/increased vaginal blood flow.
- There are rapid eye movements.
- There is a high level of brain activity.
- Sawtooth waves.
- Increased protein synthesis in animal experiments (rats).

- Sleep-walking occurs during non-REM sleep.
- Delta sleep – increased by bright light therapy in seasonal affective disorder.

Sleep, causes of – Two theories:
- Monoaminergic/biochemical/two-stage/Jouvet's model.
  - Non-REM sleep is associated with 5HT activity – raphe complex.
  - REM sleep is associated with noradrenaline activity locus caeruleus.
- Cellular model.
  - Three neuronal groups are important:
    - pontine gigantocellular tegmental fields (the nucleus reticularis pontis caudalis) – acetylcholine.
    - dorsal raphe nuclei – 5HT/serotonin.
    - locus caeruleus – noradrenaline.

Sleep deprivation – Causes hypothermia.
- Causes problems with:
  - speech
  - memory
  - eye/motor control
- Leads to increased stage 4 and REM sleep subsequently.

Sleep-walking – Is an automatism occurring during non-REM sleep, usually early in the night.
- It is most common between the ages of 5 and 12 years.
- 15% of children sleep-walk at some stage.
- May be familial.

- The most common manifestation is of the child sitting up and making repetitive movements.
- Some do walk around and appear mechanical, but avoid objects.
- They don't respond to questions and are difficult to wake.
- The episode usually lasts seconds or minutes.
- Anything increasing the depth of sleep makes the problems worse – alcohol, previous sleep deprivation, etc.
- Is associated with night terrors.

Smith – Described a number of responses in the baby's repertoire of behaviour:
- The ability to learn – especially to distinguish between parents and between other people.
- Behaviours that invite social responses.
  - Behaviours on the part of the infant which are entirely without social meaning (eg crying when hungry) become invested with social meaning as a result of adults' responses to them, from which the infant infers the social meaning of its original behaviour.
- Enjoyment of contingent responding in others.
  - The infant will behave in such a way as to start or encourage a series of interactions with an adult, whether it's by 'cooing' at an early age or by starting a game of peek-a-boo.
- Social referencing.
  - One-year-olds can judge a parent's emotional reaction to an ambiguous situation and their own reaction to it. When introduced to unfamiliar toys, the baby will look to the mother (or another adult in her absence) to determine how to respond. If the adult is positive, so the child will be.
- Social perspective taking – the ability to take the perspective of others, occurring on several levels:
  - Perceptual role taking – the ability to see how a perceptual array appears to someone with a different perspective (ie purely *physical*).
  - Cognitive role taking – the ability to take into account the thoughts of another person when they are different from one's own.
  - Affective role taking – the ability to take into account the feelings of someone else.

Social phobia – Inappropriate anxiety is experienced in situations in which the person is observed and could be criticised. These situations are avoided. There is anticipatory anxiety. Blushing and trembling are especially frequent. Alcohol and anxiolytic abuse are more common than in other phobias. The phobia can be generalised or specific (to certain situations).

Onset is between 17 and 30 years. First episode occurs in some public place, usually without any reason. Subsequent anxiety is felt in similar situations. Severity and avoidance increase. Without treatment, the condition lasts for many years.

There is a genetic component. 'Fear of negative evaluation' is the principal cognitive factor. It's not a phobia about specific people: they're worried about everyone.

Epidemiology
- equal sex incidence
- 1-year prevalence = 7% male, 9% female

There is an association with depression.
Treatment
- CBT is the treatment of choice

Psychological
- Social skills training, relaxation training and exposure *with CBT*. Exposure with CBT leads to lower relapse rates than exposure alone.
- Dynamic psychotherapy may help in those with relationship problems.

Drug
- Benzodiazepines – as temporary measure until other treatment has been effective.
- β-blockers – control tremor and palpitations.
- MAOIs – phenelzine and moclobemide (a RIMA) each have some effects.
- SSRIs – fluoxetine has some effects.

There are two special types:

Phobia of excretion
- Patients are anxious about and unable to pass urine in public lavatories.
  or
- They have frequent urges to pass urine and an associated dread of incontinence
  (a few have similar feelings about defecation).

Phobia of vomiting

- Some patients fear they will vomit in a public place and feel anxious and nauseated in these surroundings.
  or
- They fear that others will vomit in these places (less common).

Social power – Described by French and Raven.
There are five types:
- Authority – power derived from role.
- Reward – power derived from ability to allocate resources.
- Coercive – power to punish.
- Referent – charismatic and liked by others.
- Expert – power derived from skill, knowledge and experience.

Social therapy – Consists of:
- authoritarian structure
- openness
- shared examination of problems.

Socialisation – Is the process by which people acquire the rules of behaviour, systems of beliefs and attitudes of a given society or social group, so that they can function within it.
It is bidirectional.

Sopor – Is a state of marked drowsiness (ie the patient is mostly unconscious) in which the patient can only make some purposeful reaction (ie respond) to strong stimuli.

Space, personal – Hall developed a theory of 4 zones of personal space.

Span, digit – Tests immediate memory.

Speech – Pathway is:
Cognition → Wernicke's area → Broca's area → Motor speech areas → Speech

see Appendix 8.

Speech, scanning – Is a cerebellar feature and leads to difficulty in saying 'baby hippopotamus' and 'British constitution'.

Speech, schizophrenic – Includes:
- abnormal syntactic structure
- reduced quantity of speech
- use of a restricted range of words
- a tendency to repetition of syllables, words, words and phrases
- low type : token ratio (ie number of different word types : number

of words).

Spindles, sleep – Patterns on the EEG when asleep at 13–20 Hz and lasting 20 s, seen in stage 2 of sleep.

Spinocerebellar damage, lateral – Causes loss of:
- proprioception
- pressure
- touch.

Spinothalamic damage, anterior – Causes loss of:
- light touch
- pressure.

Spinothalamic damage, lateral – Causes loss of:
- pain
- temperature.

Splitting – A defence mechanism by which people deal with an emotional conflict by viewing some people as all good and others as all bad: they fail to integrate themselves or other people into complex but coherent images.

SSP – Strange Situation Procedure.

SSRI – Selective serotonin reuptake inhibitor.

Stability – Is a measure of test–retest reliability. It can be decreased by the practice effect or by inter-observer/tester variation.

Standardisation – If a test is well standardised, then the average performance of a group of people will be well known.

State, buffoonery – Seen in acute and catatonic schizophrenia.

STD – Sexually transmitted disease.

Stereognosis – The ability to recognise the 3-dimensional shape of an object by touch alone. This is a function of the association areas of the parietal lobe of the brain.

Stereotypes – Overgeneralised inferences about groups of people in which they are all assumed to have particular traits or characteristics.
or
Selective perceptions of groups of people, which exaggerate differences between them and other groups, thereby devaluing them

S

and allowing others to dismiss their concerns and requests more easily.

Occur when all members of a group are seen to have the same characteristics.
Schemata are stereotypes.

Stereotypy – Is the constant repetition of a complex action, which is carried out in the same way each time and does not appear to be goal directed.
An example is verbigeration.
It is seen in catatonia and infantile autism; sometimes it is an isolated symptom in mental retardation. It is more common in patients who live in institutions where they are bored and understimulated. It can prevent a patient from carrying on normal life, and sometimes causes physical injury to the patient.
Drugs, such as phenothiazines, and behaviour therapy are sometimes used in treating the condition.

Sternbach – Synthesised chlordiazepoxide.

Stigma – An attribute of an individual that marks them out as being unacceptable, inferior or dangerous and tarnishes their identity.
or
A sign of disgrace or discredit that sets a person apart from others.

It develops during Erikson's stage of industry vs inferiority or Freud's stage of latency.
The stigma of mental illness was first highlighted by Goffman in 1963.

Stigma, enacted – Is the experience of an individual who bears a stigma and is discriminated against as a result.

Stigma, felt – Is the fear of enacted stigma on the part of someone who bears a stigma.

Stock word – Real word used with special significance in a patient with psychosis (especially schizophrenia), in speech as cryptolalia and in writing as cryptographia.

Strange situation experiment – Is designed to provoke a response in the baby that will indicate the 1-year-old's attachment to the mother and sense of security or comfort felt in her presence. Involved 8 stages of three minutes each when mother and stranger came in and out of the room. It identified three types of attachment behaviour:
• Type A – insecure (anxious/avoidant) – 15%

the baby is not apparently distressed during mother's absence. On her return they either ignore her or greet her casually and will sometimes turn away. The stranger is treated much as the mother is.

This is caused by coldness/rejection by the mother or unresponsiveness to the baby's needs and may be a precursor of:
- Poor social functioning in later life (including Aggression).
- Type B – secure – 70%
  They explore actively in their mother's presence and are distressed when she leaves, with reduced play. They seek closeness on her return but show anger. They resist the stranger's approaches. Their mothers are sensitive and responsive to the child's needs.
- Type C – insecure (anxious-resistant *or* ambivalent) – 15%
  They are anxious before separation and don't use the mother as a secure base for exploration. They are distressed while she's away. They both seek contact with and avoid the mother on her return, by asking to be picked up and then asking to be put down.

It's caused by:
- Inconsistent mothering, with unpredictable access.

This is a precursor of:
- Childhood emotional disorders (including School refusal).
- Later disorders (eg agoraphobia).
- Depression and personality disorder in women.

Main & Solomon introduced a fourth category:

- Type D – disorganised/disoriented – 20%
  These babies don't have a strategy and show varying and incoherent responses, with incomplete movements and actions and wariness of the stranger and the mother at various times. This is caused by neglect and ill-treatment.

- Securely attached children (at 2 years) have good peer relationships, better emotional regulation and more self-confidence than insecurely attached children.
- Insecurely attached children are poorly empathetic, non-compliant and less popular.
- Security of attachment is consistent unless there is a marked change in the child's circumstances (eg parental separation, moving house, starting nursery etc, when it can change from secure to insecure or *vice versa*).
- Security of attachment is culturally dependent. Type B is always

most common, with more Type C in the East and more Type A in the West.

Structural model of the mind – Was described by Freud in *The Ego and the Id*, replacing the topographical model.
There are three parts:
- Id
  - *Mostly* unconscious – although some questions have it as *entirely* unconscious.
  - Contains primordial energy from instinctual drives.
  - Seeks to fulfil these drives and thereby maximise pleasure without concern for the consequences.
  - Most destructive element.
  - Primary source of libidinal energy.
  - Primary process thinking.
- Ego
  - Controls voluntary movement.
  - Aims for self-preservation.
  - Tests reality.
  - Operates *mainly* consciously.
  - Secondary process (ie rational) thinking.
  - External perception.
  - Brings the defence mechanisms into action.
  - Relaxed during sleep and fatigue, and when intoxicated or psychotic.
  - The centre of object-relations, in both the inner and outer worlds.
  - Can reach 3 forms of compromise between the id and the super-ego:
    - dreams
    - neurotic symptoms
    - defence mechanisms.
  - There are two aspects to the ego:
    - punitive (primitive) aspects
    - the ego-ideal (more positive).
  - Anxiety acts as a warning to the ego.
- Super-ego
  - Acts like a conscience.
  - Threatens the ego with punishment (ie guilt) if it gives in to the id.
  - Secondary process thinking.
  - Is threatened by anxiety.

Stupor –
- Mutism.
- Immobility/akinesis.
- Unresponsiveness (to environment).
- Full consciousness – eyes are open and follow moving objects (if the eyes are closed, the patient resists attempts to open them) – some books say there's usually some clouding of consciousness.
- Normal reflexes and resting posture (which may be awkward).
- Occasional periods of excitement and overactivity.

Can be caused by:
- catatonia
- depression
- mania
- epilepsy
- dissociation (hysteria)
- schizophrenia
- tumour in the diencephalon.

Features more suggestive of catatonic than depressive stupor:

- urinary incontinence
- negativism
- stereotypic hand movements
- failure to respond to painful stimuli.

Stupor, functional – Characteristic features include:
- full consciousness
- ability to follow objects with eyes (if eyes are open)
- resistance to eye opening if eyes are closed
- normal reflexes
- maintenance of resting posture
- mutism (*not* aphasia)
- immobility
- unresponsiveness.

Subarachnoid haemorrhage – May result in:
- persistent headache
- epilepsy
- organic mental symptoms, including:
  - memory impairment
  - anxiety
  - depression (common)
  - personality change (for better or worse)
- paresis.

S

Subcortical dementia – Includes:
- Parkinson's disease.

Sublimation – Described by Anna Freud. It is 'the displacement of the instinctual aim in conformity with higher social values.' It is the most mature defence mechanism and is associated with creativity.

Substance, Nissl – Is contained in dendrites, but not axons, and is involved in protein synthesis.

Substitution – Described by Carl Schneider.
Replacing one thought with an unconnected thought.

Suicide –
- 1 : 10, 000/year
- Rates are highest in spring and early summer in both hemispheres.
- Seasonal variation is more marked in females.
- Rates are higher in social classes I and V.
- Rates are lowest in the married, and then in the never-married, widowed and divorced.
- Between 1980 and 1990, rates for men increased by 1/3, and by 78% in men aged 14–24 years.
- Rates in England and Wales are highest in men older than 75 years.
- Elderly females more commonly poison themselves deliberately than young females.
- Males most commonly use CO poisoning (CO poisoning and hanging account for 2/3 of male suicides).
- Females most commonly poison themselves (overdose > 50% of female suicides).
- Hanging is the most frequent method in prisons.
- Both poisoning and hanging increase with age.
- Drowning is not common in the young and is 'more common' in the elderly.
- Men use firearms more than women, who use plastic bags more than men.
- Young people jump from high places more than old people.
- Over 50% suffer from depression.
- Of the depressed, 50% have psychomotor retardation (which is not, therefore, protective).
- Risk is increased by:
  - insomnia
  - self-neglect
  - delusions
  - hopelessness

- previous history of suicide attempt
- increasing age (>45 years)
- being male
- unemployment
- urban setting
- low social class
- mental illness.
- 20% are alcoholics.
- 5% have schizophrenia, especially young males with chronic illness who have recently been discharged, are in remission and have good insight.
- The risk in schizophrenia is increased with high premorbid academic achievement.
- 30–40% have personality disorder (especially antisocial and borderline personality disorder).
- Chronic physical illness increases risk.
- Low cholesterol levels have been reported to increase risk.
- Depressed patients who also have OCD have a 6-fold reduction in risk as a result.
- Combat-related guilt increases risk in those with PTSD.
- Strong religious beliefs are protective.
- The number of 5HT2 receptors is increased in suicidal brains.
- Violent methods are more common in
  - males
  - mental illness
- 'Self-immolation' is more common in
  - schizophrenia
  - Asian-born females
  - combined homicide–suicide.

Hostility in suicide has three components:
- wish to kill
- wish to be killed
- wish to die.

Suicide in schizophrenia –
- Risk is increased by:
  - akathisia
  - fear of disorientation
  - unemployment
  - high educational achievement.

Sulpiride – Is excreted in significant quantities in breast milk.

Super-ego – Corresponds roughly to the conscience, shame and guilt. It is the agency by which the influence of parents and others is prolonged. Their judgements and prohibitions are internalised by introjection in early childhood before the child can question them.

Supra-chiasmic nucleus – The centre of control for circadian rhythm.
* Located in the hypothalamus.
* 10, 000 small neurones acting as neurosecretory organ to send neuromodulators to many areas.
* The afferents from retina to pineal pass here.
* The main circadian regulation is in-built and autonomous.
* There are projections to the raphe nuclei.

Sympathetic nervous system –
* The adrenal medulla is a specialised sympathetic ganglion where postganglionic cells secrete into the bloodstream.
* Preganglionic adrenal medullary cells are the secretomotor supply via muscarinic acetylcholine receptors.
* Preganglionic sympathetic fibres are short and myelinated.
* Postganglionic sympathetic fibres are long and unmyelinated.

Sympathomimetic amine – These stimulate adrenergic receptors directly and include:
* dopamine
* noradrenaline
* adrenaline
* isoprenaline.

Synaesthesia – The experiencing of a stimulus in one modality in a different modality.

An example would be haptic phenomena as a result of an auditory stimulus.

Synapse, interneuronal –
* All the postsynaptic membranes in human beings are chemosensitive.
* Presynaptic inhibition occurs via axon-axonic synapses.
* Transmission is unidirectional.

Syndrome, Couvade – Occurs when the partner of a pregnant woman reports that he is experiencing some of the symptoms of pregnancy, commonly nausea, morning sickness and toothache.
* It is self-limiting.
* There are associations with ambivalence about fatherhood and

identification with the fetus.
- It is rare (but *not* very rare).
- It was described by 19th century anthropologists.
- It is a hysterical disorder.

Syndrome, Cushing's –
- Psychotic depression is most common, but paranoid symptoms are also seen.
- Depression is even more common if pituitary causes underlie the disease,
- Psychiatric problems occur in more than 50% of cases,
- Acute organic reactions are rare.
- Cerebral atrophy can be seen on CT.

Syndrome, Diogenes – *aka* senile self-neglect
Prevalence is equal in males and females.

Syndrome, dysmnesic – *aka* Korsakoff's syndrome

Syndrome, Gilles de la Tourette – Recognised features include:
- echolalia/echopraxia (10–40%)
- coprolalia (in 1/3)
- multiple tics beginning before the age of 16 years (ie *in adolescence*)
- vocal tics
- stereotyped movements (jumping/dancing)
- overactivity
- learning difficulties
- emotional disturbances
- social problems
- obsessive-compulsive symptoms (also more common in families of patients)
- Attention-Deficit/Hyperactivity Disorder more frequently than usual
- non-specific EEG changes in 30%.
  - Prevalence is 0.5/1000
  - 3–4 times more common in females
  - 10 times more common in children than in adults
  - 40% have OCD.

S

Aetiology
- Unknown, but dopamine blockers improve things.

Syndrome, Kluver–Bucy –
- Was first described in monkeys.
- Is caused by bilateral temporal lobe damage (also seen in frontal lobe damage).
- Consists of:
  - visual agnosia
  - hyperphagia
  - hypersexuality
  - hypermetamorphosis (excessive touching of objects with the hands)
  - hyperorality.

Syntactic structure – Is disordered in a different way in schizophrenia compared with mania.

Syntax – Is concerned with sentence construction and grammar. It is controlled by the left anterior hemisphere.

Syphilis, meningovascular – Pathological features include:
- cerebral periarteritis and endarteritis
- rod cells.

Syphilis, tertiary – Causes frontotemporal cortical damage.

Syringomyelia –
- Occurs between the ages of 30 and 50 years.
- Affects:
  - spinothalamic neurones
  - anterior horn cells
  - lateral corticospinal tracts.
- Causes:
  - upper limb pain
  - loss of pain and temperature sense in the upper limbs with hyporeflexia
  - finger ulcers.

Szasz –
- Belonged to the **anti-psychiatry** school.
- Said that schizophrenia was an understandable response to stress and pressure from family and society.
- Was a professor of psychiatry.

Tabes dorsalis – A type of neurosyphilis causing low-grade inflammation of the dorsal roots (ie pyramidal pathway). Features:
  • sharp/momentary stabbing pains in distinct areas of the leg(s).

Talking past the point – *aka vorbeireden*
An effect on thought/speech of loosening of associations, seen as the patient seems always about to get near to the matter in hand but never quite reaches it.

Tangentiality – An oblique verbal response that 'only glances at the gist'.
Occurs equally in manics and schizophrenics.

Tangles, neurofibrillary –
  • Are intracellular structures.
  • Are seen in a few cells of the hippocampus and entorhinal cortex in older people.
  • Are a feature of dementia pugilistica.
  • Are a feature in Alzheimer's disease.
  • Are *not* seen in LBD.

Tanycytes – Line the area over the median eminence on the floor of the third ventricle.
(Ependymocytes line the rest of the ventricles and spinal cord.)

Tardive dyskinesia – Is a disorder involving the extrapyramidal system. It involves hyperkinetic involuntary movements of the face, mouth, tongue, and also trunk and extremities. The mechanism is thought to be hypersensitivity of the dopamine receptors in the nigrostriatal system, which connects the substantia nigra in the midbrain with the striatum in the basal ganglia.

Anticholinergics make it worse. The best strategy is to stop antipsychotics and wait for it to improve.

May occur in schizophrenics who have never received antipsychotic drugs.

Characteristic features include:

- late onset
- choreoathetoid movements of lips, tongue and mouth
- hands more commonly affected than the feet
- more common in women
- more common in the elderly
- more common in patients with diffuse brain pathology
- may be aggravated by stopping antipsychotics
- is not dose- or duration (of treatment)-related.

Risk factors for tardive dyskinesia when taking antipsychotics include:
- affective illness
- mental retardation
- old age.

TB – Tuberculosis.

TCA – Tricyclic antidepressant.

Temperament – Early appearing, biologically rooted basic personality dimensions.

There are 9 categories of temperament:
- Activity level
- Rhythmicity
- Approach/withdrawal to new situations
- Adaptability in new/altered situations
- Sensory threshold/responsiveness to stimuli
- Intensity of reaction
- Quality of mood
- Distractibility
- Attention span/persistence.

The above cluster around 3 patterns:
- Easy child pattern – regularity, positive response to new stimuli, high adaptability to change, mild/moderately intense positive moods.
- Difficult child – irregularity, negative withdrawal in new situations, poor adaptability to change, intense, frequent negative expressions of mood.
- Slow-to-warm-up child – mildly negative responses to new situations and slow adaptability after repeated contact.

- Temperament influences the parent–child relationship. Laid-back infants who are difficult to unsettle may elicit more positive responses than unsettled infants.
- Temperament is a theoretical construct and it is more useful to talk in terms of the above 9 categories.
- There are 3 levels:
  - patterns of surface behaviour
  - patterns of nervous system responses
  - patterns of inborn genetic make-up.
- Temperament centres on emotion, attention and activity and is therefore determined by:
- limbic structures
- association cortex
- motor cortical areas.
- There is a correlation between temperament at 3 years and personality traits at 18 years:

3 years	18 years
Under-controlled	impulsivity
	danger seeking
	aggression
	interpersonal alienation
Inhibited	low on: the above
	social potency
Confident	impulsivity
Reserved	low on: social potency
Well-adjusted	normal

Tension – An unpleasant increase in psychomotor activity.

Test, serial sevens – Tests concentration.

Test, Wisconsin Card Sorting – Is a frontal lobe test.

Tests, intelligence – Binet devised IQ tests for children which produced an IQ (ie mental age/chronological age (180) 100) – ie they are age graded.
- IQ tests demonstrate how a person performed at that time, not how they can perform in all circumstances.
- Adult IQ tests have a mean of 100 with SD of 15.
- IQ changes reactively (decreased by institutionalisation).

Uses of IQ scores:
- Legal – IQ <70 gets you more benefits and different treatment in the criminal justice system.

- To assess overall level of function.
- Comparison with other test scores to assess possible acquired impairments.
- To gauge change over time.

IQ tests
- WAIS-III (Wechsler Adult Intelligence Scale).
  - Single IQ score
  - Separate verbal and performance IQs
  - four index scores (from subtest scores)
  - Perceptual organisation
  - Processing speed
  - Verbal comprehension
  - Working memory
  - Patterns can be interpreted
  - Subtests include:
    - verbal
    - information
    - comprehension
    - arithmetic
    - similarities
    - digit span (= immediate memory)
    - vocabulary
    - performance
    - picture completion
    - block design
    - picture arrangement
    - object assembly
    - digit symbol.
- WASI (Wechsler Abbreviated Scale of Intelligence).
- WISC-III (Wechsler Intelligence Scale for Children).
- NART (National Adult Reading Test; measures premorbid IQ).

Tests, psychological – Types of test:
- ability/IQ
- personality (correlate with theories)
- current symptomatology
- closely defined concepts (eg suggestibility)
- projective tests – Rorschach ink-blot
- composite (including Personality).

Tests, psychometric – Are used to assess personality.

Tetanus infection – Is a differential for NMS. Features include:

- hyperthermia
- autonomic lability
- sialorrhoea
- rigidity
- opisthotonos
- trismus
- diaphoresis.

Between attacks, there is a normal mental state, with clear consciousness.

Thalamus – Lesions in the dorsomedial nucleus occur in Korsakoff's psychosis and are responsible for the memory disorder.
Atrophy occurs in Pick's disease.

Thematic apperception test – When this is administered twice to the same individual, the themes of the two different stories given in response to the same cards are *not* typically similar.

Theory of mind – Is based upon the observation that human interaction often depends upon an apparent awareness or appreciation of what the person one is interacting with is thinking. The capacity to be aware of this is known as the **Theory of Mind**. Humans collect evidence about others' emotions, beliefs and wishes and use these to construct a theory that enables them to predict and explain the behaviour of others. It is developed by the age of 4 years. It's the old story about showing 3-year-olds something unexpected, only to find that they think everyone else knows it too, the 'Sally-Ann-marble test'.

An important consequence of the theory of mind is that it allows people to realise that their beliefs about the world may not be true, that they recognise the capacity for **false beliefs**.

Autism involves a deficit in theory of mind and autistic children fail the 'Sally-Ann-marble test'.

Therapeutic reaction, negative – Describes the situation in which the patient's condition gets worse, followed by an awareness by the patient or by the therapist of improvement (when the patient would normally be expected to experience relief).
It may be evoked by strong feelings of guilt. The patient seeks to reduce these feelings by getting worse.
The tendency to negative therapeutic reactions is part of the character of the patient and is not related to the psychoanalytic process.

It has not been applied extensively outside clinical psychoanalysis.

Therapy, behaviour
- Functional analysis of behaviour is an absolute necessity.
- Quantitative rating of behaviour is routinely done.
- Associated cognitions are ignored.
- Schedules of reinforcement are intermittent.

Often uses both classical and operant techniques. For example, an alcoholic is given an emetic when he drinks vodka. He will come to associate reaching for the bottle of vodka with nausea (involuntarily – this is classical conditioning) and will learn that if he takes his hand away he can avoid the aversive stimulus (voluntarily – this is operant conditioning). The nausea acts as CR to the vodka (CS). The emetic is an UCS. The vomiting is a punishment.

Therapy, Cognitive Behavioural –
- Can help in 90% of cases of phobia.
- Is the treatment of choice in social phobia.
- Is as effective as Psychodynamic Interpersonal Therapy in the treatment of depression.

Therapy, operant – Involves behavioural assessment and sometimes functional analysis.
Uses one of three main types of therapy:

- **Selective positive reinforcement**
  The therapist selects a target behaviour or adaptive behaviour which is to be increased in probability and then delivers positive reinforcement for this behaviour.
  This is used in anorexia to reward eating. The patient is only allowed to perform a favourite activity of (usually) hers if she will eat.
  The patient will often not tell the therapist what her favourite activities are, as she knows what will happen, so they are identified using the **Premack principle**, which states that activities indulged often are more rewarding/favoured.
  Basically, you only let the patient do something they want to do when they do something you want them to do.
  Shaping and chaining can be used as adjuncts.
- **Selective punishment**
  Involves identifying a maladaptive target behaviour and organising an aversive event to follow it. This is used in the treatment of self-mutilation in autistics and aggression in children.

Basically, you do something they don't want when they do something you don't want.

- **Extinction**
  Is one of the more humane methods of selective punishment. A specific maladaptive target behaviour is identified and some highly desired event is refused/omitted when it occurs.
  An example would be refusing to cuddle a child that cries at night. You need to be able to differentiate maladaptive from neutral behaviour very reliably and to provide general support and love so that the child doesn't just feel unloved/neglected.
  Basically, you don't do something they want when they do something you don't want.

Therapy, psychodynamic interpersonal – Described by RF Hobson.

- Lies between interpersonal therapy and traditional dynamic psychotherapy.
- Uses an exploratory rational approach involving staying with feelings and attaining a shared understanding.
- Has been shown to be effective in depression and IBS.
- Does *not* mainly involve the use of questions.
- Is as effective as CBT in the treatment of depression.
- Does *not* involve focusing on negative cognitions.

Thiamine – *aka* vitamin B_1
Deficiency can cause:

- Wernicke's encephalopathy
- oculomotor disturbance
- ataxia
- polyneuropathy
- nystagmus.

Thinking, concrete Described by Goldstein.

- Results in literal interpretation and understanding of metaphorical expressions.
- Is typically seen in schizophrenia.
- Not unusual in organic states.

Thinking, dereistic – Is characterised by excessive and meandering fantasy thinking.

Thinking, fantasy – Is undirected and may be used to deny painful external reality.

Thinking, flow of –

- According to Jaspers, each thought could lead to several possible

321

subsequent thoughts (ie a constellation), only one of which is actually chosen.
- The *determining tendency* is the control of the final goal in the flow of thoughts.

Thinking, imaginative – Is the use of spontaneous ideas in a constructive manner.

Thinking, over-inclusive – Described by Cameron.
Is the tendency to include items that are only remotely relevant into the stream of thoughts.
or
The inability to circumscribe a problem or retain meaningful boundaries.
- Conceptual boundaries are not preserved.
- Can be assessed by sorting tests.
- It occurs in schizophrenia.

Thioridazine – Is a phenothiazine with a piperidine side chain.
Binds dopamine D2 receptors.
Antagonises muscarinic acetylcholine receptors strongly. This is known to cause antiparkinsonian effects.

Thirst – Mediated by lateral hypothalamus.

Thought blocking – Is a sudden, unexpected interruption in the train of thought before it is completed.
- It leaves the patient 'blank' and unable to resume their train of thought.
- Occurs in schizophrenia.
- Is distinct from thought withdrawal

Thought echo – *aka echo de la pensée*/thought sonalisation/ *gedankenlautwerden*
Described by Kurt Schneider.
A phenomenon experienced when one's thoughts are perceived to be repeated audibly. This is characteristic of schizophrenia.

Thought stopping – Name given to a technique that attempts to control undesirable thinking, eg in OCD. As soon as the patient realises he/she is thinking in an undesirable manner, they apply a stimulus (eg twanging an elastic band tied around the wrist or shouting 'Stop!'), in an attempt to distract themselves.

Thoughts, negative automatic – Include:
- dichotomous reasoning.

Threshold, absolute – Minimum energy required to activate the sensory organ.

Threshold, difference – Minimum difference required to perceive two sensory sources as different.
- Weber's law – difference threshold is directly proportional to the baseline intensity. This is a poor approximation which is only good over a small range of stimulus intensities.
- Fechner's law – a better approximation, stating that sensory perception is a log function of stimulus intensity.

Thyrotoxicosis – Can be confused with generalised anxiety disorder.

Thyrotrophin releasing hormone (TRH) –
Is found throughout the CNS.
- Has general antidepressant effects.
- Inhibits sleep.
- Increases body temperature.
- Increases blood pressure.
- Decreases food consumption.

Tics – Repeated irregular movements involving a muscle group.
May be secondary to:
- encephalitis
- Huntington's disease
- Gilles de la Tourette's syndrome.

Tics, isolated –
- Affect 5–7% of children in their primary school years.

Tomography, positron emission (PET) – A nuclear medicine technique that produces an image of radioactivity in the body after the administration of a radioactive substance emitting positrons.

- Substances used include O^{15}, N^{13} and C^{11}. These are incorporated into glucose, oxygen and other molecules.
- When a positron interacts with an electron inside the tissue, two annihilation photons are emitted and these are detected by coincidence detectors.
- PET enables the study of brain blood flow and therefore of the level of oxidative metabolism.
- It has demonstrated that there are two or three times as many doamine D2 receptors in the brains of drug-naïve schizophrenics as there are in the striatums of normal control individuals.

Tomography, single positron emission – Uses lipophilic tracers

(^{99m}Tc-HMPAO) which are given iv and remain in the brain for several hours, allowing high resolution imaging with a gamma camera.

Topographical model of the mind – Was set out by Freud in *The Interpretation of Dreams* and was later replaced by the structural model of the mind.

Describes 3 components:
- **unconscious**
  - contains memories, ideas and affects that have been repressed
  - **primary process thinking**
  - motivated by the **pleasure principle**
  - access only occurs when defences are lowered by:
  - relaxing (eg daydreaming)
    - being fooled (eg joking)
    - being overpowered (eg neurosis)
  - symbolic
  - non-linear
  - timeless
  - there is no negation
  - connotative
  - image-oriented
  - beyond awareness.
- **preconscious**
  - includes memories of which we are not immediately aware, but can fairly easily bring to full consciousness
  - develops during childhood
  - maintains repression and censorship
  - **secondary process thinking**
  - is bound by time
  - is linear
  - motivated by the **reality principle**
  - it is beyond awareness
  - word oriented
  - accessed: by focused attention only.
- **conscious**
  - within awareness
  - **secondary process thinking**
  - motivated by the **reality principle**
  - easy access
  - bound by time
  - word oriented
  - declarative

- linear.

Primary process thinking features:
- displacement – an initially insignificant idea is invested with the meaning and affect originally attached to another idea.
- condensation – a variety of meanings and chains of association are intimately attached to a single idea, from which they start.
- symbolisation – use of symbols rather than words.

also:
- timelessness
- disregard of reality
- psychical reality – psychic phenomena (imaginations, real perceptions, abstract symbols) are treated as real
- absence of contradiction – contradictions are not detected and therefore are tolerated
- absence of negation.

Secondary process thinking features:
- linear flow of time
- regard for reality
- verbal form
- recognition of contradictions that are not allowed.

Pleasure principle:
- the motivating principle of the primary process
- inborn
- pain/unpleasure is avoided and pleasure sought via discharge of tension, leading to:
  - wish fulfilment
  - the discharge of instinctual drives.

Reality principle:
- the motivating principle of the secondary process
- results from acceptance of external reality
- leads to delayed gratification.

Torpor – A state of drowsiness when the patient:
- is prone to falling asleep
- shows evidence of:
  - slow thinking
  - narrowed range of perception.

TPHA – *Treponema pallidum* haemagglutination assay.

Traits – Stable and enduring aspects of personality that are reflected in people's behaviour (eg even-temperedness, liveliness).

Traits, anankastic – *see* Obsessive-compulsive traits.

Transactional Analysis – Was founded by Eric Berne.

Transference – Is the process by which the patient's feelings derived from previous figures in his life (especially childhood) are displaced onto the therapist.
or
The transferring to the therapist of feelings/attitudes originally relating to parents/others.
- Was a term first used by Freud in 1895.
- Is an unconscious process.
- Was initially thought to be an obstacle to analysis.
- Can be used to investigate aspects of the person's inner self that are otherwise inaccessible, forgotten or lost.
- Is directed towards the therapist.
- Is extensively applied outside the psychoanalytic relationship.
- An example would be a patient being hostile to me when I refuse a request because they would have been hostile to a parent in similar circumstances earlier in their life.

Transitional objects – Were described by Winnicott.

Transitional phenomena – Were described by Winnicott.

Transsexualism – More common in males than females.
- Reduced libido.
- *No* sexual arousal during cross-dressing.
- Rate of self harm is low.
- Prevalence in females is 1:110, 000.

Transvestitism –
- The individual experiences a state of appropriateness by wearing clothes of the opposite gender.
- Is *not* a form of fetish.

Trazodone –
- Has 'a major sedative effect in therapeutic doses'.
- Is an antidepressant related to the TCAs.

Treatment alliance, the –
- Can be called the working alliance.

- Can relate to the good relationship *any* two people need to have in co-operating.
- Trust is necessary (this explains incomplete development of the alliance in psychotics and people who experienced severe emotional deprivation as children).
- If based on the patient's desire to get better, it's very unreliable and the patient may break off treatment as soon as they see some improvement (the 'flight into health'),
- The patient needs to be able to tolerate a certain amount of frustration,

Triad, Kraepelin's – 3 components associated with mood:
- abnormal mood
- psychic activity (reduced in depression, increased in mania)
- motor activity (reduced in depression, increased in mania).

Tricyclic antidepressants – Plasma concentrations are increased by:
- cimetidine
- disulfiram
- phenothiazines

and reduced by:
- antiepileptics.

Trigeminal nerve – Innervates the muscles of mastication.

Tryptophan – Is the precursor of:
- serotonin/5HT.

Tuberoinfundibular system – This is a dopaminergic system blockaded by antipsychotics, with subsequent increase in prolactin.

Tyrosine – Is the precursor for:
- noradrenaline
- dopamine.

UCR – Unconditioned response.

UCS – Unconditioned stimulus.

Unconscious, the – In psychoanalytic theory, it:
- disregards the reality of the conscious world
- is the origin of basic fundamental drives
- is described in the topographical model of the mind (with the preconscious and the conscious)
- includes primitive impulses and fantasies.

Unconsciousness – A state with no subjective awareness.
Three uses clinically:
- Unconsciousness (ie coma) due to brain disease – is on a continuum between normal and death.
- (Deep) sleep – not true unconsciousness.
- Lack of awareness of environment (not often completely unconscious) – on a continuum between vigilance and relative unawareness.

Uncus – Lesions cause memory loss.

Understanding speech – Pathway is:

Ear → Auditory cortex → Auditory association cortex → Wernicke's area → Consciousness

Understanding writing – Pathway is:

Retina → Visual cortex → Visual association cortex → Angular gyrus → Wernicke's area → Consciousness

Unitary psychosis – *aka Einheitpsychose*
Described by Griesinger.

Uraemia – Can cause an acute or chronic organic reaction.

Validity – Is a property of assessment that indicates if the assessment tool measures what it's supposed to measure.

Validity, construct – Do the different items or subsets of the test measure the same thing/do they fit together?

Valproate –
- Can cause spina bifida if used in pregnancy.
- Has efficacy similar to lithium when used in mania.

Vampirism – Usually relates to schizophrenia.

Variables, qualitative – Attributes that can be categorised such that the categories do not have a numerical relationship with one another. Examples include:
- hair colour
- religion.

Variables, quantitative – Attributes that can be categorised such that the categories have a numerical relationship with one another. Examples include:
- height
- weight.

Venlafaxine – Is metabolised by:
- cytochrome p450 3A4 to an inactive metabolite
- cytochrome p450 2D6 to an active metabolite.

Ventromedial occipito-temporal regions – Bilateral lesions cause prosopagnosia.

Ventromedial tegmental area – Contains dopaminergic neurones.

Verbal associations – Clang associations, proverbs and clichés.

Verbigeration – A type of stereotypy in which sounds, words or phrases are repeated in a senseless way.
Occurs most often in schizophrenia.

Verruckheit – Described by Heinroth.
Means madness.
Characterised by delusions and auditory hallucinations.

Vicarious – Means observational.

Visual hallucinations –
- Occur in blind or partially sighted people as Bonnet's syndrome.
- Can be associated with a homonymous hemianopia.
- Can occur in narcolepsy (when they are often vivid and terrifying and accompany or precede sleep paralysis).
- Have their origin in lesions of the occipital cortex when elemental and in the temporal cortex when complex.
- They can occur in lesions of the diencephalon.

Vitamin B$_{12}$ deficiency – Can cause:
- cognitive impairment
- depression
- paranoid psychosis.

Vorbeigehen – *aka* approximate answers
Means to go past.
Seen in the Ganser syndrome.
Strongly suggests that the correct answer is known.

Vorbeireden – *aka* talking past the point
Means to talk past.

VTA – Ventral tegmental area.

Wahnstimmung – *aka* delusional mood
The first change is in mood, which may lead on to delusions.
Often causes delusional perception.

W

WAIS-III – Wechsler Adult Intelligence Scale.

WASI – Wechsler Abbreviated Scale of Intelligence.

Wallenberg's syndrome – *aka* lateral medullary syndrome

WBC – White blood corpuscle.

Weight gain – Is caused by:
- antipsychotics
- TCAs
- lithium
- venlafaxine

but *not* by:
- SSRIs
- benzodiazepines.

Wernicke's encephalopathy – *see* Appendix 1.

Westphal – Agoraphobia.

WHO – World Health Organisation.

Windigo – Is a culture-bound disorder seen in Native Americans.
- The patient comes to believe that, having undergone a transformation, they have become a monster that practices cannibalism.
- It's possible that this is a local myth rather than a real disorder.

Winnicott – Started out as a paediatrician and ended up as an object relations theorist.
He believed:
- The baby cannot be considered in isolation.
- In **objective countertransference** – that countertransference was an understandable reaction to the personality and behaviour of the subject (the analysand).

- In **countertransference hate** and said this was normal, giving reasons why a mother hates her child from the start of their relationship. The mother-child relationship was compared with the therapist-patient relationship and it was felt that countertransference hate existed here too.
- The **good-enough mother** is one who meets the baby's needs within an optimal zone of frustration and gratification.
- The **pathological mother** who imposes her needs on the baby, which develops a **false self** to protect its **true self**.
- Good parenting allows autonomy to co-exist with dependence on the mother and the child has the **capacity to be alone** in the presence of another.
- Transitional space bridges the outer and inner world.
- A **match** between outer and inner worlds facilitates the development of the true self. A **mismatch** causes a **false self** to be developed.
- In **transitional objects** that:
  - are neither oneself nor another person
  - are selected by the infant at 4–18 months
  - are used for self-soothing and anxiety reduction eg toy/blanket that helps the infant sleep)
  - help with separation/individuation
  - in adults can be music, religion or scientific creativity.
  - Separation and autonomy require aggression, which is linked to spontaneity and play.
- **Holding environments** are therapeutic ambiences or settings that allow the patient to feel safe. They make psychotherapy possible/easier.
- **Potential space** is the area of experiencing existing between the baby and the object. It is involved in play, imagination and dreams.
- **Squiggle game** is a play therapy technique.
- **At-one-ment**.
- **Primary maternal preoccupation**.
- **Regression to dependence**.
- **Going on being**.
- **Impingement**.
- **Object usage**.
- **Integration/Personalisation** – refer to the individual's development of thought processes of its being a distinct individual.

WISC – Wechsler Intelligence Scale for Children.

Witelsucht – aka fatuous euphoria
Is characteristic of frontal lobe syndrome.

Word salad – *aka* schizophasia or speech confusion
Described by Bleuler.
A type of loosening of association and stereotype seen in schizophrenia, composed of recognisable words arranged in a meaningless manner because of loss of syntax.

Writing – Pathway is:

Conscious thought → Wernicke's area → Angular gyrus → Mmotor areas → Writing

Writing, automatic – Is an automatism.

Wynn & Singer – Defective communication.

W

Yalom – Described 11 therapeutic/curative factors specific to groups:

- instillation of hope
- universality
- imparting of information
- interpersonal learning
- altruism
- the corrective recapitulation of the primary family group
- development of socialising techniques
- imitative behaviour
- group cohesiveness
- catharsis
- existential factors.

Yerkes-Dodson curve – Inverted U-shaped curve relating arousal to performance.

Zeitgebers – External cues facilitating regulation of internal timing mechanisms (ie internal clock-setters).

Zopiclone – Is a cyclopyrrolone.
- Acts at the same receptor as benzodiazepines.
- Is reversed by flumazenil.
- Has a half-life of 3–6 hours.

Appendices

Wernicke's encephalopathy and Korsakoff's psychosis

Wernicke's encephalopathy

Clinical features

diagnostic	clouding of consciousness	with confusion
	nystagmus	horizontal/vertical
	ophthalmoplegia	bilateral weakness/paralysis of lateral recti weakness of conjugate gaze
	ataxia	may be very severe
	peripheral (poly)neuropathy	
	memory disorder	difficult to assess due to confusion
	emotional disturbance	apprehension anxiety insomnia fear of the dark lability

and later:

apathy
depression
emotional lability

retrobulbar neuritis	rare and associated with peripheral neuropathy due to thiamine/B_{12} deficiency
intention tremor	rare better elicited by heel-to-toe than finger-to-nose

Mechanism

- Severe thiamine (ie vitamin B_1) deficiency.

Aetiology

- alcoholism
- hyperemesis (including hyperemesis gravidarum)
- gastric/duodenal/jejunal lesions (eg carcinoma) causing malabsorption
- starvation
- CO poisoning
- medial temporal lobe lesions
- CVA affecting specific regions (including some of those below).

Neuropathology

Lesions are seen in:
- mammillary bodies (petechiae, necrosis and gliosis)
- area adjacent to the walls of 3rd ventricle
- peri-aqueductal grey/region
- floor of 4th ventricle
- inferior colliculi
- some thalamic nuclei
- terminal portions of the fornices
- brainstem
- anterior lobe of cerebellum
- superior vermis of cerebellum – Purkinje cell layer is found here and is affected
- ventricular dilation.

Differential diagnosis

- Pellagra encephalopathy (resulting from nicotinic acid depletion).

Complications

- Progresses to Korsakoff's syndrome if untreated.

Treatment

- Intravenous thiamine
- Other B vitamins.

Notes

- Studies have been done in prisoners of war.
- A high degree of suggestibility is seen.
- It's *not* caused by B_{12} deficiency, but by B_1 (ie thiamine) deficiency.

Korsakoff's syndrome/psychosis

An abnormal state in which memory and learning are affected out of all proportion to other cognitive functions in an otherwise alert and responsive patient.

Clinical features

- retrograde amnesia
  - remote memory relatively spared
  - recent memory markedly impaired
  - immediate memory is spared
- anterograde amnesia
  - therefore impaired new learning
- disorientation in time
- inability to recall sequence of events
  - confabulation is early and reduces as intellect deteriorates
  - is *fantastic* initially and *momentary* later
- relative sparing of other cognitive functions
- peripheral neuropathy
- clear consciousness.

Mechanism

- Thiamine deficiency.

Aetiology

- Alcoholism
- Carbon monoxide poisoning.

Neuropathology

- scarring and atrophy of:
  - mammillary bodies
  - anterior thalamus

- dorsomedial thalamic nucleic lesions are seen (these are responsible for the memory disorder)
- there is substantial frontal lobe dysfunction on neuroimaging.

Treatment

- Abstinence from alcohol
- High-dose thiamine and vitamin B replacement for 6 months.

Notes

- il's an amnestic/dysmnesic syndrome.
- Perception is unimpaired.
- Implicit memory is preserved.
- Is classified according to its aetiology in ICD-10.
- Amnesia is due to failure of retrieval.
- *Jamais vu* may occur.

Spinal tracts and associated syndromes

Spinal tracts

Ascending

- Anterior
  Anterior spinothalamic tract   light touch and pressure

- Lateral
  Anterior spinocerebellar tract   proprioception, pressure and touch
  Posterior spinocerebellar tract   proprioception, pressure and touch
  Lateral spinothalamic tract   pain and temperature
  Spino-olivary tract   proprioception and cutaneous sensation
  Spinotectal tract   involved with spino-visual reflexes

- Posterior
  Fasciculus cuneatus   discriminative touch and proprioception
  Fasciculus gracilis   vibration.

Descending

- Anterior
  Anterior corticospinal tract   voluntary movement
  Reticulospinal fibres   motor function
  Vestibulospinal tract   muscle control
  Tectospinal tract   head-turning reflex and upper limb movement in response to acoustic, cutaneous and visual stimuli.

- Lateral

Lateral corticospinal tract	voluntary movement
Rubrospinal tract	muscle activity
Lateral reticulospinal tract	muscle activity
Descending autonomic fibres	visceral function control
Olivospinal tract	?muscle activity.

Associated syndromes

- Brown-Sequard syndrome

  = cordal hemisection
  ipsilateral:
  - upper motor neurone paralysis (spastic)
  - loss of proprioception
  contralateral:
  - loss of pain and temperature
  - sparing of light touch, bladder, rectum and genitalia (bilateral innervation) is rare.

- Posterior column lesions

  ipsilateral loss of:
  - vibration sense
  - proprioception
  - discriminative touch.

- Dorsal column lesions

  sensory ataxia (with positive Romberg's sign).

Some important points to note about ICD-10

F00–09 Organic including symptomatic mental disorders
- Dementias
- Amnesic syndromes } not if substance-induced
- Delirium.

F10–19 Substance abuse problems
- Includes delirium tremens.

F20–29 Schizophrenia, schizotypal and delusional disorders
- Includes an extended classification of acute and short-lived
- psychotic disorders.
- Includes schizotypal disorder.
- Includes schizoaffective disorder and post-schizophrenicdepression.
- Definition of schizophrenia is broader than that in DSM-IV.

F30–39 Affective disorders
- *Not* post-psychotic depression.

F40–48 Neurotic, stress-related and somatoform disorders
- Phobias
- Panic and anxiety disorders
- OCD
- PTSD, etc
- issociative disorders
  Include: Ganser syndrome
                   multiple personality disorder
- Somatoform disorders
  Include: hypochondriasis
- Other neurotic disorders
  Include: neurasthenia.

F50–59 Behavioural syndromes related to physiological disturbance and physical factors
- Eating disorders
- Non-organic sleep disorders
- Psychogenic sexual disorders
- Abuse of non-dependence-producing substances.

F60–69 Disorders of adult personality and behaviour
- Personality disorders, personality changes
- Habit and impulse disorders
- Disorders of gender and sexuality
- Munchausen's syndrome.

F70–79 Mental retardation.

F80–89 Developmental disorders
- Specifically
  - of speech and language
  - Scholastic
  - Motor
- Pervasive
  - autism (<3 years)
  - Other.

F90–98 Behavioural and emerging diseases of childhood and adolescence
- Hyperkinetic
- Conduct
- Emotional
- Social functioning
- Tics.

F99 Unspecified.

Classified outside the 'F' category:

Epilepsy
Wilson's disease
Thyroid diseases
Intoxication
Multiple sclerosis
Vitamin deficiencies
SLE.

Not included:

Paraphrenia.

Lobes

Frontal

Functions Sustaining of voluntary attention
Set shifting
Mental flexibility
Abstract conception
Problem solving
Initiation
Sequencing
Judgement
Error monitoring (dangerous if impaired)
Personality
Social behaviour
Motor function
Wisconsin card sorting test.

Lesions cause Frontal lobe syndrome:

- *Witzelsucht*
- impaired judgement
- impaired attention
- apathy/lack of initiative and spontaneity
- reduced motor activity
- disinhibition/reduced social awareness (but *not* hypersexuality)
- impaired behaviour
- mild euphoria
- poor insight.

Also:

- personality change
- lack of concern for others
- irritability
- perseveration

- palilalia
- Jacksonian seizures
- urinary incontinence
- contralateral spastic paresis
- primary motor aphasia
- motor agraphia
- anosmia
- ipsilateral optic atrophy
- persistent pain
- hyperalgesia
- Kluver–Bucy syndrome (includes hypersexuality)
- grasp reflex
- waxy flexibility (tumours)
- hypersexuality (uncommon, seen as part of Kluver–Bucy syndrome).

Failure of:
- cognitive estimation (eg How many pints in a bath?)
- proverb interpretation
- similarities and differences.

Occipital

Functions	Shape perception Colour perception Spatial orientation.
Lesions cause	Pseudoagnosia.

Parietal

Functions	Sensory • Stores the phonological loop • Stereognosis.
Lesions on ?which side cause	Sensory inattention.
Lesions on either side cause	Contralateral: • astereognosis • agraphognosia • atopognosia.

Lesions on both sides causes	Kluver–Bucy syndrome.
Dominant functions	Superior – production of phonemes Semantics (ie meaning of individual words).
Dominant lesions cause	Gerstman's syndrome: • Agraphia • Dyscalculia • Finger agnosia • Right–left disorientation.
Dominant functions	Assembling of the complete visual percept and attachment of meaning to it.
Non-dominant lesions cause	Constructional apraxia Topographical agnosia.

Temporal

Functions

Bilateral lesions cause	Confabulation.
Dominant lesions cause	Impaired learning of new words.
Non-dominant lesions cause	Reduced appreciation of music Difficulty planning tasks.

Developmental stage theories

Cognitive	Moral	Social/psychological	Whole life	Other
Piaget	Freud	Erikson	Levinson	Klein
	Piaget			
	Kohlberg			
	Selman			

Sigmund Freud

Birth to 15–18 months
Oral stage
Oral stimulation/feeding gives satisfaction

15–18 months to 1–3 years
Anal stage
Gratification initially from eliminating (anal-expulsive) and later from withholding (anal-retentive) of faeces

3–5 years
Phallic-Oedipal stage
Awareness of genitalia. Oedipal/Electra complex

5 years to puberty
Latency period
Quiescence

Puberty
Genital phase
Adult stage of sexual satisfaction

Jean Piaget

Birth to 2 years
Sensorimotor period
Perception of the world based on sensory information and action.
Object permanence develops at about 12–18 months – the knowledge that objects which are out of sight still exist.
Primary circular reactions (2–4 months) – reflexive, stereotyped behaviours (eg opening and closing of fingers repetitively).
Secondary circular reactions (4–8 months) – repetition of actions causing change which is interesting (eg repeatedly kicking a mobile hanging over the cot, to move it).
Tertiary circular reactions (12–18 months) – discovery of new ways to achieve goals (eg rather than moving towards a toy to pick it up, the infant will pull the pillow it is on towards himself).

2–7 years
Preoperational period
Use of words and images to represent objects
Egocentricity – unable to appreciate that there may be a perspective other than his/her own.
Realism – belief in dreams/imaginary situations.
Animism – attributes consciousness to toys, etc.
Creationism – the moon exists to provide light at night.
Artificialism – belief that natural events are caused by people, negative events seen as punishments.
Transductive reasoning – insects and birds can both fly, so they must be the same thing.
Centration – can only concentrate on one aspect of an object/situation.
Authoritarian morality – dictated by adults and rules which are not challenged.
Teleological approach – assessment of intention based on outcome not intention.
Finalism – all things have a purpose.
Precausal reasoning – based on internal schemes rather than on observation (and therefore failure of conservation).

7–11 years
Concrete operational stage
Logical thought
Understand **principles of conservation**:
- Number/liquid conservation at 6–7 years

- Substance and length at 7–8 years
- Weight at 8–10 years
- Volume at 11–12 years

Understand reversibility

Decentration – can consider more than one aspect of an object and put objects into classes based on more sophisticated things than 'colour', for example.

Can use categorical labels such as 'number' or 'animal' – ie hierarchies/relations are understood.

Ability to solve transitivity tasks using real objects – eg A is bigger than B and B is bigger than C – is A or C bigger?

11 years to adult

Formal operational stage

Hypothetico-deductive reasoning – able to formulate and test hypotheses.

Able to think hypothetically – therefore see the logical consequences of a hypothetical scenario.

Erik Erikson

Birth to 1 year   Trust vs mistrust

Consistent, stable care needed to feel secure.

Success = trust in environment, hope for future.

Failure = suspicion, insecurity and fear of the future.

1–3 years   Autonomy vs shame and doubt

Sense of independence from parents sought.

Success = sense of independence and self-esteem

Failure = shame and doubt about one's autonomy.

3–6 years   Initiative vs guilt

Exploration of environment and sexuality.

Success = enjoyment of new activities.

Failure = fear of punishment and guilt due to one's feelings.

6–11 years   Industry vs inferiority

Important cultural knowledge and skills acquired.

Success = sense of competence, achievement and confidence.

Failure = feelings of inadequacy.

12–18 years   Adolescence

Identity vs confusion

Coherent personal and vocational identity sought

Success = sense of being consistent and integrated person with

strong self-identity
Failure = confused self-identity

20s to 30 years   Young adulthood
Intimacy vs isolation
Deep and lasting relationships sought.

40–64 years   Middle adulthood
Generativity vs stagnation
Continued growth, productivity and contribution to society sought.

65+ years   Late adulthood
Integrity vs despair
Review and evaluate what's been accomplished.
Success = ego integrity, with integrated view of one's life, achievements and meaning. Mortality is accepted, one is satisfied with life and ready to face death.
Failure = despair, about one's own life's path and the way one has treated others. One feels that one's life is transient when faced with death. There is no sense of contentment and completion.

Comparative stages

Age	Erikson	Freud	Piaget
0	Trust vs Mistrust	Oral	Sensorimotor
1			
15–18 months	Autonomy vs Shame and doubt	Anal expulsive Anal retentive	
2			
3	Initiative vs Guilt	Phallic-Oedipal/Electra	Preoperational
4			
5			
6	Industry vs Inferiority	Latency (until puberty)	Concrete operational
7			
8			
9			
10			
11			
12	Identity vs Confusion	Genital (from puberty)	Formal operational
13			
14			
15			
16			
17			
18			
20s	Intimacy vs Isolation		
30s			
40s	Generativity vs Stagnation		
65	Integrity vs Despair		
>70			

Culture-bound syndromes

Amok

- Occurs in Malay men.
- Often follows an argument, insult or personal loss and social drinking.
- Consists of a period of social withdrawal followed by a sudden outburst of homicidal aggression in which the sufferer will attack anyone. This period lasts for several hours until the sufferer is overwhelmed or killed and is followed by deep sleep or stupor for several days, followed by amnesia for the episode.
- Is connected with cultural ideas about loss of self-esteem or 'face' and warfare.
- It was very common in Malaya at the start of the 19th century, but has almost disappeared today.
- Most people running amok have no mental illness,but the most common diagnosis is schizophrenia.

Brain fag syndrome

Is a culture-bound syndrome seen in many parts of Africa and New Guinea.

- It is a widespread, low-rade stress syndrome.
- Often seen among students at exam time,it consists of:
  - Head symptoms (aching, burning, crawling sensations)
  - Eye symptoms (blurring, watering, aching)
  - Difficulty in grasping the meaning of spoken or written words
  - Poor retentivity
  - Sleepiness on studying
  - Resistance to psychological interpretation of symptoms.
- More common in peasant areas, rare in upper-class areas.
- May be a form of depression, with depressive features not being articulated in Western terms.

Dhat

Is a *common* culture-bound syndrome in Asia (India, Nepal, Sri Lanka, Bangladesh, Pakistan).

- Vague somatic symptoms (eg fatigue, weakness, anxiety, loss of appetite, guilt, etc).
- Sexual dysfunction (impotence, premature ejaculation).
- It's attributed by the patient to excessive masturbation/intercourse resulting in exhaustion of one's supply of semen.
- Typical patient is rural, with conservative attitudes and lower class.
- Literacy and religion seem unimportant.
- 65% of patients in some genitourinary clinics have Dhat.
- Age of onset is early 20s.
- Most have little depression or anxiety.
- Treatment is with antianxiety or antidepressant drugs.
- It really is culture bound, because of specific beliefs about semen in Indian culture.

Koro

Common culture-bound syndrome affecting men in South-West Asia, especially the Chinese.
It is characterised by:

- periods of acute anxiety with:
  - sweating
  - palpitations
  - pericardial discomfort
  - trembling
- belief that the penis will retract into the abdomen and cause imminent death
- this belief is *not* a delusion
- it occurs mainly at night
- it occurs in the context of sexual guilt
- the man may tie his penis up with string to prevent its retraction.

It may occur in epidemics.

Latah

Is a hysterical, culture-bound condition seen in Malay women.
- onset is after a frightening experience
- there is an exaggerated response to minimal stimuli with an excessive startle reaction
- coprolalia
- echolalia
- echopraxia
- automatic obedience.

Piblokto

Is a culture-bound dissociative state seen in Inuit women.
- occurrence associated with food shortage
- associated with symptoms of depression
- clothing is torn off and the patient screams and runs about wildly, often jumping into water
- life is endangered by hypothermia
- suicidal/homicidal behaviour may also be seen.

Windigo

Is a culture-bound disorder seen in Red Indians/North American Indians/Native Americans.
- The patient comes to believe that, having undergone a transformation, they have become a monster that practices cannibalism.
- It's possible that this is a local myth rather than a real disorder.

EEG phenomena

α (alpha) rhythms
Features
* regular
* 8–13 Hz
* low amplitude

Occurrence
* seen when relaxed with eyes closed

Pathology
* completely lost in Huntington's disease

Drugs
* reduced by benzodiazepines

Notes
* arise posteriorly

β (beta) rhythms
Features
* less regular
* 13–30 Hz
* fast

Occurrence
* when awake, alert and paying attention

Pathology
* increased in delirium tremens

Drugs
* decreased by:
  * antidepressants
  * antipsychotics
* increased by:
  * anxiolytics
  * (including benzodiazepines)

δ (delta) rhythms
Features
- < 4 Hz
- high amplitude

Pathology
- increased in hepatic encephalopathy

Drugs
- increased by:
  - antidepressants
  - antipsychotics

θ (theta) rhythms
Features
- 4–8 Hz
- fairly high amplitude

Drugs
- increased by:
  - antipsychotics

λ (lambda) rhythms
Occurrence
- seen in occipital regions with the eyes open

Notes
- relate to eye movements during visual attention

v (mu) rhythms
Occurrence
- seen in motor cortex in relation to motor activity
- are *abolished* by movement of a contralateral limb

Spikes
< 80 ms duration

Waves
> 80 ms duration

Flat trace
Leads not connected
Hypothermia
Brain death

Broca's and Wernicke's areas and associated pathways and syndromes

Areas

Broca's area

- *motor* speech/speech association area
- co-ordinates the organs of speech to produce coherent sounds
- located in inferior frontal gyrus
- also involved in language production
- controls:
  - speech intonation
  - speech rhythm.

Wernicke's area

- *sensory* speech and language area, auditory association area
- processes reception of speech
- also involved in production of speech, coming earlier in the pathway than Broca's area
- occupies posterior auditory association cortex of superior temporal gyrus.

The arcuate fasciculus is the pathway between Broca's and Wernicke's areas.

Pathways

Hearing
- Auditory cortex → Auditory association cortex → Wernicke's area → Hearing/comprehension

Reading
- Visual cortex → Visual association cortex → Angular gyrus → Wernicke's area → Reading/comprehension

Speaking
- Cognition → Wernicke's area → Broca's area → Motor speech areas → Speech

Writing
- Cognition → Wernicke's area → Angular gyrus → Motor areas → Writing

Syndromes

Expressive aphasia/dysphasia, non-fluent aphasia/dysphasia, motor aphasia/dysphasia, Broca's aphasia/dysphasia
- Lesion in Broca's area.
- Disordered language production.
- Phoneme errors occur.
- Grammar is severely distorted and simplified.
- Speech is slow and hesitant.
- Rhythm and intonation are lost.
- Language comprehension is normal.
- Articulation may be affected due to proximity of Broca's area to motor areas.
- There is insight and frustration.
- Phrases can be repeated.

Receptive aphasia/dysphasia, Wernicke's aphasia/dysphasia, fluent receptive dysphasia
- Lesion in Wernicke's area.
- Disordered language comprehension (written or spoken).
- Expressive dysphasia.
- Empty words (thing, it) and paraphrasias are common.
- Normal speech intonation/rhythm.
- No insight.
- Fluent speech.
- Unable to repeat messages.

Thought disorder

Disorders of thought content
- Preoccupations
  - Hypochondriasis
  - Monomania
  - Egomania
- Obsessions
- Phobias
- Overvalued ideas
- Delusions.

Formal thought disorder (ie disorders of the form/structure of thought)
- Drivelling
- Condensation
- Flight of ideas
  Rapid, continuous, fragmentary stream of ideas, thoughts and images without any coherent pattern or focus, as expressed in speech, with the maintenance of a logical sequence but a weak determining tendency and high distractibility.
  Characteristic of mania, it features:
  - Punning
  - Rhyming
  - Clanging
- Perseveration
- Transitory thinking
- Knight's move thinking
- Word salad/schizophasia/speech confusion
- Derailment
- Woolly thinking
- Loosening of associations

  Alteration in structure of thinking such that connections between concepts are distorted.

  - Talking past the point/*vorbeireden*
  - Approximate answers/*vorbeigehen*.

Syndromes of delusional misidentification

Capgras' syndrome
- *aka* the illusion of doubles, *l'illusion des sosies*, delusion of doubles
- Occurs when the patient believes someone has been replaced by an exact double.
  Not an illusion, but a delusional perception and a delusion, it is more common in women and is usually associated with schizophrenia (or affective disorder), but may have an organic component. Any associated cerebral dysfunction is always (?) located in the non-dominant hemisphere.
  - *not* frequent
  - often implicates the spouse
  - may *not* be based on a real impostor
  - involves splitting
  - is rarely associated with organic disorder.

Fregoli syndrome
- Is the false identification of familiar people in strangers.

Intermetamorphosis
- A delusion and a delusional perception in which the patient believes that an individual has been transformed both psychologically and physically into another person.

The syndrome of subjective doubles
- Occurs when the patient believes that another person has been physically transformed into his/her own self.